Second Edition

JOINFOSTERING
Adapting Teaching for the
Multilingual Classroom

Christian J. Faltis
Arizona State University

Merrill,
an imprint of Prentice Hall
Upper Saddle River, New Jersey   *Columbus, Ohio*

Library of Congress Cataloging-in-Publication Data

Faltis, Christian

    Joinfostering : adapting teaching strategies for the multilingual classroom /
Christian J. Faltis.—2nd ed.

        p. cm.

    Includes bibliographical references and index.

    ISBN 0-13-238163-X

    1. Education, Bilingual—United States. 2. Mainstreaming in education—
United States. 3. Elementary school teachers—Training of—United States. 4. Education,
Elementary—Parent participation—United States.   I. Title.

    LC3731.F35   1997

    371.97'00973—dc20   96-22497

                                                      CIP

Editor: Bradley J. Potthoff
Production Editor: Mary M. Irvin
Design Coordinator: Julia Zonneveld Van Hook
Text Designer: Ed Horcharik
Cover Designer: Orbit Design
Production Manager: Laura Messerly
Electronic Text Management: Marilyn Wilson Phelps, Matthew Williams, Karen L. Bretz,
    Tracey Ward
Director of Marketing: Kevin Flanagan
Advertising/Marketing Coordinator: Julie Shough

This book was set in ITC New Baskerville by Prentice Hall and was printed and bound by
Quebecor Printing/Book Press. The cover was printed by Phoenix Color Corp.

 © 1997 by Prentice-Hall, Inc.
Simon & Schuster/A Viacom Company
Upper Saddle River, New Jersey 07458

Earlier edition © 1993 by Macmillan Publishing Company.

Printed in the United States of America

10 9 8 7 6 5 4 3 2

ISBN: 0-13-238163-X

Prentice-Hall International (UK) Limited, *London*
Prentice-Hall of Australia Pty. Limited, *Sydney*
Prentice-Hall of Canada, Inc., *Toronto*
Prentice-Hall Hispanoamericana, S. A., *Mexico*
Prentice-Hall of India Private Limited, *New Delhi*
Prentice-Hall of Japan, Inc., *Tokyo*
Simon & Schuster Asia Pte. Ltd., *Singapore*
Editora Prentice-Hall do Brasil, Ltda., *Rio de Janeiro*

Preface

●●●

This book was written with two audiences in mind: (1) education majors who are in the process of becoming classroom teachers, and (2) established teachers who are interested in changing the way they teach to accommodate students in their classrooms who are adding English to their already developed native language(s). As the number of students who are learning English as a second language grows in substantial proportions, regular classroom teachers must become better prepared to help these students join in all aspects of classroom and school life.

This book presents many teaching and learning strategies found in exemplary bilingual education and English-as-a-second-language (ESL) programs throughout the nation. In other words, the strategies presented in this book are derived largely from advances that have been made in bilingual education and ESL teaching. It is important to understand that exemplary teaching in a multilingual classroom differs in significant ways from exemplary teaching in a classroom where all of the students are native speakers of the same language. When students are learning the *language* of instruction in addition to the *content* of instruction, teaching them as if they were native speakers is ineffective and unacceptable. Teachers must learn to adapt teaching to ensure that these students have access to and participate in all aspects of classroom learning. Anything less means that we are denying these students the benefits of classroom learning experiences.

My experience working and teaching in bilingual and second-language education spans two decades, and I remain a strong advocate of native-language teaching in bilingual education. Over the years, however, I have come to realize that in placing all of my energies into studying and improving bilingual education, I have effectively ignored what happens to bilingually schooled children once they are placed into all-English classrooms. Virtually all children who enter a native-language bilingual education program stay in, on average, no more than two years, and most of these children receive very little ESL instruction once they are exited from the bilingual program. This means that two-thirds to three-fourths of their schooling will be in all-English classrooms with all-English teachers who have little or no idea about how to help these children join in all aspects of teaching and learning! This is a social injustice that joinfostering works against.

This book is a direct response to the critical need in teacher education for the 21st century. It is not, by any stretch of the imagination, however, a cookbook of teaching behaviors for teaching second-language learners. Joinfostering stems from a strong stance about what good teaching and learning are, a stance that is informed by research and theory and propelled by the belief that all children can learn. In the joinfostering framework, teachers are responsible for finding the means to plan and implement the conditions that will facilitate learning for the broadest range of students' abilities, needs, and interests. There are too many instances in school in which second-language learners are segregated from their native-English counterparts and placed into lower level tracks; where second-language learners are denied access to field trips, after-school events, and music lessons because of their language differences. There are too many stories about non-English-background parents not knowing what is going on in their child's classroom; about not knowing how to help their child at home; about not being included in school-related events. Joinfostering addresses these injustices by presenting ways for teachers to change the existing social organization of their classrooms to improve teaching and learning for all students and to work more effectively with parents and significant adults, regardless of their language background.

A WORD ABOUT THE SECOND EDITION

In this second edition of *Joinfostering*, I have included several new ideas and practices. You will notice that I have added a new condition to the joinfostering principles—the stance toward critical consciousness and social justice. Joinfostering goes against the grain of most teaching and learning in U.S. schools. What I hope you will understand from this new edition is that there are ways to help your students challenge and question social inequities and social hierarchies that sort people on the basis of ethnicity, class, gender, and language. I have also worked to incorporate more ideas about the role of literacy in learning. You will see many more references to oral and written language activities and ways of expression. This stems from my belief that language is literacy, not merely oral expression. Finally, I have included some new ideas about second language acquisition, ideas such as *comprehensible invite* that are closer to what I understand about how children become highly proficient bilinguals. I hope that you sense the excitement that I derived from writing this new edition.

TO THE TEACHER

This book is organized to give your students a brief introduction to language and cultural diversity and bilingual education before introducing them to adaptation strategies for teaching in whole and small groups and for small-group learning. There are many examples to draw from in the book, but undoubtedly you will want to bring in your own experiences and examples to fit your particular circumstances. The book begins by introducing Julia Felix, a first-year, third-grade teacher who is faced with learning about teaching in a multilingual classroom. As the book progresses, so does Julia by learning ways to adapt her classroom teaching to ensure that all of her students are participating. I have used lots of examples associated with the theme of elephants, and I have tried to show how to involve students in critical consciousness within this theme. You may wish to begin your class with a different theme and then, as your students move into the teaching adaptation chapters, use activities tied to the theme to illustrate the strategies and techniques as they are described and discussed. At the end of each chapter, I have included activities and exercises that help students think about and practice the ideas presented in the chapter. I suggest that your students interview teachers from multilingual classrooms to learn about their experiences and observations about what works. You may wish to arrange with one or more schools beforehand to allow your students to interview teachers over the course of the semester or quarter. Finally, it is important to stress to your students that joinfostering is more than teaching adaptations; it is a commitment to becoming a good and critical teacher for all students.

TO THE STUDENT

You are part of the next generation of teachers, the teachers who will be responsible for educating a diverse group of children, many of whom are adding English as a second language as they are learning content in your classroom. This book on joinfostering, a new term in education, is an introduction to teaching in a multilingual classroom. By reading through and practicing the teaching adaptations presented in this book, you will be prepared to enter a multilingual classroom. One of the most important goals of this book is to help you develop the following stance toward teaching, learning, and children: that all children can learn and that we are responsible for finding ways to make sure that all children do learn what they need in order to become responsible, knowledgeable, curious, and critical members of society. By the time you complete this book, you should not be fearful of entering a classroom where some of the students are second-language learners. You should welcome it.

In the next few pages, you will be introduced to Julia Felix, a first-year teacher, who lacks the knowledge and ability to teach effectively in a multilingual classroom. You will see how Julia learns to adapt in her classroom by following joinfostering principles. What Julia accomplishes within her classroom is well within your grasp as teachers. I wish you success and hope that, like Julia, you develop a commitment to joinfostering in teaching and learning.

ACKNOWLEDGMENTS

Although I tapped all of the keys that produced the words that make up this second edition of *Joinfostering*, I owe much of the credit and support for the ideas that made joinfostering possible to various individuals. I feel especially fortunate to have studied under two of the most distinguished scholars in the field of language education. To begin, I would like to gratefully acknowledge Professor Robert L. Politzer for sharing his wisdom and extraordinary insights about language teaching and language learning. Professor Shirley Brice Heath has also been a powerful inspiration in my development as a teacher. I owe much of my understanding about the cultural dimensions of language acquisition to her teaching and her writings.

Among the friends and colleagues who have influenced me over the years, I am indebted to Professors Rebecca Constantino, Sarah Hudelson, Carole Edelsky, Robert A. DeVillar, D. Scott Enright, Robert Milk, and Mary McGroarty for their enormous contributions to language education. I have co-authored many pieces with Robert A. DeVillar, Sarah Hudelson, and Rebecca Constantino. I am certain that out of our intense dialogues over the years I have incorporated many wonderful ideas without giving these individuals the credit they deserve. Carole and Rebecca have influenced my thinking about critical consciousness, and that influence shows up in this second edition. I don't think that I could have written this book without having learned from the illuminating work that Carole, Sarah, Rebecca, Scott, Robert, and Mary have produced over the last decade.

I also would like to acknowledge my friend and mentor, Professor Barbara Merino of the University of California, Davis. An exemplary teacher, an insightful scholar, and a premiere researcher, Barbara has helped me in too many ways to mention. I owe much of what I have been able to accomplish over my years in teacher education to Barbara's support and her erudite discussions about teaching and learning.

Many thanks to the reviewers of this text, whose insightful suggestions and comments I appreciate: Gina Cantoni, Northern Arizona University; John P. Milon, University of Nevada; Bertha Perez, The University of Texas, San Antonio; and Joan Wink, California State University, Stanislaus.

I would also like to acknowledge the tremendous encouragement and support that my production editor, Mary Irvin, provided me throughout the revision process for this second edition. She was a constant source of motivation and a pleasure to work with.

Finally, I could not close without acknowledging the love and intellectual support that my wife and lifelong companion, Deborah, has given me during my hours of writing. She is my inspiration.

Foreword

Henry T. Trueba
Harvard University

This book makes a plain, clear, and powerful statement of the need to reform teacher preparation if we are to succeed in American schools; it speaks to the present and future generations of American teachers and emphasizes the need to understand the role of teachers facing multiple home languages and students' difficulty in acquiring English literacy. The central issues of cultural and linguistic diversity in schools and the challenges faced by teachers seem less overwhelming in the context of *joinfostering*. Joinfostering is indeed an important modern concept with deep and old roots in the work of early sociolinguists and ethnographers of communication. It essentially recognizes that both teachers and students can jointly construct new knowledge through active, genuine, and balanced interactional participation of all students, especially those who are culturally different (and, often, not fluent in English). Joinfostering is based on the important psychological principle that cognitive development is inseparable from social and cultural development as emphasized by Vygotsky and Neo-Vygotskians. This view of learning places social interaction at the heart of learning. Joinfostering also highlights the need to capitalize on the knowledge, experience, and linguistic and cultural resources brought by students and their families to the learning process. Joinfostering is significant as a concept that can guide instructional practice because the very existence of American democracy depends on the successful schooling of the ethnic, immigrant, and the other "minority" children who are indeed now becoming the majority of school children in many urban districts.

As American society moves rapidly toward a more complex society socially, economically, and culturally, it also becomes more polarized and divided on issues of values and the meaning of democracy. It is a common belief that traditional democratic principles led this country to open its door to immigrant groups from all over the world and to create the conditions in which these groups could succeed. Success was understood by immigrants precisely as having the rights and obligations of American citizens; that is, as enjoying freedom and opportunities equal to those enjoyed by people born in America. Most ethnic groups have managed, over a period of time, to become active (and at times powerful) participants in American social institutions. The civil rights struggles of the mid-20th century clarified this interpretation of democracy and the role of schools in inculcating American democratic values among immigrant, refugee, and minority groups. Joinfostering is a powerful means to achieve democracy in and through school because its main purpose is to help language minority children, particularly those who have been disempowered, join in and participate fully in learning.

More recently, particularly after the war in Vietnam, the assassinations of John F. Kennedy, Robert F. Kennedy, and Martin Luther King, and the disappointment with the past presidents, many Americans from all socioeconomic quarters and ethnic backgrounds feel disenfranchised and angry about public policies, public institutions (especially schools), ethnic relations, and the overall role of America in the world. The infrastructure of the country, the quality of life in the cities in general, and the quality of urban schools in particular, is persuading the public that something is very wrong in America. American cultural values are changing in ways never anticipated before, and people feel disempowered.

The overall feeling of disempowerment, particularly in low income neighborhoods that are assaulted by drug dealers, homicide, prostitution, gang warfare, uncontrolled pollution, and hunger, is only the tip of the iceberg. Changes are occurring so rapidly that educators seem to be confused about what route to take, how to control the damage, how to heal our society, and how to protect our youngsters from abuse, neglect, poverty, ignorance, and alienation. Educational reform is viewed with suspicion by the right as an attempt to disperse funds provided by taxpayers to "immigrant populations," while the left disagrees with this strategy. The historical irony is that today, when the wave of intolerance for the instructional use of languages other than English is reaching its peak, is precisely when the use of home languages in public is increasing rapidly. Joinfostering offers a reform in teaching that addresses the social climate of separation and ignorance by empowering teachers with the means to socially integrate students regardless of national origin or language proficiency. These efforts also affect the ability of underrepresented students to benefit more fully from instruction and in school.

Disempowerment is essentially a process whereby ethnolinguistic, low-income, or racial groups are unable to function in mainstream institutions (especially in schools). This process has been explained in terms of macro-sociological factors that determine the status of these groups and, hence, the relative access they have to resources and other means of participation in mainstream institutions. The process has also been examined in terms of the psychosocial mechanisms resulting in "castlike" ethnic identities (those developed in opposition to that of "mainstream" persons).

It is important to point out that the reason disempowerment occurs in the context of rapid social, cultural, and linguistic change in immigrant, refugee, and the other minority children is that many of these children experience a rapid loss of their home language and culture. A child's native language is an essential instrument in the acquisition of self-identity, cultural knowledge, and cognitive skills. Sociolinguistic research and research on the ethnography of communication emphatically argue for the significance of language in the communicative process, in the construction of new knowledge, and in the transmission of cultural values. In a very real sense, the home language and culture become the "survival kit" for minority children. It is through language that they understand different scenarios and settings, different participation structures, the various usages and purposes of language, different instrumentalities and forms of communication (for example, text or face-to-face), the diverse genres (poetry, prayer, lecture, etc.), and the norms of communication associated with the various forms and usages. Faltis has made the point many times throughout this book that socially constructed language holds the key to placing learning back into the hands and minds of teachers and students. In this manner, joinfostering addresses this issue of disempowerment head on.

What goes on in the classroom must enable students of diverse social, economic, and ethnolinguistic backgrounds to participate fully in all aspects of learning. The teacher is greatly responsible for doing the work of making sure that this happens. But, as Faltis points out, the community must be involved in schools. Thus, while joinfostering places the teacher in the center of making pedagogical adaptations to counter inequitable classroom practices that can occur, it also brings in parents and family members as support agents for learning and joinfostering in general.

North America has now, as it always has, a highly diversified population. Its largest minority is the African-American group, descendants from the slaves brought during the previous two centuries. The core of European immigrants who rapidly assimilate is still very large and quite invisible. After the Hispanic population, which is the largest language minority group in the country (and now predominantly urban), the largest immigrant groups are German, French, Italian, and other European groups. After them the Asian immigrants (Chinese from mainland China and from Taiwan; Korean, Filipino, Hawaiian; and Indochinese: Vietnamese, Cambodian, Khmer, Hmong, and Laotian) are the fastest growing and rapidly becoming visible minorities. There are still numerically small communities of Native American Indians who remain highly isolated in reservations or urban areas, after having lost much of their economic self-sufficiency, their cultural traditions, and their control over land. Massive relocations and extermination policies have effectively destroyed many Indian communities and their ability to maintain a sense of peoplehood. The situation of many of the Indians and Eskimos in Alaska is comparable to that of Native Americans in the lower states. I can see how many of the joinfostering instructional adaptations can work with children from a wide range of ethnolinguistic origins.

One of America's oldest but least empowered "ethno-racial" communities is that of the African-Americans. This population is poorly understood and highly stereotyped because of its unique 250-year history of slavery and post-slavery segregation and deprivation. In general, miscegenation in the United States has been less acceptable socially—even hypergamously (i.e., where higher status males marry lower status females) than in the Latin American countries such as Brazil or Mexico where large numbers of African slaves were also brought and their descendants experienced some mobility because of a wider experience of exogamous marital choices. In America, racial discrimination against African-Americans and Asian-Americans—the latter entered the U.S. labor market as cheaply paid "sweat laborers" or "coolies" in the 19th century and came to be stigmatized under discriminatory immigration laws at the turn of the century— has continued to be manifest today against these "unmeltables" in America's melting pot. Particularly vulnerable, given their historic deprivation and the bleak contemporary employment picture, are African-American males between the ages of 15 and 25. Like Latino and Asian-American young men, they are at risk because of both limited life chances and limited education. Indeed, in some cities there may be more school-age black youngsters in jail than in the neighborhood high schools. Although joinfostering does not specifically discuss African-American children, the strong stance it takes on social integration of and communication among children of all ethnolinguistic origins leads me to believe that African-American children would have equitable opportunities to participate in learning activities with teachers who use joinfostering principles.

Chris Faltis has written a volume that offers teachers an excellent perspective on the most significant and neglected aspect of teaching and learning, on "joinfostering," which is a process of cooperative, personalized and effective teaching for all students. It is a process that will permit

Latino, Asian, African-American and mainstream students to talk and work together in all classroom activities, and to retain a high level of achievement motivation. Moreover, joinfostering goes beyond the classroom to include parents and family in social interaction and learning. In language that is understandable to teachers, and in a style that is meaningful and attractive, Faltis deals successfully with some of the most serious challenges of American schools in the 21st century.

Cambridge, Massachusetts
August, 1996

Contents

Chapter One

Expect Diversity

• •

AN OVERVIEW OF THE BOOK

This book presents a teaching framework for English-speaking teachers who will be working in linguistically and culturally diverse classrooms. The framework is organized around the notion of **joinfostering,** the organization and implementation of conditions to promote two-way communication and social integration within the linguistically diverse English-medium classroom. Joinfostering is a means for monolingual English-speaking teachers to accommodate the multiple social, intellectual, cultural, *and* language differences that children bring to class. The term *joinfostering* stems from the idea that public schools and the English-speaking teachers and students who teach and learn in them need to foster the joining in of students for whom English is an additional language in all aspects of schooling.

The effectiveness of joinfostering in English-medium classrooms containing second-language students depends on your ability as a teacher to plan for and implement five interrelated social and pedagogical conditions. These five conditions are as follows:

1. a high incidence of two-way communicative exchanges between the teacher and students and among students, regardless of their oral English-language proficiency;

2. the social integration of second-language students with native English-speaking students in all aspects of classroom learning;

3. the thoughtful integration of second-language acquisition principles with content instruction so that as second-language students experience and practice new subject-matter knowledge, they develop language as well;

4. the involvement and participation of second-language students' com-

munity in both classroom- and school-related activities;

5. the promotion of critical consciousness within the classroom, the school, and the community to oppose social stratification and promote equity in society.

A commitment to joinfostering requires that we as teachers think about ways to make classroom content authentic and language-sensitive and to teach in ways that are appropriate to the cultural groups represented in our classrooms. In addition, we must also teach against the grain of social injustice and take an active stance against education-ally sponsored means of oppression. Joinfostering is under way when classrooms are organized so that students of varying English-language abilities talk about, listen to, and work together and individually on tasks that are interesting, relevant, and intellectually challenging. Joinfostering is in motion when students have a say about topics, activities, and ways of turn-taking. Joinfostering is complete when second-language parents begin to become involved at various levels in school and classroom activities, and when teachers, students, and parents critically address issues of how perspectives and identities are constructed, how knowledge is produced, and how dominance is maintained (Edelsky, 1991).

A NOTE ABOUT LABELS: MAINSTREAM TEACHERS, ENGLISH LEARNERS, AND CULTURAL GROUPS

The classrooms that I will be referring to in this book are what I am calling *mainstream all-English* classrooms. I will often use the term *mainstream* interchangeably with and alongside *all-English* or *English-medium* to refer to grade-level classrooms taught by English-speaking teachers who have been prepared for elementary classroom teaching in an all-English teacher education program. My rationale for this is as follows: The overwhelming majority of grade-level classroom teachers are white, female, and monolingual English speakers who represent mainstream values and behaviors (Merino & Quintanar, 1988). Thus, while the schools and classrooms about which I write may not be mainstream in terms of classroom makeup, the curriculum, the teachers, and the administrators are likely to be. According to Olson (1988), relatively few minorities are choosing teaching majors in college, prompting her to conclude that it is likely that language and cultural backgrounds of classroom teachers will become even less heterogeneous in the immediate decades to come than they are at present.

The labels that mainstream teachers and administrators use to talk about students who are adding English as a second language are problematic. There are lots of labels to choose from: non-English proficient

(NEP), limited English proficient (LEP), fully English proficient (FEP), potentially English proficient (PEP), readers and writers of English as another language (REAL), monolinguals. Some are more positive than others. You should know, however, that once you designate a student by a label, you set into motion a potentially vicious cycle: The label, usually based on something the "normal" population has but that the student lacks, determines the student's schooling environment. As Wink (1993) points out, for too many students who are learning English as a second language, the environment is often in the corner of the classroom or in a remote area of the school. The cycle can become dangerous when the label highlights a deficiency, and the teacher begins to treat students differently by engaging them in fewer exchanges and by using lower-level questions and materials. (See Harklau, 1994, for a clear-cut example of differential treatment based on labels.) Once this happens, it is difficult, but not impossible, to break the cycle. We will discuss ways of going against the grain in later chapters.

To be frank, I had a very difficult time deciding which labels to use to refer to different kinds of students and different cultural groups. Most of the labels used for students have to do with language proficiency designations. It makes some sense to me to talk about students in terms of their language abilities because many of the pedagogical and social interactional decisions we make include language proficiency. With this in mind, most of the time I will use the label *second-language learner* to refer to students who are adding English to their native language. I realize, however, that that term won't work with students for whom English is a third or fourth language. Periodically, I will also reluctantly employ the U.S. government-sanctioned terms *limited English proficient* (LEP) and *non-English proficient* (NEP) because they are used widely in the literature in bilingual education and teaching English to speakers of other languages (TESOL), and they are designations that are closely tied to entry and exit testing. I dislike the terms LEP and NEP, however, because they conjure up the notion of a deficit, and as I mentioned above, negative labels can lead to undesirable teaching behaviors. In addition, the acronyms LEP and NEP are often used as labels for the children themselves, a practice that I find reprehensible.

Another set of labels that I have trouble with are labels for the ethnic groups I have included. In this book, I draw from examples of practices among Hispanic groups, Asian groups, and Native American groups. The labels *Hispanic, Asian,* and *Native American* are admittedly imprecise, and they seriously overgeneralize substantial language and cultural differences within each major group. On occasion, I use seemingly more precise labels, such as *Chinese Americans* and *Mexican Americans,* but even these are problematic because of the extensive cultural variation existing within each group. I have tried to be fairly specific when talking about immigrant vs. non-immigrant ethnic groups, and I caution you not to stereotype any individual member of an ethnic group based on the descriptions that I present. I have learned that there is no easy way to discuss the beliefs and practices of cultural groups without speaking in rather general terms.

THE NEW CHALLENGE

Many mainstream teachers have accepted the challenge of working with social, intellectual, and cultural differences and abilities. However, relatively few teachers are prepared to teach second-language children along with native English-speaking children. For example, a 1981 nationwide survey of public school grade-level teachers found that although half of all teachers had some experience with English learners in their classes, only 6% had taken one or more academic or nonacademic course to learn how to effectively teach second-language students (Waggoner & O'Malley, 1985). A more recent survey reported by Penfield (1987) showed that the majority of grade-level teachers know very little about the kinds of conditions and strategies that benefit second-language learners in their classrooms. Many teachers feared that second-language learners would do poorly in their classes because they are sorely underprepared to address these children's language and cultural needs (Penfield, 1987). A telling finding was that **all teachers expected the numbers of language-minority students in their classes to increase dramatically in the coming years**. The challenge for elementary teachers with second-language learners—novices and veteran teachers alike—is great not only because of the increase in the numbers of language-minority students, especially English learners, but also because of the tendency in schools to place students into higher or lower tracks based upon English language and literacy abilities (Harklau, 1994). Once children are tracked and segregated into these kinds of divisions, it is difficult for them to "jump the tracks" and move into higher social and academic circles (Oakes, 1986).

The joinfostering framework aims specifically at providing you with classroom conditions for meeting the social, communicative, and educational needs of native English-speakers and second-language learners of English alike. At the same time, the framework asks you to work toward social equality by directly challenging assumptions and practices concerning language, text, knowing, and learning that are often taken for granted or unscrupulously used to socially stratify children into high and low learning groups. In Chapter 1, we examine the nature and extent of linguistic and cultural variation of school-age children in the United States, with an eye toward understanding how children in different cultures are socialized to talk and how and the extent to which they are prepared for the kinds of language and literacy events stressed in school. Of particular concern is the extent to which cultural differences affect how children learn in school and whether academic success can be more adequately explained in terms of the existence of appropriate classroom conditions. The chapter begins with a brief introduction to Miss Julia Felix, a first-year teacher faced with teaching in a linguistically and culturally diverse third-grade classroom. In each of the subsequent chapters, we will see how Miss Felix adjusts her classroom to promote learning for all students and at the same time to facilitate the joining in of second-language children and their parents through appropriate communication and social integration strategies and activities. We will also see how she learns to question certain actions and behaviors that create inequities for second-language learners.

Chapter 2 introduces you to the most prevalent instructional programs for teaching second-language learners and provides a brief historical account of the political and legal decisions that led to their development. The chapter opens with Miss Felix as she examines the cumulative folders of her seven English-as-a-second-language students. She discovers that the students have experienced a variety of different school programs before entering her classroom. In an effort to learn more about their experiences, Julia gathers information on bilingual education programs, including transitional bilingual education, structured immersion education, and English-as-a-second-language pullout instruction. In this chapter we also learn about how second-language proficiency is assessed for exiting from such programs into mainstream classrooms. Chapter 3 examines the social and physical organization of the classroom to explore ways of arranging space and furniture to support social interaction and social integration. The chapter begins with a description of how most classrooms are typically organized in order to contrast them with a classroom organized to reflect joinfostering principles.

Chapters 4 and 5 introduce ways to incorporate second-language acquisition principles into the teaching of content that is taught either separately (e.g., social studies, science, or math) or as part of an integrated thematic unit. We will refer to this kind of instruction as *language-sensitive content teaching* because we will be adapting the instructional language we use for exchanging information about subject-matter content in ways that facilitate second-language acquisition. In both chapters, you will also be treated to ways of teaching against the grain to promote critical consciousness. Chapter 4 emphasizes language-sensitive content teaching and critical consciousness within the social context of whole-class instruction. In Chapter 5, we turn our attention to small-group instruction to learn how to extend this kind of teaching to learning activities that require the social integration of second-language learners with native English-speaking students. Chapter 6 suggests ways to involve second-language parents in the classroom and the school as active participants by building bridges between the home and school communities. Along with Julia, we learn how to reach out to communities that the school has largely ignored. The final chapter takes a comprehensive look at all of the joinfostering conditions and strategies that teachers can put into place to make their classroom a more enjoyable, more productive, and socially conscious environment for all children, regardless of their English-language proficiency. The conditions and strategies presented in earlier chapters are analyzed in terms of Cummins's (1986) school empowerment model, which presents four areas that are crucial to the success of language minority students in school.

EPISODE ONE: LOOK WHO'S IN YOUR CLASS

Miss Julia Felix is a first-year elementary schoolteacher, fresh out of college. She has shoulder-length auburn hair and stands about 5 and half feet tall in tennis shoes. She completed a semester of student teaching in a fifth-grade class in a small school located in a town near the college. She rode her mountain bike to the school on warm days and drove her 1969 VW bug when she had to. Her mentor teacher, Ms. Constantino, was a wonderfully talented woman who had been teaching in the small school for almost 20 years. She believed strongly in whole language and worked hard to help Julia understand how this perspective can guide the development of meaningful activities and the use of materials in ways that foster skilled and critical language use. Julia has been hired to teach in one of the two third-grade classes at Bruner Elementary School, a mid-sized school serving an ethnically mixed urban student body. To get to the school from her apartment, Julia has to drive nearly half an hour across town. Anxious to begin the school year, she picks up her key and an envelope containing her class roster 3 weeks before the first day of school and rushes with enthusiasm to inspect her new room. With the key in the doorknob, she gingerly turns the handle to the left and pulls back, opening the huge wooden door and stepping into what will be her domain for the next 9 months. It is all that she expected: a huge gray desk in the front of the room, a dark green chalkboard that covers two of the four walls, six sets of tables and chairs arranged into two rows, filing cabinets, some bookcases, a drinking fountain next to a sink with faucets, and a bathroom. She walks directly to her desk, plops herself down in the green swivel chair, and by pushing off with her red tennis shoes, spins around twice.

Rolling her chair up to the desk so that she is snuggled in tight, Julia shifts her attention to the manila envelope containing the class roster. In it, she knows, are the names of the children with whom she will spend 6 hours a day, 5 days a week for a full school year. What a moment of suspense and excitement! Pulling her hair back, she slips the ponytail holder from her wrist and fixes it tightly at the back of her head before carefully unclasping the folder. She slips her right hand in and slowly removes the computer printout. She pauses before taking it out completely and proclaims aloud: "I want to be the best teacher that I can be for these children. I want them to be excited about learning. Whoever these children are, I want to challenge their minds and make them feel good about who they are. Okay, kids, let's see who you are."

With the roster tightly held in both hands, Julia leans forward and begins reading the names of the children she will teach. The list of names she reads is as follows:

1. Brown, Leon
2. Cavenaugh, Kimberly
3. Cui, Xiancoung   X
4. Cohen, Daniel
5. Evans, Lisa
6. Fernandez, Maria Eugenia   X
7. Freeman, Jeffrey
8. Garcia, Aucencio   X
9. Gomez, Concepcion   X
10. Hamilton, Jessica
11. Mason, Tyrone
12. O'Leary, Sean
13. Pak, Kyung   X
14. Petruzzella, Gina
15. Quinn, Frank
16. Rosen, Paula
17. Robinson, Ryan
18. Rojas, Guadalupe   X
19. Sandoval, Kathy

20. Tran, Do Thi   X
21. Vasquez, Jimmy
22. Williams, Amy
23. York, Robert
24. Zbikowski, Antonin
    X = ESL student assigned to special instruction

Julia is astonished at the variety of the names on the list. Her green eyes instantly dart down to the key to learn the meaning of the "X" next to certain names. She immediately wishes that she had taken a course in bilingual education and teaching English as a second language in college, and then goes over the list again, wondering if she has pronounced all the names correctly. She pauses a few seconds to think about what she can do to accommodate her seven ESL students. Then she takes a long look around the room, stands up, and reaffirms her vow to do well in the coming year, but this time she adds, "And I especially want these seven ESL students to join in fully in everything we do in class. I really have to learn a lot about them . . . about how to get them really involved in the class. Wow, do I have a lot to learn. It's a good thing I did my student teaching with Ms. C.; all those things I learned about language and writing are really going to help. I remember what Ms. C. said about getting students to see learning everywhere and to be able to get along with and appreciate others (Edelsky, 1991). This is going to be an awesome year."

LANGUAGE AND CULTURAL DIVERSITY IN THE ALL-ENGLISH CLASSROOM

Who Are Our Second-Language Children?

For an increasing number of elementary schoolteachers, the typical classroom resembles the one just discovered by Julia Felix. Children who come from homes in which a language other than English is used for daily household communication, for shopping, for religious ceremonies, and for many other social situations are entering school in unprecedented numbers. Many of them are born in the United States to parents who immigrated to this country and continue to use their native language with their children.

In 1995, the population of school-age children (ages 5–17) living in households where a language other than English is spoken, regardless of their proficiency in English, was estimated to be just under 12 million (U.S. Bureau of the Census, 1995). In 1993, the number of school-age children whose English was not sufficiently developed to effectively participate in an English-only classroom was 2,524,592, or 6.03% of all K–12 students in school across the U.S. (W-B Olsen, 1993). Without counting the children of undocumented workers from other countries, the population of children for whom English is a second language is conservatively projected to reach 3.5 million by the year 2000 and to approach 6 million by 2020 (Pallas, Natriello, & McDill, 1989). See Figure 1.1.

In 1992, the state of California had 1,078,705 students with beginning proficiency in English as an additional language. By 1995, that number had grown to 1,262,982 (Macías, 1995). The most-spoken non-English background languages of these students were Spanish (990,801; 78%), Vietnamese (48,907; 3.9%), Cantonese (23,954; 1.9%), and Cambodian (21,765; 1.7%) (Macías, 1995). This distribution of non-English languages is also reflected in nationwide counts of speakers of languages other than English. Waggoner (1993) points out that, according to the 1990 U.S. census, "Spanish-speaking and Asian countries have replaced English-speaking countries and countries in which other European languages are spoken as the countries of birth of the largest proportion of the U.S. foreign-born population" (p. 1).

Spanish-speaking children make up the largest and fastest-growing school-age population of second-language learners in the United States. Since 1980, nearly 1.9 million legal immigrants from Spanish-speaking countries came to the United States to join the 15.5 million Hispanics who were already here. By 1987, the Hispanic population reached 18.8 million and comprises the following major subgroups (U.S. Bureau of the Census, 1988):

Figure 1.1
Projected number of children with a primary language other than English. U.S. total, 1982–2020
Source: From "The Changing Nature of the Disadvantaged Population: Current Dimensions and Future Trends" by A. Pallas, G. Natriello, and E. McDill, 1989, *Educational Research, 18,* 16–22.

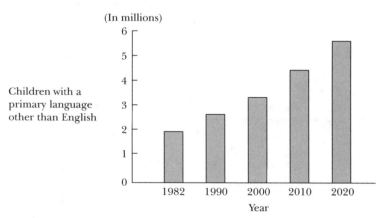

Mexican origin	13.8 million
Puerto Rican origin	2.3 million
Cuban origin	1.0 million
Central and South American origin	2.9 million
Other Hispanic origin	1.6 million

Mexican-origin population accounts for 63% of Hispanics in the United States. Among Hispanic subgroups, the highest rate of growth in numbers between 1982 and 1987 occurred in the Central American and South American population, which grew by 40%. The next highest growth rate (33%) was experienced by Other Hispanics, which the Census Bureau reported as persons "whose origins are from Spanish, or those identifying themselves generally as Spanish, Spanish-American, Hispano, Latino, etc." (U.S. Bureau of the Census, 1988). The Mexican-origin population grew by 22% and was followed by Puerto Ricans, 11%, and Cubans, 7%, who experienced the smallest growth during the period.

To give an indication of how much growth has occurred in the Hispanic population, the U.S. Bureau of the Census (1989) also reported that this population in major cities expanded rapidly between 1980 and 1985, and that as it grows, these cities will continue to experience growth at least into the 21st century. Figure 1.2 presents the metropolitan-area increases in Hispanic population from 1980 to 1985.

Hispanics have the highest birthrate of any major ethnic group in the United States. Pallas, Natriello, and McDill (1989) predict that the number of Spanish-language children will increase from 4.2 million in 1980 to 18.6 million in 2020. This expected increase of 14.4 million Hispanic children, many of whom will have Spanish as their primary language, more than offsets the expected decline of nearly 6 million native English-speaking white children over the same time period.

The second largest population of school-age second-language learners comes from Indo-Chinese and Asian-country immigrant families (e.g., Chinese from Taiwan, Hong Kong, and, more recently, Mainland China;

Figure 1.2
Metropolitan-area increases in the Hispanic population, 1980–1985

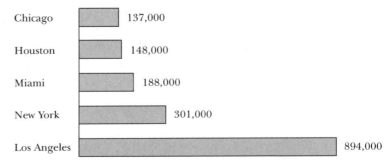

Vietnamese; Hmong; Laotians; and Cambodians). Asian-origin families began coming to the United States in large numbers in the 1960s. In 1980, three out of every five persons who identified themselves as Asian or Pacific Islander were born abroad (U.S. Bureau of Census, 1984). The children of these two groups, virtually all of whom were born in this country, made up the remaining two fifths. A majority of these children are being reared in the native language of their parents and caregivers and consequently enter school with little or no proficiency in English.

Three recent immigrant groups to the Unites States are Haitians, Russians, and Arabs (U.S. Department of Education, 1993; Carrasquillo & Rodríguez, 1996). Although immigrants have been coming to the United States from Haiti since the 1920s, a large number of wealthier and better-educated Haitians settled in New York and Florida in the early 1960s after the rise of François Duvalier, who seized power in 1957. In the 1970s another group came to the shores of Florida in an effort to escape the reign of terror of the new president, Jean-Claude Duvalier. These immigrants, most of whom speak Haitian Creole and are poor, are often referred to as "boat people." By the 1990s there were reported to be approximately 600,000 Haitians living legally in the United states (Carrasquillo & Rodríguez, 1996). A majority of the more recent immigrants, both legal and illegal, live in the Northeast and in Florida.

Another sizable group of immigrants to settle in the United States within the last 10 years are Russians. However, to label all immigrants coming from the former Soviet Union as Russian is inaccurate. Although they come from regions within what is now called Russia, many identify themselves by their country of origin and ethnicity. Accordingly, there are Armenians, Byelorussians, Estonians, Georgians, Kazakhs, Latvians, Lithuanians, Ukrainians, and Uzbeks. Delgado-Gaitán (1994) presents a fascinating account of how Russian immigrant families have adjusted to their new settings in northern California. Many of the more recently arrived Russian Jews have not been accepted by the older non-Jewish Russian immigrants and their communities.

New waves of Arab students from North Africa and the Middle East are showing up in public schools. Nearly all of them speak Arabic, and most practice the Islamic religion, which means that there are many religious and lifestyle practices that are likely to be unknown to most teachers. Carrasquillo and Rodríguez (1996) provide a number of strategies for learning about and teaching Muslim students.

LANGUAGE AND LITERACY SOCIALIZATION PRACTICES

Being born into a home in which a language other than English is used for socialization is a cultural difference that can and too often does lead to negative educational consequences. For example, among Hispanics, many of whom begin school as second-language learners of English, the number of students who do not complete high school is more than twice that of native English-speaking white counterparts (National Coalition of Advocates for Students, 1985). It is difficult to know for sure why so many ethnic-minority children leave school before graduating, but one explanation centers on the initial difference in language between the home and the school. The Language Mismatch Hypothesis predicts that children who enter school speaking a non-English language are more likely to fail than children who speak English (see Figure 1.3). Conversely, it also predicts that the greater the match between the home language and the school language, the greater the chances are that children will succeed in school. This hypothesis blames school failure on the child's lack of school-language proficiency.

In reality, however, the Language Mismatch Hypothesis is too simplistic for two reasons: (1) It fails to account for significant numbers of minority second-language children who do succeed in school without being instructed in their native language (see Ogbu & Matute-Bianchi, 1986), and (2) it fails to account for minority second-language children who do poorly in school even though they receive instruction in their native language (National Coalition of Advocates for Students, 1985). Both reasons suggest that something more profound than initially knowing or not knowing the language of the school may be influencing the success students achieve in school.

A second hypothesis is that the *language and literacy socialization practices* in certain homes may differ substantially from those expected and

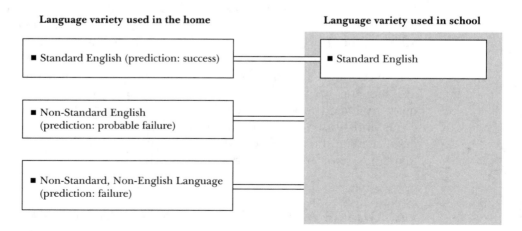

Figure 1.3
The Language Mismatch Hypothesis and predictions of school success and failure

reinforced in school, and when this occurs, the children from these homes will have difficulty in school. We will refer to this hypothesis as the Socialization Mismatch Hypothesis. This hypothesis states that the victim of unsuccessful schooling is still the culturally different child, but blames school failure on a combination of factors, including the extent to which the school accommodates for cultural diversity and the extent to which communication between the school and the child's family and community is cultivated (Sue & Padilla, 1986).

The Socialization Mismatch Hypothesis draws particular attention to the different ways that children are prepared for the kinds of language and literacy behaviors that form the foundation of classroom learning from kindergarten to 12th grade. The hypothesis is based upon two important assumptions about the relationship between language and culture: (1) that the acquisition of language and literacy uses is closely related to the process of becoming a competent member of a sociocultural group, and (2) that children learn to become competent group members by engaging in language-based activities within particular social contexts (Ochs & Schieffelin, 1982).

To investigate the Socialization Mismatch Hypothesis, let us begin by examining how mainstream caregivers socialize young children to talk and to behave as literate individuals. This account will then be contrasted with the ways children in certain second-language sociocultural groups are socialized for language and literacy. The accounts presented are meant to be illustrative and characteristic rather than precise and necessarily true for all group members, because there is always individual variation within any group. The purpose for contrasting mainstream language and literacy socialization practices with those found in the home of certain language-minority families is to show how fundamentally different the practices can be, and because, as Heath (1989) points out, "The school teaches not only language but all skills and knowledge bases from the ethnocentric biases of mainstream language acquisition and developmental perspectives" (p. 347). An awareness of the biases toward mainstream perspectives is needed before we can begin to work toward replacing them with an appreciation for the diverse experiences that children bring to the classroom.

LANGUAGE AND LITERACY SOCIALIZATION IN THE MAINSTREAM HOME

Mainstream children are socialized to develop and use language within a tradition of verbal interaction that places much of the responsibility for early language development on the primary caregiver. In the mainstream

home, the child's natural or adopted mother serves as the primary caregiver and consequently as the child's most intimate interactional partner.
Soon after a child is born, he or she is treated as a social being capable of
participating in social interaction with anyone willing to make certain linguistic adjustments. It is not uncommon, for example, for parents, grand-
parents, and friends to carry on a "conversation" with a newborn through
the nursery window as soon as he or she is brought out and placed in a
crib (Heath, 1983). In this case, the parents talk for the infant, supplying
what the infant may say in response to their questions.

The mother typically holds her newborn infant so that the baby
directly faces her. This face-to-face position allows the mother to talk to
the baby as well as to respond for the baby when the baby moves or makes
a sound. The early interactional exchanges between mother and infant
are precursors to the kinds of turn-taking procedures that will be reinforced in subsequent language-acquiring years.

Throughout the child's first few years, mainstream mothers consider
very young children as communicative partners capable of intentional
and representational speech. Treating young children as conversational
partners requires mothers and other caregivers to "take the perspective of
the child" (Ochs & Schieffelin, 1982). One strategy mothers use for taking
the child's perspective is to modify their speech to more closely match the
child's perceived verbal competence. This strategy is commonly known as
using *baby talk* or *motherese* (Cross, 1977; Ferguson, 1977). Spoken by
adults, baby talk is speech addressed to young children that has been
modified in a number of ways. It is typically spoken at a slower pace than
normal speech, and the pronunciation of certain key words is drawn out
through variations in pitch and length. A hallmark of baby talk is the use
of special terms for bodily functions, body parts, certain foods, stuffed
toys, and favorite blankets (e.g., *go potty, baba, tum tum, bear bear, blankey*).
Baby talk is considered to be simpler than normal speech, as utterances
generally are made up of simple clauses devoid of abstract vocabulary and
complex sentence structure.

A second strategy for taking the perspective of the child is to raise the
child above his competence level by richly interpreting what he is attempting to express (Ochs & Schieffelin, 1982). This strategy results from the
belief among mainstream caregivers that young children are capable of
expressing meaning and of using language to represent ideas symbolically.
Because mothers assume that the baby is attending to their talk, they interpret any utterance made by the baby in response to a question as intentional language. As such, their language needs to be interpreted verbally.
Heath (1983) provides a good example to illustrate this point: "If shortly

after one interpretation is given, the baby issues a contradictory signal, the mother may even comment on this shift as an attempt on the part of the child to clarify his intentions: 'Oh, you *didn't* like that, huh? I'm sorry, Mommy thought you liked that, I didn't mean to scare you'" (p. 248). Mothers continue to interpret their child's utterances until the child is able to more accurately express wants and needs, which normally begins between 2 and a half and 4 years of age (Lessow-Hurley, 1990).

Both strategies for taking the child's perspective encourage the use of question-and-answer routines used in certain highly ritualized language games. One of the more popular games involving such routine is the peek-aboo game (Cazden, 1983). The mother holds a blanket over her face and says "Peekaboo, where are you?" and then quickly lowers the blanket to answer "Here I am." Another early exchange pattern is the strange sound game (Heath, 1983). In this game, the mother uses a question-and-answer exchange around certain sounds that routinely appear throughout the day. For example, when the dog barks as Daddy is coming home from work, the mother may ask the child, "Who's coming?" or "Who's driving up in the driveway?" "I think it's Daddy!" In both games, the mother supplies both the question and the answer, and in this manner, models a pattern of inter-action that is crucial for literacy development.

The question-and-answer routine that drives peekaboo and other verbal interaction games also underlies much of the talk that occurs in early storybook-reading activities. Storybook reading commonly begins at birth and develops into a daily bedtime and naptime ritual that often lasts beyond the preschool years (Heath, 1982). Storybooks are given as pre-sents at baby showers, birthdays, and major religious holidays, and most mainstream caregivers enjoy reading storybooks to young children. Story-book reading is considered to be one of the most powerful means of developing literacy awareness, vocabulary and concepts, concepts of print, and a sense of story (Teale, 1984; Heath & Thomas, 1984). In addition to its role in the acquisition of fundamental literacy concepts, mainstream storybook reading inculcates the most common pattern of classroom dis-course found in all grades of schooling: the three-part sequence of teacher initiation, student response, teacher evaluation (Cazden, 1988). In storybook reading, children acquire this interactional sequence as a result of *labeling* and *clarifying* exchanges with caregivers who are con-cerned with naming objects and clarifying meaning.

The process of labeling during storybook reading depends on the use of what Mehan (1981) refers to as "known information questions." The questioner (the caregiver) already knows the information being requested of the child. Ideally, the question is posed in such a way that the child can provide an appropriate response. This enables the child to participate in a dialogue with an adult, and it allows the adult to evaluate the child's response favorably, reinforcing the value of child as knowledge-giver. Known information questions are used in many settings besides the context of storybook reading (Saville-Troike & Kleifgen, 1986).

The extent to which mainstream mothers use known information questions during storybook reading with preschool children was first explored by Ninio and Bruner (1978), who observed mothers reading with their 3- and 4-year-old children and categorized the kinds of exchanges that occurred. They found that verbal exchanges most often centered on the mother directing the child's attention to pictures in the book, followed by a request for a label of the item pointed to by the mother. Once the label was supplied, the mother responded favorably or, in the case of misinformation, gave the correct label. Ninio and Bruner categorized this labeling process into four major components: attention-getters, what-questions, labels, and feedback. Table 1.1 presents the frequency distribution of utterance types they found within each of the four major interaction components.

In addition to labeling exchanges, caregivers may also allude to the meaning of certain characters' actions and ask questions such as "Is the wolf bad? Why?" and "Why do you suppose those ducks are being so mean to the ugly duckling?" This kind of question, called a clarifying question, is typically used with children who have already learned to use connected speech. It employs the same structural format as a known information question, but because the reply is an explanation, rather than a display of knowledge, its content is relatively less predictable. In storybook reading, adults often focus the child's attention on pictures, behaviors, and story parts in order to clarify a meaning or to reinforce a value. In addition to asking for explanations of events and motivations, clarifying questions can also request the child to explain "when," "where," and "how" something happened. Adults ask clarification questions both to other adults and to children in a variety of situations outside of literacy events.

In school, teachers constantly ask children to name objects and discuss their attributes as well as to explain and clarify the meanings of words, pictures, and behaviors. The goal of using questions in such cases is to assist students to go beyond saying what something is, to attempt to express what something means, and to support the interpretation with both facts and logical reasoning. Labeling and clarifying exchanges prepare the groundwork for similar kinds of exchanges used in classroom discourse.

Beyond their value in modeling an interactional sequence found in classroom discourse, labeling and clarifying exchanges also prepare children for the major kinds of narrative discourse associated with successful

Table 1.1
Utterance types within the four stages of the labeling process

Stage/Example	Frequency	Stage/Example	Frequency
I. *Look*	65	III. *Label* (continued)	
Look!	61	More X.	3
Look at that.	4	They are X.	3
II. *What-questions*	85	These are the X.	3
What's that?	57	The X.	2
What are those?	8	You can see the X.	1
What are they doing?	6	That one is the X.	1
What is it?	5	Look at the X.	1
What are they?	1	It says: X.	1
What's on that page?	1	We'll call it X.	1
What's on the next one?	1	Kind of an X.	1
What's over there?	1	IV. *Feedback*	80
What else can you see there?	1	Yes.	50
What does that do?	1	Yes, I know.	8
What do you see there?	1	It is not an X.	5
What can you see?	1	That's it!	3
III. *Label*	216	Not an X.	2
X (= stressed label).	91	No, it's not an X.	2
It's an X.	34	Yes, it is an X.	1
That's an X.	28	That's charming.	1
There's an X.	12	No, it's an X, not a Y.	1
An X.	12	No, it's an X.	1
That's X.	6	Yes, they are (Xs).	1
There is X.	6	Yes, very good.	1
Lots of Xs.	5	That's not an X.	1
They are X-ing.	5		

Source: From "The Achievement and Antecedents of Labelling" by A. Ninio and J. Bruner, 1978, *Journal of Child Language, 5*(1), p. 7.

literacy experiences in school. Heath (1986a, 1986b) distinguishes among four kinds of narratives that occur in mainstream homes and that result from interactions between caregivers and their children: recounts, accounts, eventcasts, and stories.

Recounts are essentially extended versions of known information question-and-answer exchanges. Usually the first of the four narrative types to emerge in mainstream children, recounts require the child to retell experiences or information already known to both the child and the adult. Recounts are initiated either voluntarily or in response to questions from adults. The questions guide the child's telling so that events are linked together in sequence and tied to a central theme. For example, in the presence of a third party, a parent may ask the child to recount what happened on their outing to the zoo. The recount is typically opened with a question: "Can you tell Mrs. Taylor what happened at the zoo today, when we were visiting the seals?" As the child recounts the episode, the parent interjects questions to keep the child from veering off the theme and sequence. Questions also direct the child to include missing information or to clarify key information.

When children enter school, teachers regularly ask for recounts of stories read in reading books and of passages containing facts known to both the teacher and fellow students. Upon the teacher's request, students are expected to recount knowledge and experiences relying on information that has already been presented in class through readings or presentations. Moreover, as literature studies become increasingly popular in school, children ask other children to recount stories and to tell about what they understood from their readings of stories.

Accounts are narratives generated by the teller to provide new information to the listeners or new interpretations of information already known to the listeners. Children sharing with their parents special events of the day is an example of account. Since accounts provide new information or a novel interpretation, listeners judge them for both their truth value and their organizational structure. Thus, accounts that appear logical are accepted as truthful, while those told in an unorganized fashion are discounted. Adults model accounts for children when they narrate incidents occurring at work or other events that are out of the ordinary.

Accounts are generally initiated with a question, which signals that narrative is coming. However, unlike recounts, which typically depend on a question from an adult, accounts are started with an opening by the teller: "Wanna know what happened to the kitty cat today?" Once the opening prompt has been made and acknowledged, the child is accorded the floor until the account has been given in full. Clarifying questions are usually saved until the end of the account.

Account-giving in school is rarer than recounting, but does occur in classes that encourage student interaction and engage students in multiple writing activities. In the primary grades, students are given the opportunity to tell about their personal experiences during show-and-tell time (Michaels, 1981) and in their dialogue journals. Teachers who see their children as authors and who invite children to write stories and tell about what they see, hear, feel, and like promote account-giving. In the higher grades, accounts tend to be restricted primarily to creative writing assignments, although as more and more teachers use writing across the curriculum to foster learning, account-giving has increased. In both the primary and upper elementary grades, teachers typically measure the effectiveness of accounts in terms of their logic, truth value, and organization.

Eventcasts provide an ongoing narrative of events that currently or subsequently have the attention of both teller and listeners. Eventcasting may occur as an event is happening or may precede it. An example of simultaneous eventcasting is when children talk about how to do something as they do it. Young children commonly engage in simultaneous eventcasting during their solitary play, stating aloud what they are doing. Children also eventcast when they tell how to build a model out of Legos or when they describe what they will do when they go camping. Eventcasting also happens when children write out what they are doing for the day or as they devise or follow a sequence of events. Adults frequently model eventcasts as they discuss their vacation plans, telling where they will go and how long they will stay there.

Eventcasting is used by many teachers in school to preview lessons and to indicate what will be taking place throughout the day. In mathematics and science lessons, teachers use eventcasts to explain the steps needed to complete problems and experiments. When teachers place students in small groups to work cooperatively, eventcasts take the form of directions and descriptions of what students are expected to be doing at each step of the lesson. In turn, students may be asked to give eventcasts of each member's responsibility for completing the lesson. During reading lessons, students are often requested to predict the events of a story on the basis of the title and other key information. Some students also write out what is happening in stories or predict what will come next in a story.

Stories are the most familiar kind of narrative. A story is a fictional account in which some animate being (animal, object, or person) maneuvers through a string of events with goal-directed behavior (Stein, 1982). Stories have special conventions that set them apart from a simple account of facts in a sequence. Willy (1975) lists six conventions found in most stories told to young children: (1) a beginning title or formal opening phrase (e.g., "Once upon a time . . . "); (2) a formal closing phrase (e.g., "the end" or "happily every after"); (3) the use of a consistent past tense; (4) a variation in pitch or tone while storytelling; (5) the use of make-believe characters and events; and (6) the reoccurrence of certain stock character types and situations.

Children hear all kinds of stories, ranging from Bible stories and storybook adventures to their parents' tales of what it was like in the old days. Adults entertain children with ghost stories, war stories, and stories of real events changed slightly (e.g., naming a story character after the child) to serve as lessons for the future. Children retell these stories and others from their favorite books as well.

In school, fictional stories abound in storybooks, basal readers, and social studies textbooks. Stories are often placed within nonfictional accounts to attract students to the expository prose, and students learn to analyze fictional literary stories for morals and to identify and practice certain narrative genres. And of course, students write their own stories and publish them for their classmates, family, and teacher to read.

In all four of these types of narrative, children must learn to follow and describe events both chronologically and thematically, which requires developing each event in the proper sequence and at the same time elaborating a new aspect of the theme or situation as the story unfolds (Applebee, 1978). In mainstream homes and school alike, these narrative types are developed through interactions that occur primarily around books. Children are forever being asked to label objects both in and out of books. Adults ask children to recount stories that they have read to them. Caregivers hope that children will draw upon storybook knowledge to explain why they and others behave in a certain way. Parents enjoy hearing their children eventcast while they color in their colorbooks and build structures with their Legos and building blocks. In summary, caregivers engage children in lots of talk around books, preparing them for the kinds of literacy events that occur throughout school.

LANGUAGE AND LITERACY SOCIALIZATION IN LANGUAGE-MINORITY HOMES

Some or all of the four types of narratives and questioning routines found in mainstream homes and valued in school may also occur in language-minority homes. Language and literacy socialization may include many other patterns as well. To the extent that the mainstream patterns occur repeatedly and with some intensity, children in some language-minority families will succeed in school regardless of the language used for socialization purposes. This is because some children enter school with the scripts and discourse structures that are shared and reinforced by teachers (Saville-Troike & Kleifgen, 1986, p. 219). Recall that the Socialization Mismatch Hypothesis predicts that children are more likely to succeed in school when the home language and literacy socialization patterns are similar to those that are used and valued in school. Let us now examine how language and literacy socialization is practiced in two language-minority groups in order to see the extent to which the patterns differ from those found in mainstream homes.

A Cautionary Note

Before beginning the following section on language-minority socialization patterns, however, it is essential to remember that the descriptions to be presented are purposefully general and that any individual member of a sociocultural group may behave differently from the pattern that may characterize the group. The descriptions are based upon ethnographic research conducted specifically to learn about the language socialization practices used in the homes of certain language-minority families through long-term participant observation and careful analysis (Spradley, 1980). As descriptions, ethnographies are not deterministic. Their goal instead is to present an accurate account of life patterns of individuals belonging to the same sociocultural group (Erickson, 1986). Other group members may behave in ways similar to those described in the ethnographies, but their behavior is never determined by their group membership.

Language and Literacy Socialization in Recently Arrived Mexican-Origin Families

In the discussion that follows, the focus is restricted to Mexican families who immigrated to the United States in the last two decades, making them relatively recent arrivals. Many of these families have established themselves within communities and are part of the workforce. While the children of some of these families enter school knowing a little English, most come to school as monolingual speakers of Spanish. (See Losey, 1996; Matute-Bianchi, 1986; and Keefe & Padilla, 1987, for a fuller discussion of patterns of homelife, school, and work in Mexican-origin communities across the United States.) Recent arrivals from Mexico tend to settle in communities where other family members already reside or where there are close friends, often from the same region in Mexico. As a result, many recently arrived adults and children are likely to have contact predominantly with Mexican-origin friends and workmates of similar socioeconomic and language backgrounds (Moore & Pachón, 1985).

In terms of caregiving, young children are provided for by both family members and close friends. The responsibility for caregiving is shared among many so that young children are rarely in the company of only one adult. Young children grow up surrounded by other children and are constantly under the watchful eyes of several adults (Heath, 1986a). Children are allowed to play physically and verbally with little adult intervention. Adults talk with children primarily to praise, to scold, and to tease, and when they want to show children how something is done. Older children are immersed in the prattle of younger children and both are exposed to a rich measure of talk by an assortment of speakers who use language for many functions.

Although children grow up in a talk-filled environment, relatively little of the talk generated by adults is addressed to preschool children (Heath, 1986a). Young children are not considered to be equal conversational partners, and adults do not take the child's perspective in talking to them. While children accompany adults to most social gatherings, they are expected to talk with other children and not with adults, especially when an adult has already begun talking. Accordingly, children learn to use language with little intervention from their parents and adult relatives. The most important language instruction adults offer concerns language used for showing respect for and politeness toward elders (Heath, 1986a).

Adults ask young children for labels of objects of immediate concern, such as body parts, family members' names, and play objects. However, only rarely are children invited to label the names of objects and people in books or on television. Mothers typically do not engage in labeling exchanges with their young children, and seldom is labeling done to teach vocabulary items. Adults tend not to invite children to explain their interpretation of events to other adults. Children hear adults' interpretations of events and hear them negotiate meanings through questions, but are not invited to participate in the building of meaning or in presenting their view of the event.

Likewise, parents seldom ask questions that require children to recite the sequence of known events or to foretell their plans for the day. If parents already know the sequence for some action that the child recently experienced or will experience in the near future, they usually do not request the child to tell about the event just for the sake of recounting or forecasting. An exception might be when a third party needs to know about a special event. In this case, the parent may ask the child to talk about the event and then will fill in information as needed. Parents do request accounts from children and ask questions about the account as it is being told. Pease-Alvarez (1991) has documented the frequent use of contingency questions (questions that occur directly in response to information just given) during account episodes. Accounts are requested most often during intimate family gatherings and concern topics ranging from daily activities to unusual accomplishments.

Children learn appropriate language and other behaviors by observing and repeating actions that parents, relatives, and friends have demonstrated in highly contextualized settings. Hence, exchanges in which the child eventcasts to an adult and vice versa seldom happen. A cooperative form of eventcasting occurs when family members exchange ideas for future plans, such as returning to Mexico or how to help a relative from Mexico get situated in the neighborhood.

Of the four narrative forms, stories figure most prominently in the lives of recently arrived Mexican-origin families. There are many kinds of stories that adults enjoy telling and young children enjoy hearing. Some stories involve fantasy and tales of witches, others tell of real events and historical figures. Adolescents spend hours telling stories and giving accounts of friends' escapades. Parents and relatives occasionally read stories to young children, but most storybook reading occurs when older siblings read aloud or when children play school with other children. Spanish-language children's books are not commonly found in the home (although Moll, 1990, disputes this, claiming that many of the Mexicans he studied in Tucson, Arizona, had Spanish-language children's books). In Mexico, children's storybooks are generally not available to the masses and many recently arrived families may have little experience with Spanish-language storybooks in the home (Faltis, 1989). Adults and older children often read *novelas* (soap-opera-type magazines), comic books, and abridged novels printed in paperback. While these reading materials contain many of the features found in storybooks, they are not the kind of stories that are told and retold to young children.

Language and Literacy Socialization in Chinese-Origin Families

In this section, the discussion focuses on the language and literacy learning environment of middle- and working-class post-1965 Chinese-American families. (For a more detailed account of life, language, and work patterns of the "new" Chinese in the United States see Chen, 1981; Tsai, 1986; and Wong, 1988. Lee, 1984, provides an ethnography of East Asian student experiences.) In 1980, more than 63% of the Chinese in the United States were foreign born, and a majority lived in urban settings in California and Hawaii, which account for nearly 57% of the Chinese-American population (Wong, 1988).

In Chinese-origin families, exchanges in which caregivers request labels for items are tied primarily to the correction of errors (Heath,

1986a). Children are corrected when they misname an object that they want. Corrections occur during reading time and during creative play time. During both activities, the adult's label requests direct the child to provide the correct name of the object or attribute being focused upon.

Questions about meaning and clarification center around appropriate age- and sex-role behaviors. These questions seldom include expressions of emotional evaluation; instead their purpose is to bring attention to why it is essential to act a certain way given the child's place in the family (Heath, 1986a). Lessons about appropriate behavior often occur within the context of a written story. During storybook reading adults ask questions and provide comments about correct behavior, but almost never inquire about or interpret the emotional states of characters presented in the story.

Children are often called upon by adults to give accounts of their daily experiences. They are expected to tell new information in sequence and provide enough detail for the adults to follow without asking many questions. Recounts, which require children to tell something already known to the listener, are relatively rare since children are not ordinarily called upon to perform for adults. In fact, children are expected to remain quiet around non-intimate adults and outside the home, unless they are invited to talk (Schneider & Lee, 1990).

Eventcasts occur around activities that call for adults to model the procedure or plans for completing a task. Boys are typically engaged in fewer eventcasting episodes than girls due to the way tasks are divided between boys and girls. Girls are expected to help in the kitchen and around the house; boys run errands and look after younger children. Hence, girls are exposed to eventcasts about cooking, ironing, sewing, and cleaning, while boys, especially if the father is not at home, do routinized tasks (Heath, 1986a). Nevertheless, both boys and girls are exposed to eventcasts during family discussions of problems or when the parents are planning for outings and other sequential actions.

Adults enjoy telling and reading stories to young children; they often use book stories to tell analogous stories about special people and events from the past.

Analysis of the Differences in Socialization Practices

The ways that children are socialized for language and literacy practices clearly varies from family to family, but it is also evident that families within a particular cultural group tend to socialize their children differently from families in other cultural groups. From the discussion presented above, it can be seen that both the Mexican-origin and the Chinese-origin families exhibit socialization patterns that contrast with the mainstream pattern, though it appears that the socialization practices of Chinese-origin families are more compatible with the mainstream pattern. In fact, Schneider and Lee (1990) point out that socialization behaviors emphasized in Asian families are rewarded in school because they exemplify the desired classroom behavioral traits of being quiet, orderly, and industrious. In a similar vein, Wong Fillmore (1985) notes that mainstream teachers believe that Chinese ESL children become more attentive to classroom tasks and activities that are poorly introduced and described by the teacher.

What do the contrasts mean for the grade-level classroom teacher who has children from Mexican-origin, Asian-origin, and mainstream cultures? According to the Socialization Mismatch Hypothesis, Mexican-origin children are immediately at risk of failing academically because their socialization practices have prepared them to be competent in a set of language and literacy practices that typically are not reinforced or rewarded in school. On the contrary, the school may even discourage certain cultural literacy behaviors such as cooperative storytelling and other forms of sharing (Trueba & Delgado-Gaitán, 1983).

For the Chinese-origin children, the contrasts are less obviously drastic, but are different enough to have serious consequences as children progress through school. For example, the fact that Chinese-origin children tend to be socialized to demonstrate literal interpretations and to remain quiet in the presence of adults means that these children may have less opportunity to develop social interactional skills. One dire consequence of this practice is that Asian-origin children in general are encouraged by both their parents and the school to pursue science and technical professions that are relatively less language-based than other kinds of high-level professions (Schneider & Lee, 1990). This kind of tracking into science-oriented professions has led Asian Americans to become a "middleman minority" group (Kim, 1981; Schneider & Lee, 1990), which is allowed to rise above the professional levels of other minority groups because of a specialized skill and knowledge advantage. However, according to Blalock (1967 in Schneider & Lee, 1990), the middleman minority soon reaches a job ceiling resulting from a combination of dominant-group discrimination and persisting ethnic-group cultural values.

CONTEXTUALIZING THE SOCIALIZATION MISMATCH HYPOTHESIS

The Socialization Mismatch Hypothesis is a relatively context-free explanation for why certain language-minority groups succeed or fail in school.

The hypothesis states that the success or failure depends primarily on the goodness of fit between the language and socialization patterns of the home and those reinforced in school. One feature the hypothesis lacks is reference to the role of context in learning. In other words, consideration needs to be given to the notion that socioacademic performance and language use are also partially dependent on the social organization of learning contexts in the classroom (Erickson, 1986). Without such reference, we would not be able to account for the variable success of certain language-minority children. For example, Philips (1982) found that Native American children were performing very poorly in classroom contexts that required individualized performance and emphasized competitive tasks. These two learning contexts were culturally unfamiliar and threatening to the children: "The notion of a single individual being structurally set apart from all others, in anything other than an observer role, and yet still a part of the group organization, is one that Indian children probably encounter for the first time in school" (Philips, 1972, p. 391).

However, as a result of long-term ethnographic study, Philips learned that the children were able to perform successfully in certain kinds of contexts, particularly those in which the obligation of individual students to perform in public was minimized. Philips attributed the variable performance of the Native American children to classroom conditions that either reinforced or denied structures of participation normally demanded in the home. Drawing on Philips's findings of context-specific performance, Erickson and Mohatt (1982) examined ways to create culturally congruent contexts for learning in classrooms containing Native American and non-Native American children. They found that all students benefited from instruction when teachers learned to vary the participant structures used to activate and evaluate student participation. Moreover, they showed that mainstream Anglo teachers were capable of learning and incorporating participation structures commonly used among the Native American families whose children attended the school.

There are many other examples of context-specific learning environments that are both meaningful and appropriate for language-minority students (e.g., Au & Kawakami, 1984; Delgado-Gaitán, 1991; Gutiérrez, 1992; Macías, 1987; Moll, 1988; 1989; Moll & Díaz, 1987). In each of these studies, as in the Philips case above, notable language and cultural differences existed between the home and the school culture, yet teachers were able to change classroom contexts for learning so that language-minority students improved their socioacademic performance. Díaz, Moll, and Mehan (1986) refer to the fact that teachers can improve learning for language-minority students despite cultural differences as *pedagogically optimistic.* They agree that a measure of school failure among language-minority students can be accounted for by the mismatch between home and school language and literacy socialization patterns, but argue that school failure is also the result of classroom organization patterns that exclude language-minority children from full participation. Thus, the pedagogical optimism expressed by Díaz, Moll, and Mehan comes from the understanding that **teachers can and must change the existing social organization of their classrooms to create a variety of meaningful and culturally appropriate learning environments**.

Making changes in the mainstream all-English classroom environment to include rather than exclude second-language learners requires that we as teachers have (1) an awareness of the kinds of special instructional services that second-language learners have experienced in bilingual and English-as-a-second-language programs; (2) an understanding of how classrooms are socially and physically arranged to support different instructional strategies; (3) an understanding of second-language acquisition and participation principles and how we can incorporate these into learning activities that require two-way communicative oral and written exchanges; (4) a plan to involve the second-language community in both classroom- and school-related activities; and (5) a stance against social injustice and for questioning practices that promote social stratification. All five areas of knowledge and action, which are addressed in subsequent chapters, enable us to plan for and implement the favorable conditions needed to promote socioacademic success, critical consciousness, and equity in linguistically and culturally diverse classrooms.

CONCLUSION

In this chapter, we were introduced to Miss Julia Felix, a first-year teacher assigned to teach a 3rd-grade class of 24 students, seven of whom are second-language learners of English. This kind of classroom composition is increasingly becoming the norm across the United States as new waves of immigrants and their children seek to improve living conditions. Few mainstream all-English classroom teachers are prepared to assist second-language learners in the joining-in process required for participation in and benefit from learning activities. We want to break this pattern and move beyond the status quo! Part of the needed preparation hinges on our understanding of language and literacy socialization differences between language-minority and mainstream communities. As teachers of children from different cultural backgrounds, we need to understand that our particular language and literacy socialization in large part contributes to how we interpret and generate classroom activities. The more we learn about the diverse experiences and needs of our students, the better prepared we will be to question existing practices and create educationally and culturally appropriate activities for all of our students. In the next chapter, Julia Felix discovers that the seven second-language children assigned to her class have had distinct schooling experiences before coming to her class: Three were in bilingual education programs, two were in ESL pullout programs, and two were in classrooms with specially designed academic instruction in English (SDAIE). With Julia, we will examine the nature of these different approaches to preparing (and underpreparing) students for the transition into mainstream English-only classrooms and the historical conditions that have led to the development of educational programs for second-language learners.

ACTIVITIES

1. Observe interaction between a mainstream adult caregiver and a young child for at least 15 minutes. Jot down examples of taking the child's perspective and child-raising as described in this chapter and share them with the class.

2. Ask a mother or father with a toddler (age 2 or 3) if you can tape-record them reading a favorite story to the child. Replay the recording and look for examples of labeling as presented in Table 1.1. Share your best example of "using known information questions" with the class.

3. Select one of the following "pedagogically optimistic" studies to share with the class as a presentation: Au & Kawakami, 1984; Erickson & Mohatt, 1982; Macías, 1987; Moll, 1988, 1989; and Moll & Díaz, 1987. In the presentation, point out how teachers successfully contextualized cultural differences during lessons.

4. Have each student in your class survey at least two different mainstream teachers to find out their views on and fears of teaching limited-English-proficient students in their classrooms. Use the survey in Figure 1.4 on pp. 29–30 (adapted from Penfield, 1987) or modify it to fit your needs. As a class, tally and summarize the results for discussion.

REFERENCES

Applebee, A. (1978). *The child's concept of story.* Chicago: University of Chicago Press.

Au, K., & Kawakami, A. J. (1984). Vygotskian perspectives on discussion processes in small-group reading lessons. In P. L. Peterson, L. C. Wilkinson, & M. Hallinan (Eds.), *The social context of instruction: Group organization and group processes* (pp. 209–225). New York: Academic Press.

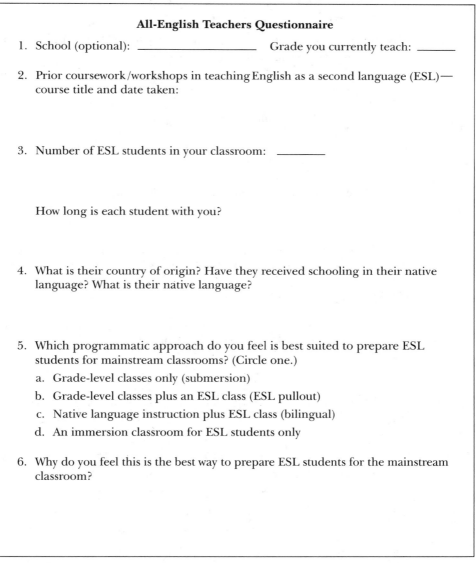

All-English Teachers Questionnaire

1. School (optional): _____ Grade you currently teach: _____

2. Prior coursework/workshops in teaching English as a second language (ESL)—course title and date taken:

3. Number of ESL students in your classroom: _____

   How long is each student with you?

4. What is their country of origin? Have they received schooling in their native language? What is their native language?

5. Which programmatic approach do you feel is best suited to prepare ESL students for mainstream classrooms? (Circle one.)
   a. Grade-level classes only (submersion)
   b. Grade-level classes plus an ESL class (ESL pullout)
   c. Native language instruction plus ESL class (bilingual)
   d. An immersion classroom for ESL students only

6. Why do you feel this is the best way to prepare ESL students for the mainstream classroom?

(continues)

Figure 1.4
Mainstream teachers questionnaire

Blalock, H. (1967). *Toward a theory of minority relations*. New York: John Wiley and Sons.

Carrasquillo, A., & Rodríguez, V. (1996). *Language minority students in the mainstream classroom*. Clevedon, England: Multilingual Matters.

Cazden, C. (1983). Peekaboo as an instructional model: Discourse development at school and at home. In B. Bain (Ed.), *The sociogenesis of language and human conduct: A multidisciplinary book of readings*. New York: Plenum.

All-English Teachers Questionnaire *(cont.)*

7. What criteria does your school use to determine when ESL students are ready for mainsteam, English-only classrooms?

8. When do *you* think they should be placed in a mainstream, English-only classroom?

9. What frustrates you most in teaching ESL students in your classroom?

10. In your opinion, how much of a limited-English-proficient student's school day should be spent with the ESL teacher?

11. In what way do you communicate with the parents of ESL students about their progress/problems in your classroom?

12. Which of the following would help you most in dealing more effectively with ESL students in your class (Choose only 3)?

    _____ Better communication between ESL teachers and regular teachers
    _____ More time to adapt lessons/tasks to ESL students
    _____ Strategies/techniques on how to teach ESL students
    _____ More familiarity with appropriate materials for ESL students
    _____ Information about cultures represented by ESL students
    _____ Materials prepared by the ESL teacher for ESL students in your class

---

Figure 1.4 *Continued*

Cazden, C. (1988). *Classroom discourse: The language of teaching and learning.* Portsmouth, NH: Heinemann.

Chen, J. (1981). *The Chinese of America.* San Francisco: Harper & Row.

Cross, T. (1977). Mothers' speech adjustments: The contributions of selected child listener variables. In C. Snow & C. Ferguson (Eds.), *Talking to children: Language input and acquisition* (pp. 151–188). New York: Cambridge University Press.

Cummins, J. (1986). Empowering minority students: A framework for intervention. *Harvard Educational Review, 56*(1), 18–36.

Delgado-Gaitán, C. (1991). Relating experience and text: Socially constituted reading activity. In M. McGroarty & C. Faltis (Eds.), *Languages in school and society: Policy and pedagogy* (pp. 512–528). Berlin: Mouton de Gruyter.

Delgado-Gaitán, C. (1994). Russian refugee families: Accommodating aspirations through education. *Anthropology and Education, 25,* 137–155.

DeVillar, R. A., & Faltis, C. (1991). *Computers and cultural diversity: Restructuring schools for socio-academic success.* Albany: State University of New York Press.

Díaz, S., Moll, L., & Mehan, H. (1986). Sociocultural resources in instruction: A context-specific approach. In California State Department of Education (Ed.), *Beyond language: Social and cultural factors in schooling language minority students* (pp. 187–230). Los Angeles: California State University, Los Angeles.

Edelsky, C. (1991). *With literacy and justice for all: Rethinking the social in language education.* New York: Falmer Press.

Erickson, F. (1986). Qualitative methods in research on teaching. In M. C. Wittrock (Ed.), *Handbook of research on teaching* (3rd ed.) (pp. 119–161). New York: Macmillan.

Erickson, F., & Mohatt, G. (1982). Cultural organization of participant structures in two classrooms of Indian students. In G. D. Spindler (Ed.), *Doing the ethnography of schooling* (pp. 132–174). New York: Holt, Rinehart & Winston.

Faltis, C. (1989). Spanish language cooperation-fostering storybooks for language minority children in bilingual programs. *Journal of Educational Issues of Language Minority Students, 5,* 46–55.

Ferguson, C. (1977). Baby talk as a simplified register. In C. Snow & C. Ferguson (Eds.), *Talking to children: Language input and acquisition* (pp. 209–237). New York: Cambridge University Press.

General Accounting Office. (1987). *Bilingual education: Information on limited English proficient students.* Washington, DC: Author.

Gutiérrez, K. D. (1992). A comparison of instructional contexts in writing process classrooms with Latino children. *Education and Urban Society, 24,* 244–262.

Harklau, L. (1994). Tracking and linguistic minority students: Consequences of ability grouping for second language learners. *Linguistics and Education, 6,* 217–244.

Heath, S. B. (1982). What no bedtime story means: Narrative skills at home and school. *Language in Society, 11*(2), 49–76.

Heath, S. B. (1983). *Ways with words: Language, life, and work in communities and classrooms.* New York: Cambridge University Press.

Heath, S. B. (1986a). Sociocultural contexts of language development. In California State Department of Education (Ed.), *Beyond language: Social and cultural factors in schooling language minority students* (pp. 143–186). Los Angeles: California State University, Los Angeles.

Heath, S. B. (1986b). Separating 'things of the imagination' from life: Learning to read and write. In W. H. Teale & E. Sulzby (Eds.), *Emergent literacy: Writing and reading* (pp. 156–172). Norwood, NJ: Ablex.

Heath, S. B. (1989). The learner as cultural member. In M. L. Rice & R. L. Schiefelbusch (Eds.), *The teachability of language* (pp. 333–350). Baltimore, MD: Paul H. Brookes.

Heath, S. B. & Thomas, C. (1984). The achievement of preschool literacy for mother and child. In H. Goelman, A. Oberg, & F. Smith (Eds.), *Awakening to literacy* (pp. 51–72). Exeter, NH: Heinemann Educational.

Keefe, S. E., & Padilla, A. M. (1987). *Chicano ethnicity.* Albuquerque, NM: University of New Mexico Press.

Kim, I. (1981). *New urban immigrants: The Korean community in New York.* Princeton, NJ: Princeton University Press.

Lee, Y. (1984). *A comparative study of East Asian American and Anglo American academic achievement: An ethnographic study.* Doctoral dissertation. Evanston, IL: Northwestern University.

Lessow-Hurley, J. (1990). *The foundations of dual language instruction.* New York: Longman.

Losey, K. (1996). *"Listen to the silences": Mexican American interaction in the composition classroom and the community.* Norwood, NJ: Ablex.

Macías, J. (1987). The hidden curriculum of Papago teachers: American Indian strategies for mitigating cultural discontinuity in early schooling. In G. Spindler & L. Spindler (Eds.), *Interpretative ethnography of education: At home and abroad* (pp. 363–380). Hillsdale, NJ: Lawrence Erlbaum Associates.

Macías, R. (1995). California LEP enrollment continues slow growth in 1995. *UC Linguistic Minority Research Institute, 5*(1), 1–2.

Matute-Bianchi, M. (1986). Ethnic identities and patterns of school success and failure among Mexican-descent and Japanese American students in a California high school: An ethnographic analysis. *American Journal of Education, 95*(1), 233–255.

Mehan, H. (1981). What time is it, Denise?: Asking known information questions in classroom discourse. *Theory into Practice, 18*(4), 285–294.

Merino, B., & Quintanar, R. (April, 1988). *The recruitment of minority students into*

teaching careers: A status report of effective approaches. Paper presented at the Far West Holmes Group Meeting, University of Colorado, Boulder.

Michaels, S. (1981). Sharing time: Children's narrative style and differential access to literacy. *Language in Society, 10*(1), 423–442.

Milk, R. (1985). The changing role of ESL in bilingual education. *TESOL Quarterly, 19*(4), 657–672.

Moll, L. (1988). Some key issues in teaching Latino students. *Language Arts, 65*(5), 465–472.

Moll, L. (1989). Teaching second language students: A Vygotskian perspective. In D. M. Johnson & D. H. Roen (Eds.), *Richness in writing: Empowering ESL students* (pp. 55–69). New York: Longman.

Moll, L. (Ed.). (1990). *Vygotsky and education.* New York: Cambridge University Press.

Moll, L., & Díaz, S. (1987). Change as the goal of educational research. *Anthropology and Education Quarterly, 18*(4), 300–311.

Moore, J., & Pachón, H. (1985). *Hispanics in the United States.* Upper Saddle River, NJ: Prentice Hall.

National Coalition of Advocates for Students. (1985). *Barriers to excellence: Our children at risk.* Boston: Author.

Ninio, A., & Bruner, J. (1978). The achievement and antecedents of labelling. *Journal of Child Language, 5*(1), 1–15.

Oakes, J. (1986). *Keeping track: How schools structure inequality.* New Haven: Yale University Press.

Ochs, E., & Schieffelin, B. (1982). Language acquisition and socialization: Three developmental stories and their implications. *Working Papers in Sociolinguistics,* Number 105. Austin, TX: Southwest Educational Development Laboratory.

Ogbu, J., & Matute-Bianchi, M. E. (1986). Understanding sociocultural factors:

Knowledge, identity, and school adjustment. In California State Department of Education (Ed.), *Beyond language: Social and cultural factors in schooling language minority students* (pp. 73–142). Los Angeles: California State University, Los Angeles.

Olson, L. (1988). Study finds few minorities reach the end of "educational pipeline." *Education Week, 8*(9), 5.

Pallas, A., Natriello, G., & McDill, E. (1989). The changing nature of the disadvantaged population: Current dimensions and future trends. *Educational Research, 18,* 16-22.

Pease-Alvarez, L. (1991). Home and school contexts for language development: The experience of two Mexican-American pre-schoolers. In M. McGroarty & C. Faltis (Eds.), *Languages in school and society: Policy and pedagogy* (pp. 487–509). Berlin: Mouton de Gruyter.

Penfield, J. (1987). ESL: The regular classroom teacher's perspective. *TESOL Quarterly, 21*(1), 21–39.

Philips, S. (1972). Participant structures and communicative competence: Warm Springs children in community and classroom. In C. Cazden, V. John, & D. Hymes (Eds.), *Functions of language in the classroom* (pp. 370–394). New York: Teachers College Press.

Philips, S. (1982). *The invisible culture: Communication in classroom and community on the Warm Springs Indian Reservation.* New York: Longman.

Saville-Troike, M., & Kleifgen, J. (1986). Scripts for school: Cross-cultural communication in elementary classrooms. *Text, 6*(2), 207–221.

Schneider, B., & Lee, Y. (1990). A model for academic success: The school and home environment of East Asian students. *Education and Anthropology Quarterly, 21*(4), 358–387.

Spradley, J. (1980). *Participant observation.* New York: Holt, Rinehart & Winston.

Stein, N. (1982). What's in a story? Interpreting the interpretations of story grammars. *Discourse Processes, 5,* 319–336.

Sue, S., & Padilla, A. M. (1986). Ethnic minority issues in the United States: Challenges for the educational system. In California State Department of Education (Ed.), *Beyond language: Social and cultural factors in schooling language minority students* (pp. 35–72). Los Angeles: California State University, Los Angeles.

Teale, W. (1984). Reading to young children: Its significance to literacy development. In H. Goelman, A. Oberg, & F. Smith (Eds.), *Awakening to literacy* (pp. 110–121). Exeter, NH: Heinemann Educational.

Trueba, H. T., & Delgado-Gaitán, C. (1983). Socialization of Mexican children for cooperation and competition: Sharing and copying. *Journal of Educational Equity and Leadership, 5*(3), 189–204.

Tsai, S. H. (1986). *The Chinese experience in America.* Bloomington: University of Indiana Press.

U.S. Bureau of the Census. (1984). *The 1980 census of the population.* Washington, DC: U.S. Government Printing Office.

U.S. Bureau of the Census. (1988). *The Hispanic population in the United States: March 1986 and 1987.* Washington, DC: U.S. Government Printing Office.

U.S. Bureau of the Census. (1989). *Population estimates by race and Hispanic origin for states, metropolitan areas, and selected counties, 1980 to 1985.* Washington, DC: U.S. Government Printing Office.

U.S. Bureau of the Census. (1995). *1990 Census of the Population, Volume I, Characteristics of the populations.* Washington, DC: U.S. Government Printing Office.

U.S. Department of Education. (1993). *Descriptive study of services to limited Eng-*

lish proficient students. Washington, DC: Planning and Evaluation Service.

W-B Olsen, Roger E. (1993). *Enrollment statistics of limited English proficient students in the United States (1985–1993)*. Alexandria, VA: TESOL.

Waggoner, D. (1993). 1993 census shows dramatic change in the foreign-born population in the US. *NABE News, 16*(7), 1, 18–20.

Waggoner, D., & O'Malley, J. M. (1985). Teachers of limited English proficient children in the United States. *NABE Journal, 9*(3), 25–42.

Willy, T. (1975). *Oral aspects in the primitive fiction of newly literate children.* ERIC document No. ED 112 381.

Wink, J. (September, 1993). Labels often reflect educators' beliefs and practices. *BEOutreach,* 28–29.

Wong, S. C. (1988). The language situation of Chinese Americans. In S. L. McKay & S. C. Wong (Eds.), *Language diversity: Problem or resource?* (pp. 193–228). New York: Newbury House.

Wong Fillmore, L. (1985). When does teacher talk work as input? In S. Gass & C. Madden (Eds.), *Input in second language acquisition* (pp. 17–50). Rowley, MA: Newbury House.

Chapter Two

Pathways to the All-English Classroom

OVERVIEW

Section 1703(f) of the Equal Educational Opportunity Act of 1974 states that schools with limited-English-proficiency students are required by federal law to "take appropriate action to overcome language barriers that impede equal participation by its students in its instructional programs." Furthermore, the *Lau Remedies* state that Section 1703(f) applies to school districts having 20 or more English learners (Avila & Godog, 1979). In this chapter, we will review the legal policies that protect language-minority students from inferior schooling practices, and we will examine the kinds of options and obligations schools have in addressing the special needs of second-language learners. Moreover, we will learn about the criteria that schools use for placing second-language learners in special language programs, for reclassifying them once in a program, and for determining when they are no longer eligible to receive such services.

EPISODE TWO: FINDING OUT ABOUT BILINGUAL PROGRAMS

In the main office, Julia Felix asks the secretary, Mrs. Contreras, if she can see the cumulative files of the seven English-as-a-second-language students assigned to her class. Obligingly, Mrs. Contreras goes directly to the green filing cabinet to search for the files. Fortunately, all of the files are there, and Julia carefully packs them into her large straw purse, thanks Mrs. Contreras, and returns to her classroom. Back at her desk, Julia neatly lays out the folders and begins looking through them, one by one. To her amazement, she notices several terms present in each folder that are completely new to her: *NEP, LEP, Transitional Bilingual Program,*

Language Assessment Scales, IDEA Test, and *ESL Pullout Program.* What in the world is a NEP? Are NEPs and LEPs somehow related? Why have some of the students been in bilingual programs and others in ESL programs? How long each day do students receive structured English-as-a-second-language instruction? How long will they continue to receive this special language instruction? Do the teachers who work with the students also speak their language? Julia knows bilingual programs are where students learn to read and write in their native language as well as learn English, but doesn't recall the technical meaning of "transitional" bilingual programs. She surmises that the Language Assessment Scales and the IDEA test must be language tests, but having never heard of them, has no idea what language abilities they test for, who administers them, and whether they are used initially for placement or terminally for exiting a program.

Where can Julia turn for help in finding answers to these questions? Her first thought is to ask the principal, remembering that she had mentioned something about special programs when she was interviewing Julia for the position. Returning to the main office, she makes an appointment for early afternoon to see Mrs. Turner, the principal.

The visit with Mrs. Turner turns out to be very informative. Julia learns that the district has operated a bilingual/ESL program for the last 10 years, and that in the last 5 years, the number of students served by the programs has tripled. Mrs. Turner talks about the criteria for entry into a bilingual/ESL program, about the major kinds of services offered, and generally about how and when children are exited from the program. At this point, Julia learns that all of the ESL students assigned to her class will continue to receive some native language and ESL instruction, most likely for the entire year, as all of them still need additional proficiency in English. Julia asks why the students aren't in bilingual classes for the entire day so they can keep up with the classwork while they are acquiring English. Mrs. Turner laments that there just aren't enough bilingual teachers beyond the 2nd grade. But on a brighter note, she adds that most of the English learners assigned to her class are pretty good readers in their native language.

Julia is puzzled and asks, "I don't understand. How does being able to read well in their first language make a difference?" "Oh, it makes a whole lot of difference," replies Mrs. Turner. "There's an old saying in education, Julia, and that is that children only learn to read once. The children who have learned to read and write for meaning in their native language will do fine in your class because they have the fundamentals of written language. In other words, they already have a pretty good idea what reading and writing are about." "That's good to hear," says Julia. "But what about the children who aren't such good readers in the first language?" Mrs. Turner pauses to think and then says, "Those children will need to be immersed in print and story reading. And I am assuming that the children will have extra help with a bilingual teacher whenever possible—and for sure, with an ESL teacher. I know the teachers in our bilingual program and they work really hard at helping the children become creative, productive, and curious learners." Mrs. Turner brings the discussion to an end by asking Julia to try and learn more about bilingual education programs to get a better picture of the kinds of experiences the English learners in her class will and won't have had.

The principal's suggestion piques Julia's curiosity about bilingual/ESL programs, prompting questions not only about its history, but also how and why it works. That very afternoon, Julia decides to detour from her normal route home and stop at the library to check out some books on bilingual education in the United States. What follows is a summary of what Julia learned from her readings on bilingual education.

A BRIEF ACCOUNT OF BILINGUAL EDUCATION IN THE UNITED STATES

The Bilingual Education Act of 1968

Broad support for bilingual education began in 1968 with the signing of the Bilingual Education Act (BEA). Prior to 1968, few school districts serving large numbers of non-English-speaking children considered implementing bilingual education to prepare these children for English-only schooling. Nearly all non-English-speaking children attending public schools were submerged in English-only classrooms, left on their own to either sink or swim. Unfortunately, many of these children sank long before finishing high school. In the mid-1960s, bilingual education began to receive national recognition because of its success with Cuban refugee children at the Coral Way School in Dade County, Florida (Mackey & Beebe, 1977). The Coral Way bilingual program soon spread to other elementary and secondary schools in Dade County, and by the late 1960s, several cities in the Southwest began to locally support bilingual education programs (Malakoff & Hakuta, 1990).

As the decade of the 1960s came to a close, the federal government was ready to accept bilingual education as a means to combat school failure among the nation's poor, many of whom were non-English-speaking children. The acceptance of bilingual education was fueled by a number of social and political events that began to surface around the mid-1960s (Judd, 1978, in August & García, 1988). First, bilingual education had been effective in Dade County with Cuban refugee children. Second, research conducted in the early and mid-1960s supported a positive relationship between bilingualism and intelligence (Lambert & Peal, 1962; Jacobs & Pierce, 1966). Third, there was a strong national move toward cultural pluralism accompanied by ethnic revitalization, both of which were fueled by the Civil Rights movement. Fourth, President Lyndon Johnson believed strongly that the way to win the War on Poverty was through increasing educational spending. Fifth, the Elementary and Secondary Education Act of 1965 had already paved the way for federal intervention in schooling efforts targeted for poor, low-achieving students. Sixth, to combat the spread of communism from Cuba, the United States stepped up its involvement in Central and South America, resulting in the need for increased numbers of bilingual government employees. Seventh, a renewed interest in foreign language instruction developed as a result of the launching of *Sputnik*. Eighth, the 1960 census data indicated that the Spanish-surnamed population had increased by more than 50%—from 2.3 million in 1950 to nearly 3.5 million in 1960. The data also indicated that Spanish-speaking children were faring poorly in school, and that education was a primary concern of Hispanics. Last, a number of powerful Hispanic interest groups had begun to support specific instructional programs, such as bilingual education, ESL, and the teaching of Hispanic culture.

So, in January 1967, when Texas Senator Ralph Yarborough introduced a four-and-a-half-page bill, known as the Bilingual Education Act, for consideration as the Title VII amendment to the Elementary and Secondary Education Act of 1965, the social and political tone of the nation was ripe for its passage. Senator Yarborough's original bill was intended to provide assistance to local education agencies for setting up bilingual programs for low-income, native Spanish-speaking children for whom English was a foreign language. By mid-year, however, there was considerable pressure placed on the Senator to expand the assistance to all low-income, non-English-speaking groups in the United States, which he did in order to pass the bill through the Senate. President Lyndon Johnson signed the bill into law on January 2, 1968, making bilingual education a federal policy for the first time in the history of the United States.

The BEA defined bilingual education as a federal policy "to provide financial assistance to local educational agencies to carry out new and imaginative elementary and secondary school programs" to meet the special educational needs of "children who are educationally disadvantaged because of their inability to speak English" (PL 90-247, Sec. 702). While the BEA of 1968 did not specifically mandate or define the kinds of programs that schools should use, grants were awarded only to applicants who (1) developed and operated bilingual programs for low-income, non-English-speaking students, (2) made efforts to attract and retain bilingual teachers, and (3) established communication between the home and the school.

Bilingual Education in the 1970s

The 1970s produced several important changes to the original BEA policy. The first major change was initiated in 1970, when the Office of Civil Rights sent a formal memorandum to school districts serving LEP students (Malakoff & Hakuta, 1990). The memorandum spelled out the conditions of Title VI of the Civil Rights Act of 1964 in relation to students of English as a second language, noting that a Title VI review team had found "a number of practices which have the effect of denying equality of educational opportunity to Spanish-surnamed pupils" and that these practices "have the effect of discrimination on the basis of national origin" (35 *Federal Register,* 11595, 1970). The memorandum also specified that the school district must take affirmative steps to rectify language deficiencies in cases where "the inability to speak and understand English excludes national origin minority group children from effective participation in the educational program" (35 *Federal Register,* 11595, 1970). The memorandum did not specify what the "affirmative steps" should be nor did it make any mention whatsoever of teaching students in their native language (Malakoff & Hakuta, 1990).

The Office of Civil Rights memorandum set the stage for a series of major legal battles over the legal obligation of school districts receiving federal funds to comply with Title VI guidelines. The single most important legal decision came from the case known as *Lau v. Nichols.* In 1970, a class-action suit filed by Chinese parents in San Francisco on behalf of their children claimed that the children were being denied equal educational opportunity. The school district had identified 2,856 non-English-speaking children, but provided ESL instruction to fewer than half of them. The school district did not dispute the number of students in need of special attention nor that it had attempted to serve the needs of this population. The issue of the suit was whether non-English-speaking children were able to receive an equal education in an English-only mainstream classroom and whether the school district had a legal obligation to provide special instructional programs to meet the needs of these children. The federal district court ruled in favor of the school district, finding that, because the non-English-speaking children were receiving the same curriculum in the same classrooms as English-speaking children, they were being treated no differently and thus were not being discriminated against by the school district. Accordingly, the court ruled that the school district was under no obligation to provide special services to non-English-speaking students. Instead, the court encouraged the school district to address the program as an educational rather than a legal obligation to the students (August & García, 1988). The ruling was appealed to the Ninth Circuit District Court of Appeals, which upheld the lower court's decision on January 8, 1973. But the dispute did not end there. The case was appealed to and eventually decided upon by the Supreme Court in the following year.

In 1972, a federal district court in New Mexico had addressed the same legal issues in a case involving Mexican-American children in the Portales Municipal School district. In *Serna v. Portales Municipal Schools,* however, the court found that non-English-speaking Mexican-American children were being treated *differently* when they received the same curriculum as native English-speaking children and thus were being discriminated against (Malakoff & Hakuta, 1990). In response to the ruling, the school district submitted a non-bilingual plan as a remedy to the problem, but the court rejected it, based on expert testimony presented at the court hearing. The school district appealed to the Tenth Circuit Court of Appeals, which in 1974 ruled in favor of the plaintiffs, finding that the students' Title VI rights had been violated and that as a result they had a right to bilingual education.

The Supreme Court handed down the *Lau v. Nichols* decision in favor of the students and their parents in 1974. The Supreme Court justices avoided the constitutional question of equal protection (the 14th Amendment), and instead, as in *Serna v. Portales Municipal Schools,* relied heavily on Title VI of the Civil Rights Act of 1964 and the Office of Civil Rights memorandum issued in 1970. The court found that guidelines outlined in the 1970 Office of Civil Rights memorandum "clearly indicate that affirmative efforts to give special training for non-English-speaking pupils are required by Title VI as a condition to federal aid to public schools" (414 U.S. 569). Moreover, the court found that students with limited knowledge of English who are submersed in mainstream classes are "effectively foreclosed from any meaningful education" (414 U.S. 566).

The *Lau* decision did not impose any particular educational remedy, such as (native language) bilingual education or English-as-a-second-language instruction. Instead, the court recommended that school districts take into account the numbers of students involved when making decisions concerning an appropriate remedy, suggesting that a remedy may differ from setting to setting.

For those school districts wishing to establish or continue with federally funded bilingual education programs, there were new guidelines to follow under the 1974 amendment to the BEA, which in effect provided the first governmental definition of bilingual education, choosing to define it in transitional terms as "instruction given in, and study of English, and to the extent necessary to allow a child to progress effectively through the education system, the native language" (Schneider, 1976, pp. 436–37).

In the same year, following the *Lau* decision, Congress legislated the Supreme Court ruling into the Equal Educational Opportunity Act (EEOA) of 1974. The major effect of this new legislation was to extend the *Lau* decision to all public school districts, not just those receiving federal funds. As of 1974, a school district with students who are speakers of languages other than English in any one of its schools is required to "take appropriate action to overcome language barriers that impede equal participation by its students in its instructional programs" (20 U.S.C. Sec. 1703(f)). Section 1703(f) of the EEOA was especially significant because it addressed the issue of "discriminatory effect" vs. "discriminatory intent" (Malakoff & Hakuta, 1990), declaring that schools could be in violation of Title VI of the Civil Rights Act if second-language students were not receiving some sort of special instructional remedy (discriminatory effect) **even if no substantial intent to discriminate was found.** Following the pattern of earlier legislation, however, the EEOA did not single out any particular instructional remedy as appropriate, leaving the choice between transitional bilingual education and English-as-a-second-language programs up to the local districts. Moreover, in the ensuing years, the power of the Section 1703(f) has become increasingly diluted as the courts have continually ruled that local districts would not be subject to taking "appropriate action" without first having the opportunity for due process; that is, to be heard on a case-by-case basis (McFadden, 1983).

Also in 1974, in the wake of the *Lau* decision, the Department of Heath, Education and Welfare appointed a task force to establish guidelines for implementing the decision. The guidelines, issued in 1975 under the name *Lau Remedies,* directed school districts having 20 or more students of the same language group having a primary language other than English (1) to establish a means for identifying all students whose primary language is not English, (2) to evaluate the English-language proficiency of these students, and (3) to provide them with appropriate bilingual education programs.

Unfortunately, since the guidelines were applied only to districts found to be out of compliance with Title VI or the EEOA, their application has not been widespread (Malakoff & Hakuta, 1990). Moreover, Avila and Godoy (1979) point out that when cases are brought to trial, the courts are inclined to examine the guidelines in terms of the ratio between the number of English learners and the total school population. Thus, a large school system may not be required to implement a bilingual program for its students who are speakers of languages other than English even though the number of these students exceeds the minimum specified in the Lau Remedies. Nonetheless, the Remedies remain in effect today, and together with Section 1703(f) of the EEOA of 1974, they continue to be a major force in supporting the rights of second-language students to have access to bilingual education programs under certain circumstances.

Bilingual Education in the 1980s

By the early 1980s bilingual education increasingly was coming under fire from anti-bilingual-education forces, including certain members of the Republican Party (Padilla, 1990; August & García, 1988, p. 84). The Office of Planning, Budget and Evaluation sponsored a report by Baker and de Kanter (1981) to review the effectiveness of bilingual education as compared to English-only approaches (structured immersion and English-as-a-second-language programs). Baker and de Kanter found that second-language children receiving English-only approaches performed as well in English and other content areas as students in bilingual education programs. The Baker and de Kanter report concluded that bilingual education, which is, in the short run, more costly to school districts, should not be the only approach for remedying the needs of second-language learners. (This study has been fiercely contested on the grounds that it was poorly designed, methodologically flawed, and extremely biased. See Willig, 1985, 1987; Yates & Ortiz, 1983; Hakuta, 1986, pp. 220–222 for criticisms of the study.)

The Baker and de Kanter report set the tone for some significant changes in bilingual education policy in the 1980s. In 1984, the BEA was amended to more strictly define the nature of transitional bilingual education programs and to allow school districts more flexibility in the kinds of educational remedies from which to choose. Transitional bilingual education programs were now required to have a structured English language component, one that was tied directly to eligibility testing and subject to approval by experts in the field. Prior to 1984, an English language component had been required, but there were no controls on the kinds of programs that school districts could use. Under the 1984 amendment to the BEA, special alternative instructional programs not requiring the use of a child's native language were now allowed and even encouraged for certain populations. However, the special alternative programs had several guidelines to follow to receive Title VII funding: (1) They needed to have specifically designed curricula; (2) they had to be appropriate for the language and educational needs of the students; and (3) they had to provide structured English language instruction to enable a child to achieve competence in English. The amended BEA of 1984 also established an Office of Bilingual Education and Minority Language Affairs and appointed a director to oversee it.

A major policy change to the BEA occurred in 1988. The amended act requires that federal monies to support bilingual education programs be divided between transitional bilingual education programs (75%) and special alternative instruction programs (25%). This represents the greatest percentage of federal support for nonnative language instruction programs to date. The 1988 BEA also limits the amount of time that a student can spend in a transitional bilingual or a special alternative instruction program to 3 years. Students can be enrolled for a fourth or fifth year "only if teachers and school personnel familiar with the students' overall academic progress have conducted an evaluation. The results of the evaluation must be made available to students' parents. The fourth and fifth year emphasis must be on English acquisition" (August & García, 1988, p. 92). This particular requirement calls special attention to the exit criteria used to declare students ineligible for special instructional services. Finally, the 1988 BEA obliges schools to make every effort to provide information to students' parents in a language they understand—a requirement that is specifically addressed in the joinfostering framework.

Several important court cases involving bilingual education were decided throughout the 1980s. In *Castañeda v. Pickard* (1981), the Fifth Circuit Court of Appeals once again found that schools must address the special language needs of students who are adding English as a second language. But the central issue of this Arizona case was really whether the court has the authority to direct a school to use a specific educational remedy. The plaintiffs argued for transitional bilingual education as the "appropriate action" for students of Mexican or Yaqui ancestry, citing Section 1703(f) of the Equal Educational Opportunity Act of 1974. The court responded that Section 1703(f) did not require any particular form of remedy, and so the task of determining the appropriateness of a given program for a given school district was up to the particular judge presiding over the case. However, in an unprecedented move, the court presented three criteria that judges should use for determining the "appropriateness" of a particular remedy in subsequent cases:

1. The program must be based on sound educational theory;
2. the program must be implemented in a effective manner;
3. the program, after a period of "reasonable implementation," must produce results to substantiate that language barriers are being overcome (August & García, 1988).

Criterion number two was especially significant because it spoke to the need for capable educational personnel, materials, and other relevant support needed to ensure effective program implementation. In other words, for whatever program model a school district chooses to address the needs of second-language students, the district must provide evidence that the staff and materials are suitable for the program. An unanticipated result of *Castañeda v. Pickard*, therefore, was support for the idea that teaching staff working in bilingual and ESL programs must be specialists in bilingual and second-language teaching and learning. Implicit in this ruling was the need to create new state-approved credential and endorsement programs for ESL teachers and to upgrade professional coursework in existing bilingual teacher education programs to reflect the changing role of ESL instruction in bilingual education. (See Faltis, 1993b, for an overview of practices in bilingual/ESL K–12 instruction and Kreidler, 1987, for a description of nationwide ESL endorsement and credential program requirements.)

Teacher abilities were also a major concern in *Keyes v. School District No. 1* (1983). The suit was originally filed in 1969 as a class action of minority parents on behalf of their children attending the Denver Public Schools, which segregated them on the basis of their ethnic background. The plaintiffs won their case in 1974 but, at the urging of the Congress of Hispanic Educators, they returned to court to argue that years of segregation and inferior education required a special remedy above and beyond the school district's desegregation efforts. In late 1983, the court, following the three criteria presented in the *Castañeda v. Pickard* decision, ruled in favor of the plaintiffs, stating that the school district had failed to develop an educationally sound program for its language-minority students and that teachers in the existing programs were pedagogically underprepared.

The issue of teacher preparation in transitional bilingual and special alternative instruction programs was again brought up in a class-action suit known as *Teresa P. et al. v. Berkeley Unified School District* (1989). In this case the plaintiffs alleged that the rights of students who were adding English as a second language were being violated by the Berkeley, California, USD because the students were being taught by teachers who did not have bilingual or ESL teaching credentials. However, at the heart of the case was the plaintiffs' assertion that English learners were being exited too quickly from the bilingual programs and that students placed in the district's English-only (ESL) program were being denied comprehensible instruction precisely because teachers lacked the necessary preparation in second-language methodology. The court ruled that Berkeley's programs for ESL students satisfied Section 1703(f) of the Equal Education Opportunity Act of 1974. Ruling in favor of the defendants, the court found that Berkeley's English-only (ESL) program was no less effective than the native-language transitional program in developing students' English-language proficiency. Moreover, the court found that federal standards concerning the effective delivery of programs outlined in *Castañeda v. Pickard* did not require teachers of ESL students to have special credentials.

Teresa P. v. Berkeley USD may have serious consequences for both native-language bilingual and ESL instruction in the future. If school districts decide to follow the ruling, the quality of instruction provided second-language learners in both bilingual and ESL classrooms will probably diminish, since greater numbers of poorly prepared teachers will be teaching in bilingual and ESL classrooms. (See Sánchez & Walker de Felix, 1986, for an account of how untrained and inept teachers were routinely placed in ESL classrooms.) Consequently, fewer students will be exiting with higher levels of English proficiency. Moreover, because the ruling concludes that bilingual education is no more effective than English-only instruction, and the latter is hailed as less expensive than the former, it is likely that more school districts will apply for Title VII money under the 1988 provision that set aside 25% of funding for special alternative instruction programs. Finally, as nonnative-language approaches to bilingual education gain in popularity, it is possible that the next amendment to Title VII will increase the percentage of support for special alternative instruction programs and decrease support for transitional bilingual education.

Bilingual Education in the 1990s

There have been many changes in funding patterns, legal decisions, and public opinion since the birth of bilingual education. While funding did not significantly diminish in the 1970s and 1980s, it is clear that the proportion of funding for nonbilingual special alternative instruction (English-only) programs has increased significantly, from zero to 25%. At the same time, the proportion of funding for native-language bilingual instruction has decreased from 100% to 75%. The shift in funding emphasis is also showing up in the number of English learners being served by bilingual education programs as compared with ESL students in nonbilingual programs. A study conducted by the National Education Association (Rodríguez, 1990) found that in the 1989 academic year, bilingual education programs served only an estimated 5.6% of all students who were speakers of languages other than English. The rest were presumably served either by special English instruction (ESL) or provided no help at all (submersion). The number of students served by bilingual programs has decreased considerably from 1980, when Stein (1986) estimated that bilingual programs served approximately 10% of all students in need of bilingual education.

The legal system has consistently decided in favor of second-language learners' right to equal educational opportunities, but has repeatedly resisted handing down a ruling that prescribes a particular remedy as more appropriate than another. The effect of leaving the decision up to the district has been that many districts are choosing bilingual education programs over other forms of instruction. But the pressure has been great to switch to English-only remedies. As of 1988, only 22 states even allowed native-language use for instruction in bilingual programs (August & García, 1988). In the late 1980s, a newly formed group calling itself "U.S. English" began to mount a large-scale attack on any attempt to use languages other than English for schooling and governmental affairs. (See Rossell, 1989, as an example of anti-bilingual education research and propaganda.) This group is also responsible for introducing and passing official English-language amendments in several states having large bilingual populations.

Public opinion generally favors bilingual education over English-only special instruction for language-minority children (Hakuta, 1986). Yet there are reports of increasing numbers of non-English-speaking parents specifically requesting English-as-a-second-language programs rather than native-language bilingual programs. For example, Spanish-speaking parents at a school in urban Phoenix, Arizona, which in 1995 had an ESL program, were vociferously opposed to starting up a Spanish-English bilingual program because most of the bilingual teachers were not native speakers of Spanish and, according to the parents, had inadequate proficiency in Spanish to teach content and literacy in that language.

As we move closer to the 21st century, it appears certain that fewer students who are speakers of languages other than English will receive native-language bilingual instruction than ever before. It remains to be seen, however, what role the courts, especially the higher courts, will have in reversing this apparent trend. The matter of whether English-only instruction is an "appropriate remedy" for educating language-minority students or whether other approaches are more suitable under certain conditions will surely continue to be contested as a civil rights issue in the years to come (Daniels, 1990).

In the first half of the 1990s, bilingual education witnessed a rash of pro-English-only propaganda aimed at obliterating the use of languages other than English in the schools. Several of the major Republican candidates for the 1996 presidential election, for example, were openly opposed to bilingual education and the use of non-English languages in public places. In a similar vein, states' rights advocates have continually argued that states should be able to determine for themselves how to educate children who enter school not speaking English.

Bilingual education advocates have mounted an equally energetic counterattack to convince educators and the public that learning through the native language is an effective and equitable means for schooling large numbers of language-minority students. Ramírez, Yuen, and Ramey (1991) and Rosier and Holm (1980) found long-term benefits of late-exit bilingual programs. Christian (1994) has also found language and academic benefits for two-way bilingual education programs. Moreover, the Office of Bilingual Education and Minority Language Affairs, under the direction of Eugene García from 1993 to 1995, made the granting of Title VII monies to schools and school districts contingent upon *school-wide* plans for the incorporation of English learners into all aspects of schooling. This reform is very much in line with joinfostering principles. That is, the entire school has to show how it is involved in the education of English learners, in helping them join in the schooling activities and receive the benefits that schools, as opposed to special programs, have to offer them. One significant result of this reform in Title VII is that all teachers may need to be prepared to work with children who are learning English as an additional language.

PROGRAM DESIGNS

Throughout the preceding section on the history of bilingual education in the United States, mention was made of transitional bilingual education and special alternative (nonnative) language instruction programs. In this section, we will look more closely at the meaning of these program types as well as at the various ways that program designs can be distinguished.

There are lots of ways to organize a discussion on the bilingual education program types (Hornberger, 1991). A reasonable starting distinction is whether the program leads to *additive* or *subtractive* bilingualism (August & García, 1988). The distinction has to do with one of the goals of bilingual education: to add a second language or to minimize the use and importance of the first language. Additive bilingualism is the result of programs that honor and use the student's native language for language arts, literacy, and subject matter instruction along with English for all or most of schooling. In an additive bilingual program, there is an effort to develop in students high levels of proficiency in two languages—the student's native language and English. Additive bilingualism is based on the theory of "less English initially means more English later." The "less equals more" argument derives from the idea that students who acquire high levels of literacy and develop content and discourse knowledge in their native language before acquiring English will not only acquire high levels of English, but will also be able to participate well in English settings because they have the academic base to do so (Cummins, 1979).

Subtractive bilingualism, in contrast, results from programs that provide minimal instruction in the student's native language and do so for a limited amount of time. In this case, the goal is to get students to become English proficient as quickly as possible without developing the native language in the process. One of the eventual results of subtractive bilingualism, therefore, is monolingualism. For this reason alone, subtractive bilingualism is indefensible as a goal, and needs to be questioned and battled whenever possible.

Additive and subtractive bilingual programs can be further distinguished by the manner in which language is distributed during and for instruction. Jacobson (1990) differentiates bilingual instructional methodology in terms of whether the two languages of instruction are used concurrently or separately, yielding eight types of bilingual instructional methodology:

Concurrent Language Models	Separate Language Models
Preview-Review	Content
Concurrent translation	Person
Flip-flopping	Time
New Concurrent Approach	Place

Generally speaking, separate language model methodology is found most often in additive-oriented bilingual programs; concurrent language methodology, in subtractive-oriented programs. The reason is that separate model programs aim toward a distribution of the two languages for distinct purposes, and thus tend to use the native language for longer periods of time and for a wider range of functions than do concurrent language models.

Concurrent Language Models

Preview-Review.   In the preview-review instructional model, the teacher previews and reviews subject matter content in one language (usually the native language) and interacts with students during the main part of the lesson (including practice activities) in the other language (Moll & Díaz, 1985; Delgado-Gaitán, 1991). So, for instance, if you were in a Spanish-English bilingual class talking with students about Thanksgiving and how Native Americans are often misrepresented during this holiday, you would talk about the major ideas and encourage students to discuss major ideas in Spanish. Then you might have them work in small groups to read a variety of stories about Native Americans in English and discuss in English with their fellow students the ways Native American children and the community are portrayed in books. Finally, you would lead a discussion about the major points presented in the preview, and relate them to what students learned in their small groups. This review phase would be conducted in Spanish.

Concurrent Translation.   Concurrent translation is when the teacher presents information in one language and then translates it word for word into the other language. Ostensibly, the purpose of concurrent translation is to ensure that all the students in the class understand what is being said. However, because students usually ignore the second language and wait instead for information to be provided in their native language (Saville & Troike, 1971), they are less likely to develop high levels of English-language proficiency when instruction is presented through this model, and their native language is likely to suffer as well. Consider this: When teachers use concurrent translation to interact with students at any point of a lesson, they are taking twice as much time, and students are paying attention only half of the time. For this reason alone, the detriment of concurrent translation outweighs the benefit of student comprehension. There are other, better ways to invite students into the discourse of the lesson without resorting to translation all the time.

Flip-flopping.   Flip-flopping from one language to the other is when the teacher switches from one language to the other within a sentence or between several sentences of the same thought. Flip-flopping, also known as intralingual code-switching, reflects a back-and-forth switching strategy used for informal interaction among some bilingual adolescents and adults in U.S. bilingual communities (Faltis, 1989) and thus may be useful for learning subject matter content because it ties in to community language practices. Flip-flopping looks something like this:

(Spanish to English) *Andale, Gerardo,* why don't you tie your shoe, *porque si no, te vas a caer.* [Hey, Gerardo, why don't you tie your shoe, because if you don't, you'll fall.]

(English to Spanish) Okay, class *quiero que escuchen* really hard right now because I am going to explain *cómo vamos a hacer el dibujo.* [Okay, class I want you to listen really hard right now because I am going to explain how we are going to do the drawing.]

If language development is the primary goal of instruction, however, this language alternation approach may be totally inappropriate, since students are rarely exposed to full ideas in one language or the other. They need opportunities to hear, read, use, and write both languages for extended stretches of meaning to acquire high levels of proficiency.

New Concurrent Approach.   One approach to language switching that does aim to provide bilingual students with extended use of both languages in a way that promotes dual language and content learning is the New Concurrent Approach (Jacobson, 1982), a nontranslation bilingual methodology that systematically incorporates the reasons proficient bilingual speakers switch languages. An NCA teacher learns to alternate from one language to the other between thought units and in response to consciously identified sociolinguistic cues (Faltis, 1989). NCA teachers can also incorporate critical reasons for language switching in order to engage students in politically oriented discussions. Here is an example of using NCA to engage students in a bilingual discussion about war, in this case, the Gulf War (Morgan, 1992/93).

After a general discussion about the Bosnian War and how war can change people's lives, the teacher asked her 6th-grade students to consider the Gulf War, in which the U.S. attacked Iraq to stop the Iraqi military advancement in Kuwait:

Teacher: *¿Cómo cambiaría el mundo si Saddam Hussein controlara el mundo? ¿Tendríamos los mismos derechos?* [How would the world change if Saddam Hussein controlled the world? Would we have the same rights?]

Student 1: *Sería totalmente diferente, pero yo no creo que la guerra contra Saddam sea justa. No es justo bombardear Iraq.* [It would be completely different, but I don't think that the war against Saddam was fair. It isn't fair to bomb Iraq.]

Student 2: *Sí es justo porque Saddam invadó a Kuwait.* [Yes, it is fair because Saddam invaded Kuwait.]

Teacher: What do you think, class? Did Saddam invade Kuwait? Was there a reason for the invasion? Was the U.S. right to attack Iraq?

Student 3: (to Student 1) What would you do if a robber came to your house and attacked your family and stole your property? Wouldn't you try to stop him?

Student 2: I agree. We have to protect what is ours.

Student 1: Yes, but the U.S. was protecting oil, not people.

Teacher: *Ahora llegamos al problema: ¿Estaban los Estados Unidos protejiendo su fuente de petroleo o estaban ayudando a su amigo Kuwait?* [Now we are getting to the problem: Was the U.S. protecting its oil source or was it helping its friend Kuwait?]

Student 1: *Ya sabemos que Kuwait tiene mucho petroleo. ¿Por qué no se mete los Estados Unidos en otras guerras, y no más en ésta?* [We already know that Kuwait has lots of oil. Why doesn't the U.S. get involved in other wars, not only this one?]

In this NCA exchange, the students follow the teacher's lead and stay in the language she speaks. They and the teacher switch from one language to the other as they carry on a discussion of ideas. One feature to notice is that the students are listening to and speaking both languages about equally.

Separate Language Models

Content. One way to separate languages for instruction is to assign one language for certain academic subjects and the other language for the rest. The decision can be made on a content-free basis by randomly assigning each of the languages to a particular set of subjects or on a content-sensitive basis where each language is judged to be more appropriate for teaching certain subjects. (See Wong Fillmore and Valadez, 1986, pp. 660–664, for a discussion of the issues involved in separating languages by content.) Some bilingual educators believe that language arts, mathematics, and social studies should first be taught in the students' native language, and that art, science, and music should be taught in the students' new language. However, as elementary school teaching becomes increasing integrated and less focused on discrete subject matter areas, language separation by content seems out of touch.

Person. Some bilingual programs separate language teaching by having two individuals in the classroom; one speaks in one language, and the second speaks in the other. There are several ways of organizing for this kind of separation-by-person bilingual instruction. Team teaching and use of a teacher's aide are the two most common practices. The goal in classes where two adults consistently teach in different languages is to accustom students to use the language of the adult to whom they are speaking and/or listening.

Time. The two languages of a bilingual program can also be separated by time so that one language is used on one day and the other is used on the next day. This is called the alternate-days approach. Or the teacher can designate one language for morning use and the other for afternoon use. Ordinarily, language use separated by time factors is achieved by posting signs at the classroom door so that when students enter, they are reminded as to which language will be used that day or during a certain block of time.

Place. The physical location of the classroom may also signal to students which language will be used for instruction. In certain bilingual programs, the classrooms in which native language and English medium classwork occur are physically separated. This means that students change classrooms for the native language and English parts of the school day once English is introduced into the curriculum. In this manner, students learn to associate language use with a particular physical setting. Occasionally, when separate classrooms are unavailable, clearly marked activity centers serve the same purpose (Jacobson, 1990).

Additive Bilingual Education

In the United States, there is basically only one type of additive bilingual program: Bilingual maintenance education, also known as bilingual immersion education (Lindholm, 1990) or two-way bilingual education (Christian, 1994). In bilingual maintenance programs, non-English-speaking students receive instruction in their native language along with English, and native English-proficient students receive instruction in English along with the second language of limited-English-proficient students. Bilingual maintenance programs typically maintain a strict separation of language use according to time, content, place, and/or teacher (Christian, 1994). Typically, after an initial year or two of total minority-language instruction, the two languages are distributed so that the minority language is used 60% of the time up to the 4th grade, and then the two languages are used for equal amounts of time through the 6th grade. After the 6th grade, the minority language may be offered as a subject up through 12th grade. Figure 2.1 presents a graphic representation of the percentage of time spent in the two languages over time in a program

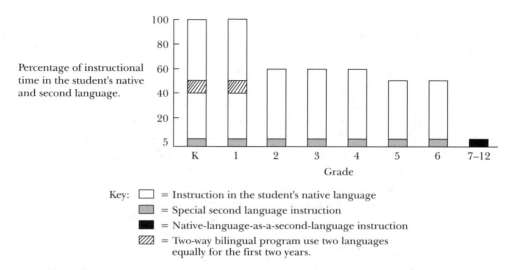

Figure 2.1
Bilingual maintenance education programs

such as the one described above. Bilingual maintenance programs, which are extraordinarily rare in the U.S., promote cultural pluralism, language enrichment, and language restoration (Baker, 1988 p. 47). Krashen and Biber (1988) describe several exemplary bilingual maintenance programs in California. Lindholm (1987) and Christian (1994) provide a directory of bilingual maintenance programs throughout the United States.

Subtractive Bilingual Programs

The overwhelming majority of bilingual education programs throughout the United States, however, lead to subtractive bilingualism in conformance with assimilationist goals. Subtractive bilingual programs "are designed to help students make the transition from one language to another; that is, they take monolinguals and produce monolinguals" (Malakoff & Hakuta, 1990, p. 39).

The most commonly practiced subtractive educational program is transitional bilingual education. Following the definition spelled out in the 1974 amendment to Title VII, this kind of program uses the native language for some or all subject matter instruction, usually for no more than three academic years, while the student is acquiring English as a second language. In other words, the native language is used temporarily as a bridge to English.

Programs that use the native language for part of instruction for less than two years are called *early-exit transitional programs* (Ramírez &

Merino, 1990). Students in these programs may continue to have structured English instruction even after they no longer receive native language instruction, usually for an additional year. Thus, a student entering the program in kindergarten would be exited at the end of 1st or 2nd grade. Programs that offer native language instruction from kindergarten through the upper elementary grades are called *late-exit transitional programs* (Ramírez & Merino, 1990). Students stay in late-exit programs even after they have learned enough English to succeed academically in a mainstream classroom. In both types of programs, students who fall too far behind in academic achievement after being placed in a mainstream classroom for the entire day may be reclassified as limited English proficient and become re-eligible for English-as-a-second-language instruction for up to two years. See Figures 2.2 and 2.3 for a graphic representation of early-exit and late-exit transitional bilingual education programs.

Transitional bilingual education is primarily practiced in schools serving large numbers of English learners who speak and understand the same minority language (Faltis, 1989). Such programs can be designed so that the two languages are used separately or concurrently for instruction. However, even in programs organized to separate language use according to content, time, person, and/or place, there is little to prevent teachers from using both languages concurrently (usually by translating back and forth) in an effort to reach all students in the class (Faltis, 1990). Moreover, given the tremendous push to use English and the major objectives of transitional programs, teachers tend to use more English than the native language, regardless of whether the two languages are allocated for concurrent or separate use (Halcón, 1983; Milk, 1986).

Figure 2.2
Early-exit transitional bilingual
education programs

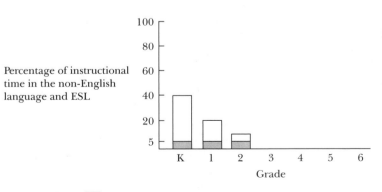

Key: ☐ = Instruction in the student's native language
▨ = English-as-a-second-language instruction

Figure 2.3
Late-exit transitional bilingual
education programs

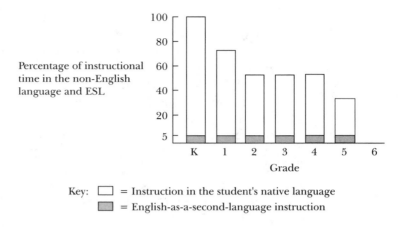

Percentage of instructional
time in the non-English
language and ESL

Key: ☐ = Instruction in the student's native language
      ▧ = English-as-a-second-language instruction

Three other common programs that lead to subtractive bilingualism, or eventual monolingualism, are *submersion, ESL pullout,* and *ESL push in.* In a submersion program, students are placed in mainstream classrooms and are given no special assistance or English language instruction. Teachers may try to help by assigning a buddy to work with individual students, but by and large, no other adjustments are made. Students are expected to sink or swim. In ESL pullout programs, second-language students leave their mainstream classes at certain times during the day to receive structured ESL instruction in a separate classroom (Richard-Amato, 1988). The instruction ranges from 15 to 50 minutes daily. ESL pullout programs are frequently used in schools where native language bilingual instruction is difficult to implement; for example, in schools serving second-language students from different language backgrounds or where there are a small number of second-language students. Teachers in ESL pullout programs may or may not have an endorsement or certification to teach ESL to children. Such endorsement usually entails at least 12 credits of college-level courses in the areas of ESL methodology, second-language curriculum and materials development, second-language acquisition theory, and second-language testing and assessment. Few states offer certification in teaching English as a second language because this specialty is generally not recognized as a discipline.

A more recent English medium approach to helping ESL students who find themselves placed in mainstream all-English classrooms is ESL push in. The idea here is to keep English learners in the mainstream class and have an ESL teacher or aide come into the class on a daily basis to work with ESL students on specific class assignments. This approach has more support than pullout programs because the ESL teachers work more closely with the regular classroom teacher. Moreover, the students remain in the mainstream class for the entire day.

A less common subtractive program that is slowly gaining in popularity is *structured immersion* (Ramírez & Merino, 1990), which is modeled after the Canadian French-immersion programs for middle-class language-majority students (English speakers in Quebec). In the Canadian model, language-majority students who volunteer for the program receive all or part of their instruction in French for the first few years of schooling and then at least 50% of their studies are conducted in English, their native language, up through secondary school (Genesee, 1987). In contrast, in the U.S. model, minority students who are limited English proficient are assigned to self-contained classrooms in which English is the only language of instruction. When students exit from the program, they enter mainstream classrooms where the remainder of their education is conducted through the English language. Structured immersion teachers are often functionally bilingual, but avoid using the students' native language in class for anything other than emergencies. Native language use among students is tolerated initially, but students are openly encouraged to use English for classroom interaction. Structured immersion students are taught the same subject matter content as their native-English-proficient peers in regular classrooms. Structured immersion teachers adjust their vocabulary, discourse, and pacing to enhance comprehension so that students can understand the material and participate in classroom activities.

Structured immersion education is designed primarily for early elementary grades. At the higher grades of elementary school and at the secondary level, a variation of structured immersion has developed under the name of *sheltered content teaching* (Faltis, 1993a). Only English learners attend sheltered content classes, where they do not have to compete with native speakers of English. Such classes enable English learners to study important subject matter because teachers use comprehension-oriented teaching methodology and teach students study skill strategies to prepare them for mainstream classes.

ENTRY, RECLASSIFICATION, AND EXIT CRITERIA

Let us now turn to the questions of who is eligible for special language instructional services, how and how often language proficiency is assessed, and when and how a student becomes ineligible for special language instruction services once the services have begun. Getting in and out of special language programs is largely determined by tests. Accordingly, it is important for us to learn how language test scores are used to determine program eligibility as well as program ineligibility. As joinfostering teachers, we need to join forces with bilingual and ESL teachers as advocates for second-language students to ensure that they are not exited from special language programs before they are ready for all-English instruction (Cazden, 1986). In the following section, we will examine the kinds of procedures and tests that are commonly used for identifying eligible students, for assessing their language proficiency, for reclassifying them once they are in a program, and finally, for exiting them from the program. All of the tests that we examine are worthy of criticism; they can hardly be called authentic assessments of how students use language for communication with a variety of audiences. Nonetheless, we will learn about them and then look for other ways of making sense about how well students use language for oral and written communication.

Determining Program Eligibility

The Lau Remedies of 1974 made the identification of students whose primary language is not English and the evaluation of their English language proficiency mandatory in all school districts. The first step in determining program eligibility is to identify students whose first language is not English. Most school districts in multilingual cities administer a survey to parents upon the enrollment of children in school. The survey commonly contains four questions:

1. Was your child's first language a language other than English?
2. Is a language other than English spoken in the home?
3. Is the language most often spoken by your child a language other than English?
4. Do you speak a language other than English to your child most of the time?

An answer of "yes" to any of these four questions by parents indicates that the student's primary home language is other than English. Once this has been determined, the next step is to find out whether the student has limited English proficiency and thus, whether he or she is eligible for bilingual or English-only special language instruction.

The criteria for entering a special instructional program vary from state to state, but most states determine entry eligibility on the basis of oral English proficiency test scores, English reading test scores, and native language reading test scores (Canales, 1992). The three most popular oral English proficiency tests are the Language Assessment Scales (LAS), the

Bilingual Syntax Measure II (BSM), and the Language Assessment Battery (LAB). Other frequently used tests are the Basic Inventory of Natural Language (BINL) and the Individualized Developmental English Activities (IDEA) Placement Test. The most commonly used English reading tests are the Comprehensive Test of Basic Skills (CTBS) and the California Achievement Test (CAT). When available, schools most often choose the following native-language reading tests: the Spanish version of LAS and the Spanish version of BSM (Cardoza, 1986).

To get an idea of what oral English proficiency tests actually measure and how they distinguish levels of proficiency, we will examine three popular tests, the LAS, the BSM, and the IDEA test, in greater detail. (For a review of all of the tests mentioned as well as many others, see Alderson, Krahnke, and Stansfield, 1987.)

The Language Assessment Scales. The LAS is an individually administered test that was developed by Edward DeAvila and Sharon Duncan in the late 1970s (McGroarty, 1987). There are two versions: LAS I for grades 2 through 5, and LAS II for grade 6 and up. Both versions measure oral language skills in English and in Spanish based on a student's performance on four linguistic subsystems, which include the sound system, vocabulary, syntax, and pragmatics (the ability to complete certain tasks in the language). The sound system is assessed by having students indicate whether minimal pairs of words sound the same or different (30 items) and by having them repeat certain sounds of the language (36 items). Vocabulary is tested by having the student name items pictured in the test (20 items). Syntax is measured through two subscales, oral comprehension and oral production of a story presented on an audiocassette. The assessment of pragmatic ability is optional and consists of 10 questions that draw out the student's ability to use language for describing and narrating without the use of story props.

Students are assigned to one of five proficiency levels on the basis of total correct responses that are converted to weighted scores. Table 2.1 presents the scores and the corresponding proficiency levels.

Level 1 indicates that the student is non-English-proficient (NEP). Level 2 is also non-English-proficient with some isolated language abilities. Level 3 students are designated as limited-English-proficient (LEP), while levels 4 and 5 mean that students are fully English-proficient (FEP) and highly articulate, respectively.

The Bilingual Syntax Measure. The BSM has two versions, one for K through 2 (BSM I) and one for grades 3 through 12 (BSM II). Developed by Marina Burt, Heidi Dulay, and Eduardo Hernandez-Chavez in the mid

Table 2.1
Scoring and proficiency levels for the Language Assessment Scales I and II

Total Score		LAS Oral Proficiency Level	
LAS I	LAS II		
85–100	92–100	5	Fully English Proficient, highly articulate (FEP)
75–84	82–91	4	Fully English Proficient (FEP)
65–74	72–81	3	Limited English Proficient (LEP)
55–64	62–71	2	Non-English Proficient, isolated language ability (NEP)
0–54	0–61	1	Non-English Proficient (NEP)

Source: From "Language Assessment Scales" by M. McGroarty in *Reviews of English Language Proficiency Tests* by J. C. Alderson, K. J. Krahnke, and C. W. Stansfield (Eds.), 1987, Washington, DC: Teachers of English to Speakers of Other Languages (p. 51).

and late 1970s, both versions are individually administered (Cziko, 1987; Hayes-Brown, 1987). The BSM provides a direct measure of syntactic proficiency in Spanish or English by stimulating natural conversation through a structured interview. The student and the examiner engage in a conversation about a story depicted by the test's cartoon characters. Students are asked a total of 25 questions based on seven cartoon drawings. The examiner writes down each student response in the test booklet and later scores them as correct or incorrect according to whether the student has produced to target form in an obligatory instance.

The number of correct responses is used to determine proficiency level assignment. For BSM I there are five levels (Cziko, 1987): Level 1 (no English or Spanish); Level 2 (receptive English or Spanish only); Level 3 (survival English or Spanish); Level 4 (intermediate English or Spanish); and Level 5 (fully English or Spanish proficient—FEP). Levels 1 through 4 are considered to indicate limited English proficiency. BSM II has six levels (Hayes-Brown, 1987). As in BSM I, students scoring in Levels 1 through 4 are classified as limited-English-proficient (LEP). Level 5 can indicate either full English proficiency (FEP) or high limited English or Spanish proficiency, depending on school district policy (Hayes-Brown, 1987). Level 6 indicates native-like proficiency in English or Spanish.

The IDEA Placement Test. The IPT was developed by Wanda Ballard and Phyllis Tighe in 1982. The test is designed to assess oral proficiency in English or Spanish for grades K through 6. Both the English and the Spanish versions consist of 83 items divided among the areas of vocabulary, syntax, comprehension, and verbal expression spread over seven proficiency levels (McCollum, 1987). Thirty-five items require students to respond to questions about figure drawings. The rest of the items measure the student's ability to (a) discriminate between minimal pairs, (b) respond to verbal commands, (c) retell a short story, (d) describe a common object, and (e) identify the main idea from a passage that is read to the student.

The IPT has seven levels of oral proficiency attainment, Levels A/B to F. Each level corresponds to a series of structured English language lessons provided through the IDEA Language Program. Students answering fewer than 50% of the 12 items on Level B are automatically placed in Level A to work on language activities designed specifically for that level. For any level above Level B, students are assigned to the corresponding level when they are unable to answer correctly at least 80% of the items at that level (McCollum, 1987). The IPT uses NEP/LEP/FEP designations, and students are placed in bilingual or ESL programs if they are classified as either NEP or LEP. However, proficiency designations are tied directly to grade-level considerations so that higher levels are required for each of the designations as students progress through the grades. For example, 2nd-grade students who score at Level D might be considered to be fully English proficient. The same students in the 6th grade would need to complete Level F to be classified as FEP; Level D students could still be considered to be LEP.

All three of these tests are old (originally from the 1970s and 1980s) and, frankly, provide little information that is useful to teachers who are interested in how well children can use English to write and talk about things that interest them and about school-related topics. These tests assess things that really don't count as speaking and writing in school settings. They assess how well children can respond to and pick out things that the test developers thought represented language proficiency. None of the tests present language as a whole system, one that cannot be fragmented into minimal pairs, sentence patterns, and recall formats. My suggestion is that if you have to use any of these tests, use them judiciously, look for additional ways of assessing language ability, and pay lots of attention to how children use language within diverse settings.

Reclassification and Exit Criteria

Reclassification refers to the practice of regularly assessing students to determine continued eligibility for language-related instructional assistance. Reclassification is used primarily in late-exit and maintenance bilingual programs. Accordingly, a student could be reclassified as fully English proficient (FEP) and still remain in the bilingual program as high up in grade level as the program goes. In transitional early-exit bilingual programs as well as in English-only programs, reclassifying a student as FEP usually means that the student is ready to exit out of the special program. In this manner, exiting and reclassification are not distinguished in a majority of cases (Cardoza, 1986).

Assessing students to determine continued eligibility is usually done once a year, in the final weeks of school. Most school districts assess English oral language proficiency as a part of their exit criteria, and most use the same tests employed for entry eligibility. The cutoff scores used for program exit are usually those recommended by the test publisher. When standardized English tests are used for exit purposes, there is considerable variation across states as to the cutoff percentile score used for discontinuing program eligibility (Walton, 1989). New York, for example, uses the 40th percentile. Arizona exits LEP students from programs when they score at or above the 36th percentile on a standardized English test. In Texas, students are exited from the program when they score between the 23rd and the 40th percentile on a standardized English test.

In addition to English oral proficiency testing, many school districts that have bilingual and/or ESL programs rely on other information to determine when to exit a student out of a program. In California, for example, exit decisions for students in bilingual and ESL programs are based on five criteria (Walton, 1989): (1) teacher evaluation of the student's oral English language proficiency; (2) assessment of English oral language proficiency as measured by state-designated proficiency tests (LAS, BSM, and IDEA); (3) assessment of writing ability as measured by teacher-scored writing samples or standardized tests; (4) assessment of English language arts (spelling, punctuation, and reading comprehension); and (5) consultation with parents to ensure that final classification is appropriate. Most states that have multiple exit criteria, however, rely primarily on the first three areas of assessment (Cardoza, 1986). Few states assess native language literacy as part of the exit battery of tests.

It is important to note that in recent years several states have begun to raise the cutoff scores for exit criteria based on the finding that nearly 40% of elementary students in programs with low exit cutoff scores required remediation after being placed in mainstream classes. In contrast, fewer than 20% of students in programs with exit cutoff scores at or above the 40th percentile required additional language remediation (Lee, 1989; Nadeau & Miramontes, 1988). The reason for raising the exit cutoff scores is to ensure that students are not exited prematurely, before they have developed the requisite language proficiency to progress in an English-only instructional setting.

Increasingly, in addition to standardized tests, many teachers have begun to use alternative assessment strategies for both native English-speaking and English-learning students. One of the most promising alternative assessment strategies is portfolio assessment. A portfolio is "a purposeful, chronological collection of student work, designed to reflect student development in one or more areas over time" (French, 1992). Ideally, the teacher and students work together to generate lists of written and artistic tasks, projects, or exhibits for agreed-upon learning areas. Portfolio assessment can be highly structured for specific area evaluation, or it can be highly reflective, emphasizing students' perceptions, interpretations, and strategies used in acquiring knowledge. (See Gottlieb, 1995, for the CRADLE approach to Portfolio Development.) The main idea in portfolio assessment is to let students and the teacher collect, develop, and link students' work over time to show how and the extent to which multiple learning has occurred. When students select a sample of their work to be included in their portfolio, the teacher might ask them to write a reflective statement explaining why the piece was important and why they chose it for the portfolio. This helps students develop self-assessment strategies as well as providing you with information about how they see themselves as learners in the class (Smolen, Newman, Wathen, & Lee, 1995). The teacher can have students do this once a week or every two weeks. Some English learners may need help developing explanations for why they select items to showcase in their portfolios, but over time and with practice, all students are able to give reasons for selecting materials.

In addition to student self-selected work, the teacher can also select and place in the portfolio pieces of the student's work that provide evidence of understanding as well as producing knowledge through computations, writing, and art. The teacher might look for examples of invented spelling to show phonics knowledge and can put in pieces that include thematic vocabulary knowledge. The teacher, like the student, may also want to jot down why the work is important and how it shows growth and student awareness of what is happening in class and in the community.

In addition, the teacher should try to include evidence of students' critical understanding of social consciousness. For example, suppose the class were having a discussion of historical and visual inaccuracies of *Pocahontas*, the Disney film, based on Cornel Pewewardy's review of the film (Pewewardy, 1995), and then several of the students wrote on their own why the film negatively stereotypes Native Americans and uses racist terms such as *savages, devils,* and *primitive*. This work might be something that would be placed in the students' portfolios.

CONCLUSION

This chapter presented a history of the legal and political events that have influenced the development of bilingual and other forms of special language instruction for students who enter school speaking a language other than English. We were introduced to the ways that bilingual education programs vary in terms of whether the native language is being maintained or lost and whether the languages of instruction are used concurrently or separately. Also presented were the various nonnative-language instructional programs that serve increasing numbers of children who are learning English as an additional language. Knowing about these programs helps us gain an appreciation of the time and effort it takes to acquire enough English along with academic knowledge to be able to function without assistance in a mainstream classroom. Finally, we examined the entry and exit criteria used in bilingual and English-as-a-second-language programs throughout the United States. Of particular importance to all-English teachers is understanding the criteria used to determine when a student is ready for all-English instruction without continuation of special English-language instruction. You may have to join forces with other teachers to make sure that students are not being pulled out of bilingual programs too quickly and that alternative ways of assessing readiness for all-English classes are taken into consideration.

In the case of Julia Felix, all seven of the ESL students in her class will continue to receive some kind of English-language help for one hour daily until the end of the school year, at which time their English proficiency and achievement will be evaluated for reclassification. Knowing this, and having reviewed the history and types of bilingual programs, Julia is now ready to begin organizing her classroom to ensure that she provides an optimal learning environment for all of her students, regardless of their oral and written English-language proficiency. Accordingly, in the next chapter, we will learn how to organize the social and physical environment of classrooms in line with joinfostering principles.

ACTIVITIES

1. Using the 1992 Winter/Spring, Vol. 16, Nos. 1 & 2 of the *Bilingual Research Journal,* all students read and discuss the Executive Summary by J. David Ramírez, and then divide the class into two groups to present a debate over the Ramírez Report. One side argues in favor of the report; the other against it. Support for and against the Ramírez report is found in the remaining articles of the volume.

2. Observe and describe a bilingual classroom in which the teacher and

students use a non-English language. Observe the class at least twice for no less than one hour each time. Note how students are physically arranged, whether student materials are displayed on the walls, and whether the teacher and the students primarily use one language or two for teaching and communication. Interview the teacher about his or her views on native-language instruction and concurrent vs. separate language use for teaching. Remember that any time you set foot on school grounds you need to check in at the main office before going to the classroom in which you plan to observe.

3. Observe and describe an English-as-a-second-language classroom or an ESL pullout class, following the instructions in activity 2. Talk with several of the students and ask them about their likes and dislikes, their hobbies, and their families. Find out whether and how their interests and hobbies are used as topics for learning in their classrooms. Remember that any time you set foot on school grounds you need to check in at the main office before going to the classroom in which you plan to observe.

4. Explain the difference between an ESL credential and an ESL endorsement. If your state offers either or both, summarize the kinds of required coursework needed to obtain them. If your state offers a bilingual teaching credential, summarize the required coursework and then compare and contrast it with the ESL coursework. Write to a neighboring state's department of education and inquire about their ESL credential/endorsement and bilingual credential requirements. You might wish to consult Kreidler (1987) and ERIC document No. ED 400-86-0019 for some initial information and comparison data.

5. Following the lessons presented in Jacobson (1990), write out new lessons, using any content area to demonstrate the major ways of allocating language for instruction concurrently or separately. This activity requires individuals with fluency in two languages.

6. Invite the language testing specialist from your local school district to give an in-class demonstration of the kinds of assessment and other criteria used for bilingual or ESL program entry, reclassification, and exit. Try to locate someone who has knowledge of and practice in portfolio assessment.

REFERENCES

Alderson, J. C., Krahnke, K. J., & Stansfield, C. W. (Eds.). (1987). *Reviews of English language proficiency tests.* Washington, DC: TESOL.

August, D., & García, E. (1988). *Language minority education in the United States.* Springfield, IL: Charles C. Thomas.

Avila, J. G., & Godoy, R. (1979). Bilingual/bicultural education and the law. In National Dissemination and Assessment Center (Ed.), *Language development in a bilingual setting* (pp. 15–33). Los Angeles: California State University.

Baker, C. (1988). *Key issues in bilingualism and bilingual education.* Clevedon, England: Multilingual Matters Ltd.

Baker, K. A., & de Kanter, A. A. (1981). *Effectiveness of bilingual education: A review of the literature.* Washington, DC: Office of Planning, Budget and Evaluation, U.S. Department of Education.

Canales, J. (1992). Innovative practices in the identification of LEP students. *Proceedings of the second National Research Symposium on limited English proficient student issues: Focus on evaluation and measurement,* Vol. 2 (pp. 89–122). Washington, DC: U.S. Department of Education.

Cardoza, D. (1986). The identification and reclassification of limited English proficient students: A study of entry and exit classification procedures. *NABE Journal, 11*(1), 21–45.

Cazden, C. (1986). ESL teachers as language advocates for children. In P. Rigg & D. S. Enright (Eds.). *Children and ESL: Integrating perspectives* (pp. 7–21). Washington, DC: TESOL.

Christian, D. (1994). *Two-way bilingual education: Students learning through two languages.* Santa Cruz, CA: The National Center for Research on Cultural Diversity and Second Language Learning.

Cummins, J. (1979). Linguistic interdependence of the educational development of bilingual children. *Review of Educational Research, 19,* 222–251.

Cziko, G. (1987). Bilingual syntax measure I. In J. C. Alderson, K. J. Krahnke, & C. W. Stanfield, (Eds.), *Reviews of English language proficiency tests* (pp. 12–14). Washington, DC: TESOL.

Daniels, H. A. (1990). *Not only English: Affirming America's multicultural heritage.* Urbana, IL: NCTE.

Delgado-Gaitán, C. (1991). Relating experience and text: Socially constituted reading activity. In M. McGroarty & C. Faltis (Eds.), *Languages in school and society: Policy and pedagogy* (pp. 512–528). Berlin: Mouton de Gruyter.

Faltis, C. (1989). Code-switching and bilingual schooling: An examination of Jacobson's new concurrent approach. *Journal of Multilingual and Multicultural Development, 10*(2), 117–127.

Faltis, C. (1990). New directions in bilingual research design: The study of interactive decision making. In R. Jacobson & C. Faltis (Eds.), *Language distribution issues in bilingual schooling* (pp. 45–57). Clevedon, England: Multilingual Matters Ltd.

Faltis, C. (1993a). Critical issues in the use of sheltered content teaching in high school bilingual programs. *Peabody Journal of Education, 69*(1), 136–151.

Faltis, C. (1993b). From kindergarten to high school: Teaching and learning English as a second language in the U.S. In S. Silberstein (Ed.), *State of the art TESOL essays: Celebrating 25 years of the discipline* (pp. 91–114). Alexandria, VA: TESOL.

French, R. (1992). Portfolio assessment and LEP students. In *Proceedings of the second National Research Symposium on limited English proficient student issues: Focus on evaluation and measurement,* Vol. 1 (pp. 249–272). Washington, DC: U.S. Department of Education.

Genesee, F. (1987). *Learning through two languages: Studies of immersion and bilingual education.* New York: Newbury House.

Gottlieb, M. (1995). Nurturing student learning through portfolios. *TESOL Journal, 5*(1), 12–14.

Halcón, J. J. (1983). A structural profile of basic Title VII (Spanish-English) bilingual bicultural education programs. *NABE Journal, 7*(3), 55–73.

Hakuta, K. (1986). *Mirror of language: The debate on bilingualism.* New York: Basic Books.

Hayes-Brown, Z. (1987). Bilingual syntax measure II. In J. C. Alderson, K. J.

Krahnke, & C. W. Stanfield, (Eds.), *Reviews of English language proficiency tests* (pp. 14–17). Washington, DC: TESOL.

Hornberger, N. (1991). Extending enrichment bilingual education: Revisiting typologies and redirecting policy. In O. García (Ed.), *Bilingual education: Focusschrift in honor of Joshua A. Fishman* (pp. 215–234). Philadelphia: John Benjamins.

Jacobs, J. F., & Pierce, M. L. (1966). Bilingualism and creativity. *Elementary English, 43,* 1390–1400.

Jacobson, R. (1982). The implementation of a bilingual instructional model—The new concurrent approach. In R. Padilla (Ed.), *Ethnoperspectives in bilingual education research,* Vol. III (pp. 14–29). Ypsilanti, MI: Eastern Michigan University.

Jacobson, R. (1990). Allocating two languages as a key feature of a bilingual methodology. In R. Jacobson & C. Faltis (Eds.), *Language distribution issues in bilingual schooling* (pp. 3–17). Clevedon, England: Multilingual Matters Ltd.

Judd, E. L. (1978). *Factors affecting the passage of the Bilingual Education Act of 1967.* Doctoral dissertation. New York University.

Krashen, S., & Biber, D. (1988). *On course: Bilingual education's success in California.* Sacramento, CA: California Association for Bilingual Education.

Kreidler, C. (1987). *ESL teacher education.* Washington, DC: Center for Applied Linguistics.

Lambert, W. E., & Peal, E. (1962). The relationship of bilingualism to intelligence. *Psychological Monographs, 76,* 1–23.

Lee, E. (1989). Chinese American fluent English proficient students and school achievement. *NABE Journal, 13*(2), 95–111.

Lindholm, K. (1990). Bilingual immersion education: Criteria for program development. In A. M. Padilla, H. H. Fairchild, & C. M. Valadez (Eds.), *Bilingual education: Issues and strategies* (pp. 91–105). Newbury Park, CA: Sage.

Mackey, W. F., & Beebe, V. N. (1977). *Bilingual schools for a bicultural community: Miami's adaptation to the Cuban refugees.* Rowley, MA: Newbury House.

Malakoff, M., & Hakuta, K. (1990). History of language minority education in the United State. In A. M. Padilla, H. H. Fairchild, & C. M. Valadez (Eds.), *Bilingual education: Issues and strategies* (pp. 27–44). Newbury Park, CA: Sage.

McCollum, P. (1987). IDEA oral language proficiency test. In J. C. Alderson, K. J. Krahnke, & C. W. Stanfield, (Eds.), *Reviews of English language proficiency tests* (pp. 37–39). Washington, DC: TESOL.

McFadden, B. J. (1983). Bilingual education and the law. *Journal of Law and Education, 12*(1), 1–27.

McGroarty, M. (1987). Language assessment scales. In J. C. Alderson, K. J. Krahnke, & C. W. Stanfield, (Eds.), *Reviews of English language proficiency tests* (pp. 51–53). Washington, DC: TESOL.

Milk, R. (1986). The issue of language separation in bilingual methodology. In E. García & B. Flores (Eds.), *Language and literacy research in bilingual education* (pp. 67–86). Tempe: Arizona State University Press.

Moll, L., & Díaz, E. (1985). *Ethnographic pedagogy: Promoting effective bilingual instruction.* In E. García & R. Padilla (Eds.), *Advances in bilingual education research* (pp. 127–149), Tucson: University of Arizona Press.

Morgan, B. (1992/93). Teaching the Gulf War in an ESL classroom. *TESOL Journal, 2*(2), 13–17.

Nadeau, A., & Miramontes, O. (1988). The reclassification of limited English proficient students: Assessing the inter-relationship of selected variables. *NABE Journal, 12*(3), 219–242.

Padilla, A. M. (1990). Bilingual education: Issues and perspectives. In A. M. Padilla, H. H. Fairchild, & C. M. Valadez (Eds.), *Bilingual education: Issues and strategies* (pp. 15–26). Newbury Park, CA: Sage.

Pewewardy, C. (1995). Why one can't ignore *Pocahontas. Rethinking Schools, 10*(1), 19.

Ramírez, J. D., & Merino, B. (1990). Classroom talk in English immersion, early-exit and late-exit transitional bilingual education programs. In R. Jacobson & C. Faltis (Eds.), *Language distribution issues in bilingual schooling* (pp. 61–103). Clevedon, England: Multilingual Matters Ltd.

Ramírez, J. D., Yuen, S. D., & Ramey, D. R. (1991). *Longitudinal study of structured English immersion strategy, early-exit and late-exit transitional bilingual education programs for language-minority children. Final report to the U.S. Department of Education. Executive Summary and Vols. I and II.* San Mateo, CA: Aguirre International.

Richard-Amato, P. (1988). *Making it happen: Interaction in the second language classroom.* New York: Longman.

Rodríguez, R. (1990, July 1). Escasez de maestros bilingües en una etapa crítica [A paucity of bilingual teachers in a critical period]. Los Angeles: *La Opinión*, 5.

Rosier, P., & Holm, W. (1980). *The Rock Point experience: A longitudinal study of Navajo school programs.* Washington: Center for Applied Linguistics.

Rossell, C. H. (1989). The effectiveness of educational alternatives for limited English proficient children. In G. Imhoff (Ed.), *The social and cultural context of instruction in two languages: From conflict and controversy to cooperative reor-ganization of schools.* New York: Transaction Books.

Sánchez, K., & Walker de Felix, J. (1986). Second language teachers' abilities: Some equity concerns. *Journal of Educational Equity and Leadership, 6*(4), 313–321.

Saville, M., & Troike, R. C. (1971). *Handbook of bilingual education.* Washington, DC: TESOL.

Schneider, S. G. (1976). *Revolution, reaction or reform: The 1974 bilingual education act.* New York: Las Americas.

Smolen, L., Newman, C., Wathen, T., & Lee, D. (1995). Developing student self-assessment strategies. *TESOL Journal, 5*(1), 22–27.

Stein, C. B. (1986). *Sink or swim, the politics of bilingual education.* New York: Praeger.

Walton, A. L. (1989). *Exit criteria for limited English proficient students: A memorandum to the honorable members of the Board of Regents, The University of the State of New York, Albany.* Albany, NY: The State Department of Education.

Willig, A. (1985). A meta-analysis of selected studies on the effectiveness of bilingual education. *Review of Educational Research, 55,* 269–317.

Willig, A. (1987). Examining bilingual education research through meta-analysis and narrative review: A response to Baker. *Review of educational research, 55,* 363–376.

Wong Fillmore, L., & Valadez, C. (1986). Teaching bilingual learners. In M. C. Wittrock (Ed.), *Handbook of research on teaching,* 3rd ed. (pp. 648–685). New York: Macmillan.

Yates, J. R., & Ortiz, A. A. (1983). Baker-de Kanter review: Inappropriate conclusions on the efficacy of bilingual education. *NABE Journal, 7*(3), 75–84.

Chapter Three

Arranging the All-English Classroom Environment for Communication and Social Integration

OVERVIEW

The bulk of what and how children learn in school takes place inside the four walls of the classroom. Within this physical setting, the teacher is solely responsible for organizing the environment so that students have multiple opportunities to participate and have some control over the selection of topics, ways of interacting with peers, and the audiences to whom they talk and write. In linguistically diverse all-English classrooms, this responsibility is especially important because second-language learners can easily be left out of decisions about topic selection, interaction exchanges, and types of audiences. English learners need to hear and use English to talk about topics that interest them and to participate in academic discourses to develop high levels of social and academic proficiency in English (Saville-Troike, 1984). As teachers, we need to organize the environment so that second-language students have opportunities for social interaction about many topics with the teacher and their native English-speaking classmates in the three major social contexts that support language (including literacy) and content learning:

1. teacher-led whole-class teaching
2. teacher-led small-group teaching
3. teacher-delegated small-group projects in which students work together on their own.

Organizing the classroom so that students experience these three major learning contexts helps ensure that we are reaching a wide range of cultural and individual learning styles. Accomplishing this goal requires the support of classroom norms for participation and a physical arrangement that permits talking, writing, listening, reading, and multiple forms of collaboration.

The focus of this chapter will be on how to organize the social environment—how students participate—and to support the physical environment—the classroom furniture, pathways, learning space, and distribution of learning materials—so that students can successfully be a part of all three social contexts and, in addition, have opportunities for individual reading, writing, and thinking about ideas and information presented in small-group work. Let's begin by looking into Julia's classroom as she prepares it for her opening day.

EPISODE THREE: SOCIAL INTERACTION AND THE PHYSICAL ENVIRONMENT

With the start of the school year less than two weeks away, Julia anxiously begins the process of organizing and decorating her classroom. She has an idea of how she wants it to be, but she's having trouble figuring out exactly how to arrange the furniture to match the idea. Moreover, as a new teacher she is a little worried that her plans are going to diverge too much from what teachers in neighboring classrooms have already done: placed student desks in rows, with the teacher's desk to one side, in the front of the room; set up the computers against the wall in the back of the room, one right next to the other. Exactly the way someone left her room from the year before! "I don't like this arrangement," Julia thinks to herself, "and I'm going to fix it." She wants a more integrated classroom, one in which students will be moving around the room throughout the day, at times working in pairs and small groups, and at other times as a whole class. She also wants to have ample space set aside for individual reading, writing, thinking, and practice time, places where students can settle in for comfortable learning. In her class, students will be doing lots of reading and writing and talking, that's for sure.

Julia has always been interested in art. Since she was very young, she has loved drawing, painting, and working on crafts. In college, Julia made a little extra money selling silver jewelry, mostly earrings and bracelets and, on occasion, a painting or two. Now she wants artwork and decorations to abound in her classroom. She wants them to be unconventional and for the most part to be works that the students create. She recalls that in her student teaching classroom, there were all kinds of neat things around the room, and the children loved that. In her room, Julia wants designs and pictures hanging from the ceiling, posters dotting the walls, and special locations devoted to highlighting story books, community projects, and multicultural events. But most of all, she wants the room to be a setting that offers purpose for learning, captures students' interests, and allows for both planned and spontaneous uses of language and literacy throughout the day.

Julia decides that one of her first tasks should be to consider how to arrange the desks, including her own, as well as the few tables and chairs so that students can interact verbally and collaborate socially. She plans to tackle the decorations and related stuff later, after she figures out how to arrange the room. She remembers talking about how to arrange the classroom with her cooperating teacher during her student teaching experience, but didn't accord it much importance at the time. She recalls her cooperating teacher mentioning how important it is to begin by visualizing which parts of the room will be used for student activities and which parts will be associated with teacher space. So before attempting to move anything, she goes to the chalkboard and begins sketching out a diagram of her room, including all of the fixed and movable furniture.

Just as Julia is about to finish the drawing she hears an unfamiliar voice coming from the side classroom door: "How's it going? I'm Rudy Jacobson; I'm a bilingual teacher. Thought I'd stop by and introduce myself. Most people call me Jake." Jake, a tall man with long brown hair in a ponytail, is beginning his fourth year as a bilingual teacher at Bruner Elementary. A native speaker of English born and reared in Northern California, Jake also speaks and writes Spanish fluently and knows enough words and phrases in Vietnamese and Chinese to interact a bit with students who speak these languages. Jake lived in Mexico as a child, attending Mexican schools up to the 6th grade before returning to the States.

With the back of her left hand, Julia wipes her forehead and wisps several strands of her auburn hair away and simultaneously extends her right hand to Jake and says, "Nice to meet you, Jake. I'm Julia Felix. Your class is down by the cafeteria, isn't it? I guess you know by now that I have seven bilingual students in my class." "Sure do, and you know what? They're all really neat children; they'll add a lot to your class." Jake goes on to say something pleasant about several of the children and how hard they have worked to do well in school. He cautions Julia that it may take a little time for the children to become attuned and adjusted to an all-English class after having spent the summer in their native language. Explaining that a "silent period" is common among second-language children and that the period varies for each child, Jake assures Julia that if she pays attention to how well children are attending to lessons throughout the day she will see that they will join in and participate right along with their peers.

Turning toward the door, Jake bids Julia good-bye and wishes her well: "I look forward to working with you, Julia. If there's anything I can do for you, let me know."

Julia at once senses that Jake will be a valuable source of help during the year and doesn't want him to leave without asking for his advice about arranging her room. "That's really nice—thanks, Jake. You're totally lucky to be able to understand and talk with most of the kids. Hey, before you leave, maybe you can help me out a bit. I'm working on how to organize the furniture in my classroom to make sure the children get to talk and write a lot and work in small groups throughout the day. But the thing is that I also want to, you know, be able to teach to the class as a whole group lots of times as well." Julia goes on to explain some of her ideas and concerns about how she wants to arrange the classroom and about how she plans to place the English learners with native English students for small-group work. She also mentions that she needs special places for her African Emperor scorpion (nonpoisonous), her baby Texas Indigo snake, and her two guinea pigs, Salt and Pepper.

"Wow, I can't wait to meet all your animals. Tell you what, Julia, your classroom sounds cool. It sounds like you know what you're doing, 'cuz I know these things work. All I would say is when you think about where you're going to place the furniture and desks and stuff, try to think about pathways and where the learning materials might go. Also, it can get like totally crazy if you don't have some way to let the kids know what's cool to do and not to do when they are talking, listening, and working together. I'd put the animals where they'll be easy to watch."

Jake decides to stay a few minutes longer to exchange ideas with Julia about how to organize her classroom in line with what she has planned for her students. Together they conclude that whatever physical arrangement Julia ultimately designs, it must be supported by social norms of participation that allow the teacher and the students to share in the decisions about opportunities for social interaction and in the development of topics for learning. Jake and Julia say good-bye for now, but you can be sure that they will talk again. Let's learn about their ideas now, but first, let's contrast them with what many elementary classrooms in the United States look like. This will help us affirm what we don't want our classrooms to be like!

THE ORGANIZATION OF MANY U.S. CLASSROOMS

The physical and social arrangement of classroom life in the majority of American public schools has been remarkably consistent across time and space. Today's classrooms hardly vary at all from classrooms found in the beginning of the century. Classrooms in the city are extraordinarily similar in their physical layout and social organization to classrooms in rural areas. The social and physical patterns of interaction of classrooms in big schools resemble those found in classrooms in small schools. The classrooms that the children of the wealthy attend are organized and run pretty much the same way as those attended by the children of the poor. Life in bilingual classrooms is virtually indistinguishable from what takes place in all-English classrooms.

In the following two sections, we will discover how most classrooms are arranged for instruction by paying attention to the ways talk and literacy are managed in the classroom. The amount and quality of social interaction and authentic literacy activities in the classroom are a reliable indication of how teachers organize classrooms for learning. For example, if teachers do virtually all of the talking, and student talk and writing is restricted to short, factual responses, we can assume that the physical environment is organized to block two-way communication between the teacher and the students and among the students. Whenever possible, direct reference will be made to the physical arrangement of the classroom; when this information is not available, we will be drawing inferences about how classrooms are organized on the basis of the nature of classroom talk.

All-English Classrooms

Furst and Amidon (1962) were among the first to conduct a nationwide study on social interaction in American classrooms. They observed social interaction in 160 1st- through 6th-grade classrooms in low-socioeconomic urban, middle-socioeconomic urban, and suburban elementary schools. They found that most teachers taught to the entire class and that teachers did most of the talking. Within whole-class instruction, the student talk that did occur was brief and usually related to what the teacher had already presented. One of the more interesting findings was that student talk during whole-class instruction tended to decline as students progressed through the grades, decreasing from a high of 39% in the primary grades to 27% in the upper elementary grades. Furst and Amidon also reported that the prevailing interaction pattern characteristic of the upper elementary grades was fairly well established by the 3rd grade. Accordingly, in the 3rd grade they found a marked increase in teacher talk and corresponding decrease in student-generated ideas. The nature of teacher talk also changed, with a greater proportion of it now devoted to giving instructions. Students also received less teacher praise for their contributions, which by this time were expected to be short and already known by the teacher. In short, students talk quantitatively and qualitatively less.

Some 20 years later, Sirotnik (1983), in an equally ambitious nationwide study involving 129 elementary school all-English classrooms, found that students spent about 70% of their time in class listening to the teacher, who taught mostly to the class as a whole group. Verbal interaction with students in this setting most frequently entailed asking for and answering known information, factual questions. Nearly all of the classrooms had a combination of fixed and movable chairs, but students were almost never observed talking or working together on learning tasks. Fewer than half of the classrooms had separate learning centers that had been arranged by the teacher. Although a majority of the classrooms had some alteration of the physical environment, the alteration mainly consisted of having plants, area rugs, and unusual bulletin boards. Summarizing the findings, Sirotnik (1983) offered the following dismal image of the typical all-English elementary classroom:

> Consider again the model classroom picture presented here: a lot of teacher talk and a lot of student listening, unless students are responding to teachers' questions or working on written assignments; almost invariably closed and factual questions; little corrective feedback and no guidance; and predominately total class instructional configurations around traditional activities—all in a virtually affectless environment. (p. 29)

Both this and the depiction of the typical all-English classroom given by Furst and Amidon are prime examples of what Paulo Freire (1970) refers to as the *banking concept* of education, in which the teacher as holder of knowledge presents information as deposits to students. Both depictions exemplify a pedagogical pattern that has persisted in U.S. education since the turn of the century. According to Kliebard (1989), who refers to this preferred pattern as *recitation education,* it is a manner of instruction based on the control of knowledge through a pattern of social interaction that restricts student talk. It occurs primarily in classrooms where teachers decide which, when, and how much students will talk. Kliebard suggests that the reason the recitation mode of instruction is so persistent in U.S. classrooms has to do with the need for keeping order. As Kliebard (1989) explains:

> The teacher as question-asker and the student as responder is a way of ensuring teacher dominance in the classroom situation. If students asked the questions or if they addressed one another rather than the teacher or if they engaged independently in discovery practices, the risk of disorder would be introduced, and the structure of school organization will not tolerate that kind of risk. (p. 10)

In recitation-oriented classrooms, teaching is perceived as unidirectional, from the teacher to the students, and students are essentially denied the use of language to mediate social and academic learning. This environment is especially detrimental to English-as-a-second-language students for two reasons: first, it denies them access to language that is geared to their needs, and second, it restricts the context of learning to the teacher-led whole class. Figure 3.1 illustrates a recitation-oriented classroom.

To summarize up to this point, many all-English classrooms are typically arranged so that the bulk of teaching occurs in a whole-class "no talking" environment (Enright & McCloskey, 1985). The arrangement of furniture and space in this prevailing environment is easy to imagine. Student desks, though movable, are placed in stationary positions, facing forward toward the front of the class, often for the duration of the year. There is well-defined "teacher space" and "student space." Teacher space consists of a U-shaped area covering about one third of the classroom; it includes the teacher's desk, perhaps an extra table, a bookshelf, and a storage area. Student space is the part of the classroom containing the students' desks and perhaps the computer area. Students are expected to do most of their seatwork in this space. Moving into teacher space or out of student space (e.g., to go the bathroom, to sharpen a pencil, to consult a resource book) ordinarily requires permission from the teacher. Moreover, social interaction within the student space is teacher-controlled. Student-to-student communicative exchanges within the student space are discouraged because, as Kliebard (1989) reminds us, this would increase the risk of creating disorder in the classroom.

Another well-established use for student space within the all-English classroom just described is to have students work individually, especially immediately following whole-class instruction (DeVillar & Faltis, 1991). This practice has come into favor over the past 20 years ostensibly as a means to address individual differences in learning aptitudes and learning styles. Goodlad (1984) reported, however, that teachers rarely customize learning materials for individual seatwork, since all tasks assigned to students for individual completion were essentially identical. Thus, individualized instruction amounts to little more than seatwork in which students complete prefabricated worksheets and other forms of ersatz busywork. More important, however, is the fact that individualized instruction requires students to be working alone at their seats or desks. Accordingly, this particular practice offers little opportunity for communicative exchange of information for students who are learning English as a second language. It is not hard to imagine the kind of physical classroom arrangement needed to support this approach to instruction.

Bilingual/English-as-a-Second-Language Classrooms

So far, we have considered only the typical all-English classroom. What about bilingual and English-as-a-second-language classrooms, where con-

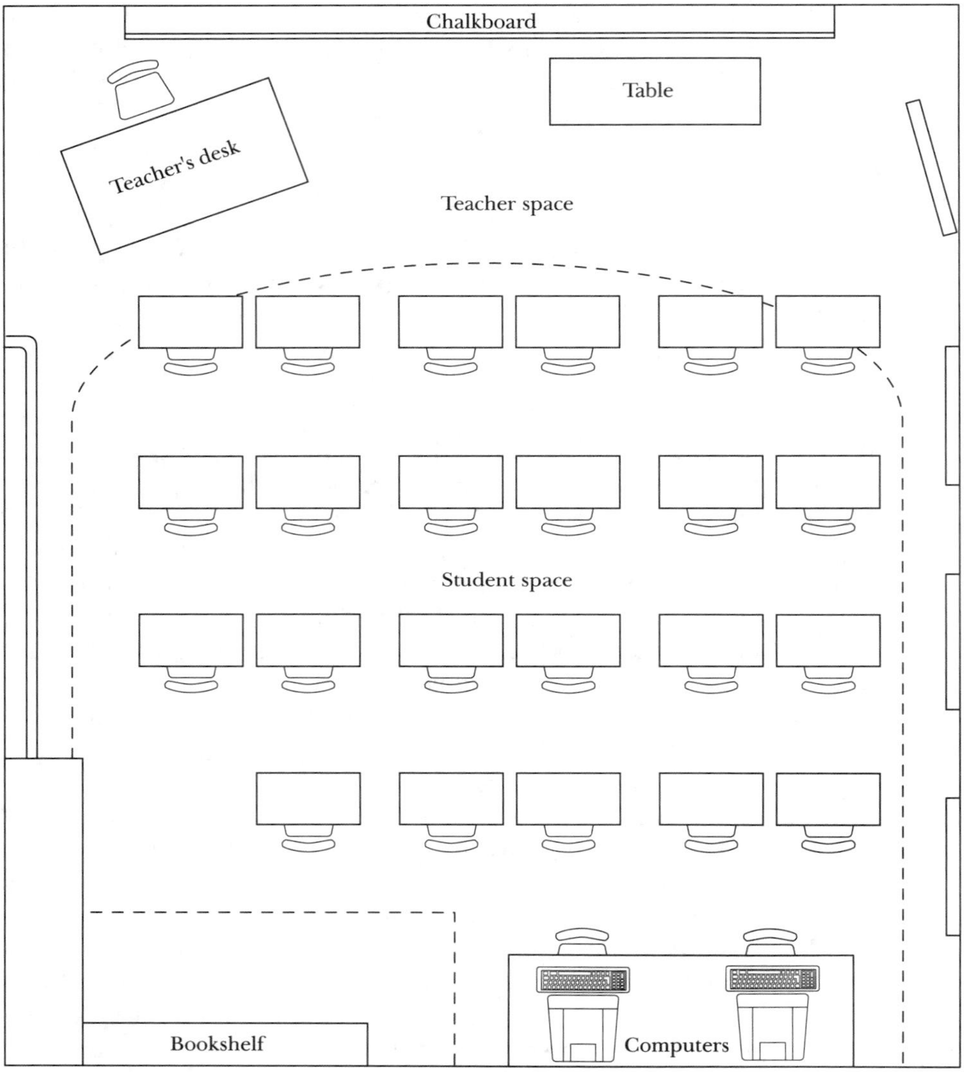

Figure 3.1
Teacher space and student space in a recitation-oriented classroom

scious attention is paid to assisting English-language development? Are these classrooms arranged any differently to accommodate the language and cultural needs of the students in them? Ramírez and Merino (1990) investigated the nature of classroom interaction in three types of bilingual education program models: (a) structured English immersion, (b) early-exit transitional bilingual, and (c) late-exit transitional bilingual (see

Chapter 2 for descriptions of these program types). Using a systematic observation instrument, they observed social interaction in 103 1st- and 2nd-grade classrooms at eight sites in California, Florida, New Jersey, New York, and Texas. Their findings indicated the following patterns of interaction and classroom organization across programs and grades:

1. instruction was conducted mainly in large groups, typically in a whole-class setting;
2. teachers generated two to three times more talk than students;
3. over 75% of student-initiated utterances were made in response to teacher initiations;
4. student interactions with teachers were mainly for the purpose of providing expected responses;
5. less than 10% of student-initiated language was in the form of a free response or a free comment, not controlled by the teacher.

These findings are strikingly similar to the patterns of little student talk and the use of whole-group instruction generally found in all-English mainstream classrooms. Ramírez and Merino (1990) suggest that students' language abilities coupled with cultural rules governing the appropriateness of talk could have contributed to the low incidence of student talk. However, it seems more plausible that the physical and social arrangements of the classrooms were largely responsible for the limited occurrence of authentic communication among students of varying language proficiency.

In summary, both the all-English and the bilingual/ESL classrooms are essentially one-dimensional, teacher-controlled social and physical learning environments. Students have little say in determining classroom content or in using authentic language to communicate ideas with the teacher or peers. Teachers rely on the whole class as the chief physical environment for teaching, virtually excluding the contexts of teacher-led small-group teaching and small-group learning from their teaching repertoire. Thus, neither the all-English nor the bilingual/ESL classrooms appear to accommodate socially or physically the language and/or educational needs of students in the process of acquiring English as a second language.

PLANNING A JOINFOSTERING CLASSROOM

In a joinfostering classroom, the social and physical environment must allow students of varying English-language proficiency to interact meaningfully with the teacher and with peers. The pattern of studentless talk found in most classrooms is often a direct result of a social environment that curbs student participation and a physical arrangement that divides the room into teacher space and individual student space. In this kind of classroom environment there are few opportunities for students to exchange ideas or to present different points of view. In short, students are prohibited from communicating authentically about topics that matter to them. This pattern may also prevent some students from interacting in ways that are culturally familiar to them (Trueba & Delgado-Gaitán, 1983).

In planning a joinfostering classroom, we need to consider the social and physical environments in tandem, since each contributes to the efficacy of the other. The social environment concerns the ways students participate in social interaction throughout the day. Organizing the classroom so that at times students talk and work among themselves requires certain social rules of behavior and a physical environment arranged in such a way that students can collaborate without interrupting the work of others. Let's discuss the social rules of classroom behavior first and then examine ways to reinforce them through the physical arrangement of furniture, paths, and learning materials.

In the typical all-English classroom, the social organization of the classroom into rows of students being taught in whole groups supports a participation structure in which the teacher has exclusive rights over who is granted permission to talk and what they are allowed to say (Au & Mason, 1981). In this arrangement, students who wish to respond to the teacher's question must raise their hands and wait until the teacher calls on them, reinforcing competition among students (Kohn, 1986). While this participation structure may have a place in whole-group instruction, it is inappropriate for a joinfostering classroom because it severely limits the range of participant structures that must be present for social interaction in the three major social contexts for learning.

The Balance of Rights of Participation

In classrooms organized around joinfostering principles, we need to consider three dimensions used to differentiate access to classroom participation. The three dimensions of control, which can occur in any of the three pedagogical contexts that support language and content learning, are as follows (Au & Mason, 1981):

1. *Control of turn-taking:* The teacher can allow more than one student to speak contemporaneously, rather than limiting the floor to one student at a time;

2. *Control of topic:* The teacher can allow the students to dictate the topic to be studied, discussed, or written about, rather than insisting that they stay on a prescribed topic;

3. *Control of talk and writing audiences:* The teacher can allow the students to talk among themselves and write to a variety of audiences, rather than insisting that they address their talk and written work only to the teacher.

Within any social context of classroom learning, a *balance of rights* of participation occurs when neither the teacher nor the students control more than two dimensions at any one time (Au & Mason, 1981). For example, in small-group literature study, we may allow the students to talk or write only about the story or story-related ideas (teacher control of topic). The students, however, may be allowed to talk freely with one another throughout the story (student control of talk opportunities) without raising their hands (student control of turn-taking). Talking freely supports the integration of listening and talking or what Heath (1985) refers to as the "tie-in" strategy of developing new language abilities. In a whole-group setting, we may require students to raise their hands before talking (teacher control of turn-taking), but encourage them to bring their own experiences into the discussion or the writing activity (teacher-student shared control of topic), and at key points in the lesson ask them to share ideas in pairs (teacher-student control of talk and writing audiences). Bringing in past experiences is what Heath (1985) calls the "tie-back" strategy for making classwork meaningful. When students share ideas in pairs they are also employing the tie-in strategy.

Both lesson samples achieve a balance between speaking and turn-taking rights of the teacher and the students. However, if either the teacher or the students have exclusive control over all three dimensions, we can no longer speak of a balance of rights for participation. Once this happens, all meaningful interaction between the teacher and the students ceases, as do opportunities for capitalizing on tie-in and tie-back learning strategies.

Support for Language and Content Learning

A balance of rights provides support for second-language development and content learning in ways that are not so obvious. For instance, allowing more than one student to talk at a time essentially means that students are talking to one another and perhaps to the teacher, using language that more closely resembles naturally occurring communicative exchanges. In addition, when students are talking to one another, they also have a chance to take turns listening to one another and thus to tie in several language skills at once. In both cases, the result is increased frequency and variety of second-language practice as students talk about and work on topics of mutual interest (McGroarty, 1989).

Being able to decide on and control the topic of a conversation can also facilitate second-language acquisition (Ellis, 1984). Topics that are initiated by students rather than by the teacher are often of greater interest to students and are more likely to have genuine purposes because students can tie back to prior experiences. For example, a teacher may generate some interest on the topic of earthquakes when it comes up in a chapter in science, but after experiencing one, students will have a million questions. When students are truly interested in the topic, the language and interaction that occurs around it are immediately more meaningful and thus most likely to facilitate second-language acquisition (Enright, 1991).

A balance of rights also encourages discourse types that expose second-language students to multiple uses of language during content learning. For example, when students are allowed to talk among themselves to accomplish a goal, they are using "share discourse" (Enright & McCloskey, 1988). Share discourse occurs frequently in classrooms rife with collaboration. Pease-Alvarez and Vásquez (1990) attest to the power of share discourse in their study on the value of social interaction for learning to use computers to enhance learning. They found that language-minority students who talked about ways to use the computer and who wrote personal messages to one another on the computer showed substantial gains in both language development and computer knowledge. Another type of discourse that is practiced when students are allowed to talk freely in class is "fact discourse" (Enright & McCloskey, 1988), which involves language that is used in the discovery and creation of new knowledge. An example of fact discourse is language that would be learned in collecting information and then preparing a classroom newscast about a topic decided upon by the students. Last, when students are encouraged to exchange ideas, their imaginations are also inspired. Language that is used in the service of imagination to create and organize new ideas is "thought discourse" (Enright & McCloskey, 1988). Students meeting to decide on ways to help the homeless or how to program Logo on the computer to draw a mermaid are examples of thought discourse. These examples are possible only in classrooms where joinfostering is supported by a balance of rights of participation between the students and the teacher. A more complete discussion on the relationship between interaction and second-language acquisition is presented in Chapters 4 and 5.

Classroom Norms for Participation

In the joinfostering classroom, students need to feel that talking and collaboration are acceptable ways of behavior. If we as teachers wish to achieve a balance-of-rights classroom atmosphere, we must establish a set of rules or *norms* of participation that guide our own and the students' behavior within the three major pedagogical contexts (teacher-led large group, teacher-led small group, and teacher-delegated small group). Cohen (1986) defines a norm as a rule for how students ought to behave. In the three social contexts for learning, students must learn norms of participation that require them to listen to their teacher and other students, to give others a chance to talk, to ask for others' opinions, and to make meaningful contributions during both large- and small-group work.

Examples of norms of participation that support the balance of rights hypothesis are:

1. Listen when the teacher or your classmates are talking to you.
2. Give your classmates a chance to talk.
3. Ask your classmates for their ideas.
4. Say your own ideas (Morris, 1977).
5. Try to figure things out for yourself. When you can't, ask the teacher or a classmate for help (Enright & McCloskey, 1988).

These norms of behavior are general enough to be applicable to multiple ways of organizing participation within a balance-of-rights perspective. Moreover, the norms reflect the conviction that learning occurs through both social and individual efforts and thus are likely to be culturally relevant to a wide range of student backgrounds. Once you have established a set of classroom rules to support joinfostering principles, it is helpful to talk with students about them and remind them of them as the need arises. You can also explicitly model classroom rules for your students, using both positive and negative examples. (See Enright & McCloskey, 1988, pp. 72–78, for additional information on developing socially oriented classroom rules.) Although there is really no need to post the rules on a wall, some teachers like to do this at the beginning of the school year, for reference purposes.

The Physical Arrangement of the Classroom

As we have already stated, the social environment of the classroom needs to be reinforced by a physical arrangement that allows students to talk and collaborate for part of the day and to learn in a whole-class setting or individually the rest of the time. This requires the thoughtful organization of furniture, of space for movement, and of learning materials.

Regardless of the dimension and size of your classroom, arranging the physical environment to reinforce the social needs is a difficult task that is never complete. The arrangement at the beginning of the school year will not necessarily accommodate the wide range of tasks and supporting group activities coming later in the year (Loughlin & Suina, 1982). Given that the physical arrangement of the classroom is temporary, let's start by considering how to arrange the furniture so that students can experience all three social contexts for learning. This means that we will need to set up an arrangement that allows us to teach to the whole class and to small groups part of the time as well as allowing students to collaborate in small groups and work individually part of the time. Moreover, it means that students will have to be able to move to, from, and around the spaces that we arrange for them without disrupting the general flow of instruction.

Learning to Revisualize Classroom Space. A first step in arranging the physical environment to enable all three social learning contexts is to learn how to visualize classroom space (Loughlin & Suina, 1982). Many teachers see the classroom only as teacher space and student space and thus overlook valuable learning space. The way we look at classrooms is partly a function of our own experiences as students and partly a result of our preparation for teaching. For example, a common practice in teacher preparation programs is to have students conduct micro-teaching lessons in front of the room so that they can demonstrate effective teaching behaviors. Moreover, teaching in the teacher zone is abundantly reinforced when students go out into the schools to do practica for their methods courses. Both of these practices hamper the way that we visualize the use of space.

In a joinfostering classroom, teaching and learning take place in many areas of the classroom: in the corners, in group areas, in a converted storage closet, at learning centers, at the back of the room, around the piano, on the carpet, under the window, on an old couch, around the computer screen, and at students' desks. A primary goal of arranging a joinfostering classroom is to visualize and then create multiple learning areas in places that are not necessarily bordered only by the corners of the classroom and still maintain a functional whole-class environment.

A good place to start is to make a floor plan of the classroom showing the size and location of all of the built-in features. Next, by sketching in all of the furniture as close to scale as possible, we can begin to get a realistic picture of spaces, pathways, and room for activities. Once we have the finished floor plan in hand, we are ready to consider the following basic questions:

1. What learning spaces are available for students? Are there both small and large activity spaces?
2. Which spaces are occasionally used by the students? Which are seldom used? Which are never used?
3. Where are the crowded areas of the classroom?
4. Which spaces serve as pathways for movement?
5. Which spaces are used by students to relax?
6. Which spaces are used for noisy activities? Which are used for quiet activities?

Answers to these questions reveal where and under what conditions students spend most of their time in class, which areas they use occasionally, and which areas are never used at all. In other words, the answers tell us whether, in general, the physical arrangement supports the variety and kinds of communication and social integration features we wish to incorporate into the daily routines of our classroom.

A general picture of the physical arrangement also helps us think about the places that we have or have not provided for student activities. If the picture that emerges is one in which the majority of student activities occur either in a large-group area or individually at student desks, and that space has not been arranged to allow for variation in the amount of student interaction, then clearly students are not engaging in the kinds of activities that support two-way communication and social integration!

In a joinfostering classroom, students need certain places to talk, listen, read, and write together in a host of activities and certain other places to work alone. Accordingly, it is important to bear in mind the noise level that an activity will probably generate (small-group work is noisy!) as well as the amount of traffic in and out of the learning space. Noisy activity centers and places with lots of student traffic should be located a good distance from learning activity space designed for quieter activities. In addition, it is a good idea to locate small animals away from noisy areas. These requirements need to be considered as furniture is arranged and learning activity spaces and pathways are defined.

Multiple Uses for Classroom Furniture.   Furniture obviously designed for student use consists primarily of desks or tables and chairs, computer booths, and, frequently, in the lower primary grades, a rug or two. To this basic student furniture, we can add new furniture in order to break up classroom space and at the same time create new space. It is best to use furniture that can be easily rearranged and that can serve a variety of purposes (Enright & McCloskey, 1988). Another feature to consider in acquiring new furniture is whether it can help define learning activity space. For example, low tables can be used to define an area out from a corner or along the wall by providing one- or two-side protection. If we place the low table within a small area designed for three or four students, they can use it for written work while they sit on cushions (Loughlin & Suina, 1982). On other occasions, students can use the same table for teamwork on math problems, art construction, and bookmaking.

Other furniture pieces that can serve a variety of purposes and define learning space as well are large milk crates, bookshelves on wheels, revolving bookcases, bookracks, message boards, couches, chalkboards on wheels, throw rugs, and seat cushions. Low bookcases can be placed down the middle of the room, for example, to immediately divide the room into two halves. Add a message board at a right angle to the bookcase and you create an additional space. A revolving bookcase placed on a small tiled area of the room can form part of a classroom library. A chalkboard on wheels can be moved around the room for teacher-led small-group work. Placed perpendicular to the wall, the chalkboard provides a relatively secluded learning space, the size of which can be adjusted by moving the chalkboard closer to or farther from any other piece of furniture that happens to be serving as the third side of the area. Large milk crates can be stacked to form a wall or be used to keep journals, magazines, and paper. Different-color rugs can be used to designate talk areas, quiet areas, be-alone areas. The possibilities are endless.

In addition to movable furniture, we can also learn to use the space in and around the permanent fixtures of our classrooms: the storage shelves, the storage closet, the coat room, the windows, and the bookcases. Once filled, storage shelves are rarely used throughout the year. So instead of viewing them as teacher space (because they are filled with your junk!) look at them as walls to be covered or as the back side of a learning activity space. Try placing a table against them. If the shelves are low enough and strong enough, consider using them as a kind of bench to use during singing and for watching a classroom play.

The storage closet and the coat room can also be made into excellent learning activity spaces. The storage closet can be converted into a special place for reading or studying individually. Loughlin and Suina (1982), for example, relate the story of a teacher whose lighted storage closet so attracted the attention of her students that she reorganized the higher levels for storage purposes and then added a small table and lots of books and pictures for students' use. Now the closet has become a special place for enjoying reading! On the door of the closet, you can tape a height chart to keep track of student growth or a long poem written by your students.

If the coat room is well-lighted and within your view, you may wish to consider adding a small table and chairs and equipping the space with tape recorders so that students can listen to taped versions of their favorite storybooks. Windows are also great learning spaces. You can maintain small gardens and observation charts near the windows. Students can record growth and weather information to share with the class throughout the week. As these examples illustrate, there are many ways to take advantage of permanent classroom furniture. The idea is to organize and arrange the room so that students have lots of activity spaces for talking, listening, reading, and writing about a variety of interesting topics.

Movement In and Around the Classroom.   Every learning activity space in your classroom requires some empty surrounding space for movement (Loughlin & Martin, 1987). Students need to be able to get to and from the learning space and be able to move around it without bumping into one another or interfering with activities occurring in adjoining space. Moreover, there must be clearly defined pathways that enable students to get from one learning activity site to another. To function effectively, a path should be visible at several different eye-levels; students should be able see it just as clearly from their chairs or floor-level angles as they do from their standing and walking heights.

In addition, the space arranged for paths should not be available for other uses. Paths should be vacant at all times. Students can interfere with the work of others if the pathways cross into learning activity space or vice versa. Thus, it is important to make sure that students are working within designated learning spaces and also that the paths to, from, and around the learning spaces remain empty to facilitate movement through the environment.

Paths are important not only because they can lead students to and from learning activities, but also because they provide access to valuable learning materials that support the activities. In classrooms with multiple contexts for learning, students will need to make use of raw materials (construction materials, fabrics, cords, papers), tools (for measuring, joining, computing, cutting, observing, viewing, recording, heating, expressing, and communicating), containers (flat and deep boxes, watertight pails, cages, racks, envelopes), and information sources (references, pictures, recordings, natural specimens, labels, books, magazines, models, charts, living things) at different times in the day for different purposes. (See Loughlin & Suina, 1982, pp. 78–101; Loughlin & Martin, 1987, pp. 19–26 for additional examples.) To ensure that all students have access to the available support materials, we need to make certain that there are clear and visible pathways to the materials. However, it is equally important to consider the distribution of learning materials, since although some materials are best stored at centralized locations, other materials should be recentralized to minimize traffic problems and to get materials into students' hands when and where they need them (Loughlin & Suina, 1982).

The Distribution of Learning Materials.   There are essentially two ways to distribute learning materials. Each way regulates when and where students locate the learning materials and may also determine whether they are used at all (Loughlin & Martin, 1987). One way to distribute learning materials is to place them in *centralized* locations throughout the classroom (Loughlin & Suina, 1982). The most common way of centralized materials distribution is to store learning material by categories, such as art materials, reference books, writing and bookmaking materials, and recording tools. Each category of material is located and stored at a specific site. This means that when items from any of the categories are needed for a learning activity, students must travel to the site to gather the material.

Imagine the amount of traffic and the traffic jams that could easily result from students going after learning items located at a few centralized distribution sites in different parts of the room! Too often, the result is that students spend time doing things that are completely unrelated to the activity at hand. Moreover, once an activity has begun, there always seem to be students who realize they forgot to pick up a certain item or need more of something, so they get up to walk across the room while classmates are working and end up interrupting them. For example, on the way to and from the materials storage site(s), a student may stop and talk with friends or get caught up in events at other locations and eventually lose sight of the original reason for leaving his or her seat in the first place. The students who talk with their wandering classmate(s) may also veer from their work. In any event, there is a good chance that both parties will lose valuable time when materials are distributed only at centralized locations.

This is not to say, however, that getting up and moving around in the classroom is wholly undesirable. At times, moving about can be productive because it gives students a chance to see what their classmates are doing and to exchange ideas with them. They should have opportunities to consult with one another, to check out each other's projects, and to learn from one another, especially during small-group work, because it is through such genuine exchanges that students participate in share, fact, and thought discourse.

A way to allow students to talk and collaborate freely without having to move about the room to fetch individual materials at different centralized locations is to divide commonly used materials into smaller quantities and *recentralize* them. (Loughlin and Suina, 1982, refer to recentralizing as *decentralizing*.) Recentralizing learning materials means that collections of learning tools and materials are placed at or near individual learning areas before the activity begins. The closer the combinations of tools and materials are to where the students will be using them, the better. Students are most likely to use the learning materials they can see and reach as they work (Loughlin & Suina, 1982).

Recentralizing learning materials according to their role in the task at hand also reduces traffic and interruption problems. Since the key learning materials needed for the activities are within the students' reach, movement to and from centralized storage areas is reduced; hence, there are fewer instances of students interfering with the work of their classmates. Ample opportunities remain, nonetheless, for students to talk and work together and to share ideas.

CONCLUSION

There are many social and physical adjustments to consider in organizing a joinfostering classroom. Julia Felix's concern over arranging the physical environment to support joinfostering principles is a real one that we will have to address many times over in our own classrooms. If Julia is going to design a social environment that supports a balance of rights between her own and her students' need to talk and decide on what to talk about, she must also have a physical environment that not only permits but also encourages a balance of talking and writing audiences, topic selection, and turn-taking rights.

We know from having read this chapter that many (probably too many) classrooms in the United States are organized to suppress two-way communication, social integration, and opportunities for authentic writing and that many eschew a balance of rights, favoring

instead a recitation mode where participation and interaction are controlled exclusively by the teacher. One of our first challenges, then, is to modify the existing social and physical organization patterns to include, in addition to teacher-led whole-class instruction, small-group work (both teacher-led and teacher-delegated) and individual learning. Each of the major social contexts for learning must allow second-language learners the opportunity to participate in lessons to the fullest extent possible. Moreover, we must be able to incorporate the conditions that are most favorable for second-language acquisition during content instruction. In the next two chapters, therefore, we will examine the nature of classroom interaction to learn about ways to facilitate second-language acquisition within the major social contexts of content instruction, beginning with the whole-class setting.

ACTIVITIES

1. Interview two experienced elementary classroom teachers to find out how they differentiate access to classroom participation according to the balance of rights of participation model. Ask each teacher the following questions:

   A. How do you handle turn-taking in your classroom? Are there certain times when you allow students to speak at the same time?

   B. How are the topics for learning selected in your classroom? Are there times when students choose topics?

   C. Are there certain times during the day when students are allowed to talk among themselves to work on problems?

   D. What kinds of opportunities are there for students to write to real audiences, such as children in other grades, peers, the teacher as a trusted adult, other adults?

   Based on the answers you receive, try to determine whether participation is balanced in favor of the teacher or the students or whether the teacher attempts to share the rights of participation with students.

2. Write out a set of classroom rules that you feel best reflect norms of participation that would require students to listen to their teacher and other students, to give others a chance to talk, to ask for others' ideas and opinions, and to make meaningful contributions during whole-class and small-group instruction. Share your ideas with classmates and discuss them.

3. Visit a local elementary school and draw the floor plan of a classroom that you feel best supports the variety and kinds of communication and social integration features you would like to incorporate into your classroom.

4. Interview two experienced elementary classroom teachers to find out (a) how they arrange and use furniture in their classroom; (b) where they collect learning materials and the kinds of things they look for; and (c) how they organize learning materials in their classroom. If there are animals in the class, tell where they are located and why.

REFERENCES

Au, K. H., & Mason, J. M. (1981). Social organizational factors in learning to read: The balance of rights hypothesis. *Reading Research Quarterly, 17*(1), 115–152.

Cohen, E. G. (1986). *Designing groupwork: Strategies for the heterogeneous classroom.* New York: Teachers College Press.

DeVillar, R. A., & Faltis, C. J. (1991). *Computers and cultural diversity: Restructuring for school success.* Albany, NY: SUNY Press.

Ellis, R. (1984). *Classroom second language development.* Oxford: Pergamon Press.

Enright, D. S. (1991). Tapping the peer interaction resource. In M. McGroarty

& C. Faltis (Eds.), *Languages in school and society: Policy and pedagogy* (pp. 209–232). Berlin: Mouton de Gruyter.

Enright, D. S., & McCloskey, M. L. (1988). *Integrating English: Developing English language and literacy in the multilingual classroom.* Reading, MA: Addison-Wesley.

Enright, D. S., & McCloskey, M. L. (1985). Yes talking!: Organizing the classroom environment to promote second language learning. *TESOL Quarterly, 19*(3), 431–453.

Freire, P. (1970). *Pedagogy of the oppressed.* New York: Herder and Herder.

Furst, N., & Amidon, E. (1962). Teacher-pupil interaction patterns in the elementary school. In E. Amidon & E. J. Hough (Eds.), *Interaction analysis: Theory, research and application* (pp. 167–175). Reading, MA: Addison-Wesley.

Goodlad, J. (1984). *A place called school: Prospects for the future.* New York: McGraw-Hill.

Heath, S. B. (1985). Literacy or literate skills? Considerations for ESL/EFL learners. In P. Larson, E. L. Judd, & D. S. Messerschmitt (Eds.), *One TESOL '84* (pp. 15–28). Washington, DC: TESOL.

Kliebard, H. M. (1989). Success and failure in educational reform: Are there historical lessons? *Occasional Papers,* The Holmes Group, East Lansing, MI: Michigan State University.

Kohn, A. (1986). *No contest.* Boston: Houghton Mifflin.

Loughlin, C. E., & Martin, M. (1987). *Supporting literacy: Developing effective learning environments.* New York: Teachers College Press.

Loughlin, C. E., & Suina, J. (1982). *The learning environment: An instructional strategy.* New York: Teachers College Press.

McGroarty, M. (1989). The benefits of cooperative learning arrangement in second language instruction. *NABE Journal, 13*(2), 127–142.

Morris, R. A. (1977). *A normative intervention to equalize participation in task-oriented groups.* Unpublished doctoral dissertation, Stanford University.

Pease-Alvarez, L., & Vásquez, O. (1990). Sharing language and technical expertise around the computer. In C. Faltis & R. A. DeVillar (Eds.), *Language minority students and computers* (pp. 91–107). Binghamton, NY: Haworth Press.

Ramírez, J. D., & Merino, B. J. (1990). Classroom talk in English immersion, early-exit and late-exit transitional bilingual education programs. In R. Jacobson & C. Faltis (Eds.), *Language distribution issues in bilingual schooling* (pp. 61–103). Clevedon, England: Multilingual Matters Ltd.

Saville-Troike, M. (1984). What *really* matters in second language learning for academic achievement? *TESOL Quarterly 17*(2), 199–219.

Sirotnik, K. (1983). What you see is what you get—Consistency, persistency, and mediocrity in classrooms. *Harvard Educational Review, 53*(1), 16–31.

Trueba, H. T., & Delgado-Gaitán, C. (1983). Socialization of Mexican children for cooperation and competition: Sharing and copying. *Journal of Educational Equity and Leadership, 5*(3), 189–204.

Chapter Four

Integrating Language and Content Teaching in the Whole-Class Setting

● ●

OVERVIEW

The joinfostering framework is built on the premise that second-language students need a variety of opportunities in the classroom for two-way communication (oral as well as written) about content and readings that combines authentic language and language uses with interesting topics. Furthermore, the topics at some point should inevitably enable students to question and discuss critically issues that surface in their lives. As was discussed in Chapter 3, there are three major social contexts in which these conditions take place. This chapter focuses primarily on the first social context for language and content learning: teacher-led whole-class teaching. There are a couple of good reasons for starting with this instructional context. First, whole-class teaching is thoroughly familiar to virtually all teachers (Goodlad, 1984; Ramírez & Merino, 1990; Sirotnik, 1983). In fact, this social context is so familiar that few teachers take notice of the extent to which they control (1) student talk and writing opportunities, (2)

the topic of discussion, and (3) turn-taking rights. One of our goals, therefore, is to make this familiar teaching context seem strange (Spindler, 1982) by consciously attending to these three dimensions of participation as we plan for and carry out lessons within this context.

A second reason for beginning with the social context of whole-classroom teaching is that it is in this setting that the teacher has to attend to the widest range of language abilities. That is, when second-language learners and native speakers of English are mixed in the same large teaching setting, the teacher is constantly faced with the difficult problem of tailoring instructional language to the needs of the language learners without losing the attention and interest of the native English-speaking students and vice versa.

Knowing how to tailor pedagogical language in the whole-class context requires a working knowledge of effective teaching strategies for facilitating second-language acquisition and participation as students exchange information with the teacher and peers about subject matter content (Faltis & Merino, 1992). As we have already learned, few teachers possess this knowledge base (Penfield, 1987). What most all-English teachers do when faced with teaching to a mixed-language whole class is gear their language to the students who readily understand rather than consciously using language in ways that enable the greatest number of students to join in (Wong Fillmore, 1982a). An unfortunate result of this tendency is that the second-language students participate considerably less than their native English-speaking counterparts because much of what the teacher says makes little sense to them (Schinke-Llano, 1983). It is in this circumstance that students become bored and inattentive at best and feel alienated and traumatized at worst (Trueba, 1988). In both cases, students are effectively denied the opportunity to participate so that little, if any, language acquisition or content learning takes place. To counteract this tendency and its undesirable effects, we must learn to facilitate language acquisition during content teaching involving students of diverse English-language abilities. This amounts to a commitment to go beyond the basics of what works for native English-speaking students and incorporate new teaching and learning strategies that work in mixed language-ability settings.

As we learned in Episode One, Julia made a commitment to be the best teacher that she could be for all of her students, to help them see learning everywhere, and to help them appreciate and get along with others. She made a commitment to learn about her students' prior schooling experiences and put a good deal of thought and effort into organizing her classroom so that her students would experience a variety of social settings and literacy experiences that would pique their curiosity. However, like many teachers, she has much to learn about adjusting her teaching to accommodate diverse language abilities during subject matter instruction. Julia came into teaching with a solid communicative stance toward classroom learning and literacy, a stance she relies on frequently for planning and carrying out lessons. But she is often frustrated when she senses that the second-language students are not joining in as well as they could be. She is beginning to suspect that good content teaching is not necessarily the same as good language teaching (Swain, 1988). Therefore, let's begin this chapter by stepping into Julia's classroom to see how she is faring as she learns to integrate language and content teaching. We will follow the episode with a general discussion on how to integrate language teaching and content instruction by adapting the pedagogical language we use for exchanging information about the content and the discourse structures that organize the content in ways that facilitate second-language acquisition.

EPISODE FOUR: STRETCHING THE BASICS OF GOOD BEGINNING TEACHING

The first couple of months have passed by quickly and the students in Julia's class are showing signs that they have internalized many of the social norms for participating appropriately while still being curious, playful, and thoughtful in the variety of social contexts that Julia and the students have implemented. The classroom is arranged so that students work part of the day as a whole group and the rest of the day in small groups or individually. From garage sales and scrounging around the school, Julia has acquired some additional movable furniture to break up the classroom into learning centers, workspaces, and quiet reading and writing spaces. During whole-class teaching sessions, students are seated at their tables, four students to a table. Each table is provisioned with crayons, pencils, erasers, scissors, paper, and a picture dictionary. The walls of the classroom and several bulletin boards used as space dividers are decorated with students' artwork and writings that reflect their interests in current learning topics. At the beginning of the school year Julia decided to post the classroom rules for talking and listening near the water fountain. These are written in large letters and are accompanied by rebus symbols to support their meaning. Now she plans to replace them with student artwork. Julia wanted students to think about what they were doing, to do what works, and to not try to get out of being responsible in and out of class.

Virtually all of the furniture and provisions for learning are labeled with rebus pictures, words, or both. There is also a large map of the world with the birthplaces of all the students marked. Julia has placed individual photographs of the students around the map and used thick red yarn to connect the birthplace on the map to the photograph of the corresponding student. In a number of special places around the room, Julia has organized literacy support materials, including puppets, tape recorders, wordless storybooks, comic books, picture books, and biographies of people from many different walks of life. She also has a special spot for Authors of the Week. These are authors of children's books that she or the students select on a weekly basis. This week Julia is featuring books by authors who write about children as helpers of older people. (See Hudelson & Rigg, 1994/95; Rigg, Kazemek, & Hudelson, 1993, for references.) She uses an old magazine rack for this, and she includes student-authored books in the rack as well.

Julia's teaching units are organized so that most of the content-learning activities relate to a theme that unites concepts across the content areas and ties in the four language processes of speaking, listening, reading, and writing. She believes strongly that language is for constructing meaning, that written language is language, and that context is paramount for making sense of and with language (Edelsky, 1991).

So far in the year, Julia has developed two thematic units and has just begun the third—on elephants, a theme suggested by the students as a result of an intriguing story about how much elephants weigh. Through brainstorming with the students, she has established some of the areas of interest and knowledge that they already have about elephants and has a full set of questions about elephants that they would like to have answered. A very important goal of Julia's thematic units is to engage the students in critical thinking about some aspect of the major topics to be covered in the unit. In this manner, she uses themes as a way to get students to problematize issues associated with the theme. As Ms. Constantino showed her during her student teaching, helping students problematize issues takes a lot of work; students need to read, discuss, and write lots to get a sense of the issues and how to pose them.

The students are excited about making elephant footprints, about finding out how much water an elephant's trunk can hold, about learning to do the elephant walk, about why elephants live in herds, and about helping to stop elephant poaching. They have decided to develop a skit about elephants and their phenomenal memories, to design posters that urge people not to buy ivory products, and to learn about the role of elephants in several different cultures. Several students have even volunteered to find out if elephants are related to pigs! What do you think?

Although the level of participation is generally high, Julia is still frustrated at times that inevitably, some of the second-language students appear lost during whole-class teaching, especially when she is introducing and explaining new topics or when she is giving instructions about the learning activities. One afternoon after the students have left for the day, while Julia is arranging some slides on elephant poaching for tomorrow's class, Jake stops by to see how things are going. "Hey, Julia, what's happening? Everything cool?" "Oh, hi, Jake, come in. Yeah, everything's going pretty well, in general. I'm glad you stopped by because maybe you can help me out." Julia describes what she has been doing in her class and shows Jake around the room to give him a sense of the kinds of activities that students have been involved in. "Here's my concern, Jake. It seems to me that uh, sometimes my ESL students don't understand what I'm saying to them when I'm talking with the whole class; then there are other times when they're working in small groups that seem to be lost. And another thing: Sometimes they don't say anything! Interestingly, they do try to write and stuff, and that's good, but I worry when they don't talk. I want them to feel comfortable talking in this class. Am I being too pushy? Is there something I can do that I'm not doing now to help them understand better and to help them join in and contribute more to the class?"

"Well, Julia, I'll tell you, there are no easy answers to your questions, for sure. But, in my mind, the way you've organized your classroom to include the students' interests is bound to benefit the second-language students. You're giving them all kinds of opportunities to hear and use English while they're learning other stuff. What's fresh is that there's like a bunch of strategies you can learn to use that will really help your students. You might want to start by noticing how you and the students use language when you're going through a lesson with them. You know, like, pay attention to the kinds of questions you and they use in writing and when you're talking with them. Your goal is for you and your students to find ways to use language in a variety of ways for making sense of content. I mean, like, you gotta adjust how you interact with students, and you gotta invite them into the interaction. Help them *see* and *touch* what you're talking about. Let 'em write, let 'em talk, let 'em draw. It's all communication, for sure." "Yeah," says Julia, "I'm with you. That sounds really great. I'm gonna keep workin' on that."

In the following sections, let's pursue Jake's advice and consider ways to plan for and use language during whole-class content teaching, ways that will facilitate second-language acquisition and at the same time enable second-language students to join in learning activities with their native English-speaking classmates. Remember that "what is true for language in general is true for written language" (Edelsky, 1991, p. 97). I refer to teaching that incorporates second-language acquisition principles and includes written language as *language-sensitive content teaching.* This kind of teaching is necessary whenever you as the teacher are primarily responsible for the pedagogical language used in the learning activity. Two special abilities underlie language-sensitive content teaching: (1) taking notice of content language and the kinds of discourse that organize the content and (2) adapting that discourse so that students can comprehend the content and express knowledge about it both orally and in writing.

LANGUAGE-SENSITIVE CONTENT TEACHING

Noticing the Language of Content Teaching

Content instruction in the elementary grades is ordinarily tied to a curriculum design that prescribes the scope and sequence of learning objectives for the subject-matter areas taught at each grade level. Thus, for example, the learning objectives for language arts, science, social studies, science, and mathematics for the 2nd grade may differ in terms of both emphasis and order of presentation from those prescribed for the 3rd grade and so on. Typically, the curriculum is organized so that topics presented in the primary grades are repeated in the upper elementary grades, this time with learning activities that incorporate more sophisticated concepts requiring higher levels of knowledge processing. Moreover, as students progress through the grades, the language of content learning becomes increasingly more context-reduced and more discourse-specific, reflecting a greater demand for academic language abilities and an expanding reliance on written text for learning support. Accordingly, an emphasis in the primary grades on skilled language use through myriad whole-language activities, rather than getting students to practice using language skills, prepares children for the predominately literacy-based learning that prevails in the upper grades (Edelsky, 1993; Edelsky, Altwerger, & Flores, 1990).

The fact that content instruction, particularly in the whole-class context, depends almost exclusively on oral and written language means that content learning is a formidable task for second-language students who are also in the process of acquiring the language of that instruction. Bear in mind that language use becomes more complex and less supported by visual and other real contexts as students move through the grades. One of our challenges, then, is to learn ways to use language during content teaching not only to assist content learning, but also to facilitate second-language acquisition. Let's begin to address this challenge by considering dimensions of language during content instruction, with an eye toward understanding how the language of content teaching interacts with cognitive demands of the tasks we provide our students. In subsequent sections, we will weave into the discussion ways to promote second-language acquisition and participation when students are studying content by first noticing language use and then adapting it to increase student comprehension and expression of ideas.

Dimensions of Language in Content Instruction

Cummins (1981) presents a theoretical framework to help explain why second-language children may have difficulty learning content in an all-English classroom. Cummins proposes that classroom language used in content teaching can be organized along two dimensions, each on a continuum. One dimension concerns the cognitive activity involved in the learning activity and spans from cognitively demanding to cognitively undemanding instruction. A cognitively demanding learning activity might entail the classification of elephant feeding behaviors or the formulation and testing of hypotheses about the various feeding behaviors. Conversely, a less cognitively demanding activity might be listening to or recounting a favorite story about Dumbo the Elephant.

The second dimension addresses the extent of contextual assistance that is provided to a particular learning activity and spans from context-embedded to context-reduced instructional support. For example, the classification activity above could be contextualized by using visuals and other extralinguistic support. Likewise, the Dumbo story could be helped along by using drawings or pictures to support the sequence of the story. Context-reduced learning activities, on the other hand, rely mainly on written text or verbal instructions accompanied by little or no extralinguistic support. Figure 4.1 presents a graphic representation of the intersection of the two continua to show how we can divide classroom language into four quadrants that reflect differing demands on language users.

An important implication of the Cummins framework is that for any content learning activity, we can roughly estimate its potential difficulty for second-language learners according to which quadrant it falls into. We can consider a learning activity to be difficult if the student is required to process and manipulate content knowledge that is largely unfamiliar and/or almost exclusively dependent on linguistic cues, verbal or in text. Thus, learning activities in quadrant A are the least difficult; those falling into quadrant D, the most difficult. Quadrant D activities are difficult because the learners cannot re-embed or call up pre-existing knowledge and language to make sense of them. Learning activities associated with quadrant B are cognitively difficult, but because of opportunities to negotiate meanings through interactions with the teacher and/or peers and

Figure 4.1
Range of contextual support and degree of cognitive involvement in communicative exchanges and classroom lessons
Source: From "The Role of Primary Language Development in Promoting Educational Success for Language Minority Students" by J. Cummins, in *Schooling and Language Minority Students: A Theoretical Framework* (p. 21) by California State Department of Education, 1981, Los Angeles: Evaluation, Dissemination and Assessment Center, California State University, Los Angeles. Reprinted by permission.

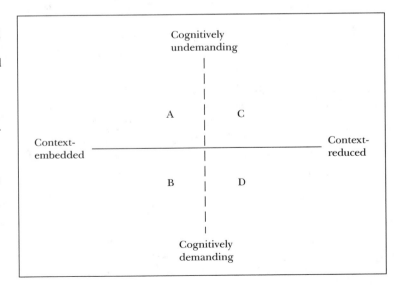

availability of varied extralinguistic cues, second-language students can still participate in them. Quadrant C learning activities deal with content knowledge with which students have already been acquainted, but it is presented without reference to extralinguistic cues from the immediate surroundings. Students are expected to understand the content knowledge in terms of the language used to introduce and explain it without the added support of negotiated language and/or extralinguistic visual and other nonverbal cues. For example, the teacher might verbally review social studies concepts that all students have mastered and then use one or two key concepts and examples to introduce and tie in a related topic that is likely to be less familiar to the students.

The Cummins framework on the dimensions of language in content instruction allows us to take a macro-level view of the language demands placed on second-language learners and to use this information accordingly for selecting learning activities to reflect and support learning objectives. So, for example, if in conjunction with students you decided to plan and implement a thematic unit on recycling (see Irujo, 1990; Gianelli, 1991) or to prepare a lesson from existing content materials on measuring precipitation, we could notice the extent to which the learning activities were contextualized and generally how cognitively demanding they might be given the prior experiences and knowledge processes required for understanding.

I should note here that there is some debate about whether Cummins's two-dimensional framework of classroom language use is realistic. The idea for the framework evolved from Cummins's earlier distinction between BICS (basic interpersonal communication skills) and CALP (cognitive academic language proficiency) (Cummins, 1979), a distinction that for many is based on faulty assumptions about language. As a result of considerable criticism by Edelsky and her colleagues (Edelsky, 1991; Edelsky et al., 1983) Cummins stopped using the terms BICS and CALP in the early 1980s and replaced them with the more sophisticated two-dimensional model that integrates context with how cognitively difficult a school task might be. However, Edelsky (1991) cautions teachers that the newer version retains the basic misconception of language the original distinction carried: That reading is basically a skill and that doing well at skill-based activities is what constitutes CALP-like or cognitively demanding, context-reduced language. Moreover, many teachers in bilingual education still use the terms BICS and CALP to explain differences in language ability. I leave it up to you as critical readers to judge for yourselves whether Cummins's work misrepresents language. (See Activity 5 at the end of the chapter for further discussion of this debate.)

The Language of Teaching Content.   A second feature of language that we can notice is the language of content instruction. Whenever you present content orally or in written form in any of the social contexts of learning, how well students make sense of what you say or write depends greatly on their ability to use the cuing systems of language (phonology in spoken language, orthography in written language, morphology, syntax, semantics, and pragmatics) and to express their meaning. In the teacher-led whole-class context, you typically use language to motivate students about topics of interest, to introduce advance organizers and other information about topics of interest, to elicit and evaluate student exchanges, and to regulate student behavior during the lesson. Students use language to clarify meaning, to inquire about meaning, and to add meaningful information.

Taking notice of the language of content instruction requires an understanding of (1) the kinds of language teachers use for content instruction, (2) the kinds of knowledge structures that underlie content instruction, and (3) the kinds of language students use to make sense of content. In other words, teaching content involves using language to present knowledge structures that support the content of interest and understanding students' meanings of that content. For example, suppose you were introducing a lesson on elephant tusks to a whole class of 3rd graders, some of whom were second-language learners. If you were to start out the lesson by having the class look at a number of slides on elephants and follow this by working together on describing the tusks and then on generating some hypotheses about the function of tusks, you would be engaging students in description and principle formation, two knowledge structures that require very different cognitive processing. Description involves the observation and identification of distinct features; principle formation, by contrast, invokes the use of explanation, prediction, cause and effect, means and ends, and general rules. While both may be cognitively demanding, depending on prior experiences with them, principle formation is especially difficult because it deals with more general, theoretical aspects of knowledge that account for phenomena across time and space (Mohan, 1986). Students may need to inquire about meaning in multiple ways to make sense of how to form principles and, therefore, might use lots of questions and guessing.

Mohan (1986) proposes that subject-matter content includes, but is not limited to, six major types of knowledge structures, which can be further classified into two groups: structures that deal primarily with specific aspects of knowledge and structures that deal with general, more theoretical features. We can identify the knowledge structures underlying any content by asking about the kinds of specific and general information students need to know to understand the topic. The six major kinds of knowledge structure that cut across subject matter content are:

A. Particular aspects of knowledge about the topic
    1. *Description*—The who, what, and where of persons, objects, and events.
    2. *Sequence*—The temporal process, cycle, and procedure of events.
    3. *Choice*—The alternatives, choices, and decisions people make about objects and events.
B. General concepts, principles, and values within the topic
    4. *Classification*—The definition and classification of words, concepts, and events.
    5. *Principles*—The explanation, interpretation, and application of data in order to develop generalizations and draw conclusions.
    6. *Evaluation*—The judging, appreciation, and critique of objects, actions, and events using opinions and other evaluative criteria.

Using the Cummins framework, we could say that the six knowledge structures span across the cognitive activity axis, with description being closest to the cognitively undemanding endpoint and evaluation being closest to the cognitively demanding endpoint. In fact, however, each one of the knowledge structures can be cognitively easier or more difficult depending on the familiarity of the topic and the number of elements, relationships, and properties involved. For example, knowledge structures containing features that are few in number and easily distinguishable from one another are less difficult than structures having many features that are not easily distinguishable from one another (Brown & Yule, 1983). Thus, a short description involving a single person and only one or two major features is considerably easier to comprehend and express than a description involving several persons and covering many details.

Moreover, the Cummins framework also informs us that the knowledge structures can be either context-embedded or context-reduced according to the amount of extralinguistic support used in conjunction with them. Thus, without lowering the cognitive demands of a knowledge structure, context can be added to or subtracted from content to affect the understanding of the lesson and the production of language for expressing meaning and evaluating content understanding. For example, we can use pictures and realia to build background knowledge before and during a discussion or a reading of a sequential narrative on elephant feeding habits. Likewise, students can be helped to talk about the life cycle of elephants by using a chart that diagrams major stages.

A major idea here is that children need to be invited into the discourse of the various knowledge structures, because the knowledge structures are interconnected with content, which in turn is organized around recognizable discourses. As Gee (1992, p. 107) points out, knowledge structures are embedded in secondary discourses, which are "ways of displaying (through words, actions, values, and beliefs) *membership* in a particular social group or social network (people who associate with each other around a common set of interests, goals, and activities)." A secondary discourse is a tradition of talking, writing, being that is passed down through time. When we invite children into a secondary discourse, such as the classification of elephant types, we are reenacting a discourse performance. The performance must be similar enough to how those who do such work (for example, scientists) classify and talk about classification for it to be recognized as such. But how the children classify and what they focus on as distinguishing features can be novel in the sense that their ways may differ from what a more capable member of the discourse would use. The point is that children are entering a secondary discourse. It is in this sense that a secondary discourse acquires the learner or that members of secondary discourses acquire the learner.

As teachers, we are members of certain secondary discourses (math, history, children's literature, art, science), all of which are organized around knowledge structures. When you invite children to participate in various knowledge structures, you are simultaneously engaging them in secondary discourses, which necessarily entails getting them to use academic language and literacy in accordance with the knowledge structure and content area(s) involved (Solomon & Rhodes, 1995). Mathematics, for example, necessarily uses comparison (greater than/less than) and logical connectors (if . . . then, given that) for extended discourse (Spanos, Rhodes, Dale, & Crandell, 1988). Becoming a member of the discourse of science entails formulating hypotheses, describing, classifying, predicting, and revealing findings (National Science Teachers Association, 1991). Moreover, science as well as math discourses require that members present information in the proper sequence, usually in the passive voice (Lemke, 1990). In the social studies, you need to be able to explain, describe, define, give examples, sequence, compare, and evaluate (Short, 1994). History, in particular, relies a great deal on time-specific language, comparing and contrasting, and cause-and-effect relationships (Coelho, 1982).

Assuming that content instruction involves inviting children into knowledge that is organized around Mohan's six categories and that these knowledge structures represent secondary discourses, what other kinds of language do second-language students need to comprehend and participate in whole-class instruction? Up to this point, we have discussed content teaching as if it entailed only informative sequences in which we as teachers present subject-matter content to students. Clearly, however, instructional language in a joinfostering classroom must engage students in two-way interaction about content and within secondary discourses. Not only do you exchange and negotiate meaning in discourse with students, but you also use language to regulate interaction with them, to sustain your invitation to learning. Figures 4.2 and 4.3 illustrate the kinds of language uses students need to deal with during content instruction (Wong Fillmore, 1982b). Figure 4.2 shows the kinds of language that students need to com-

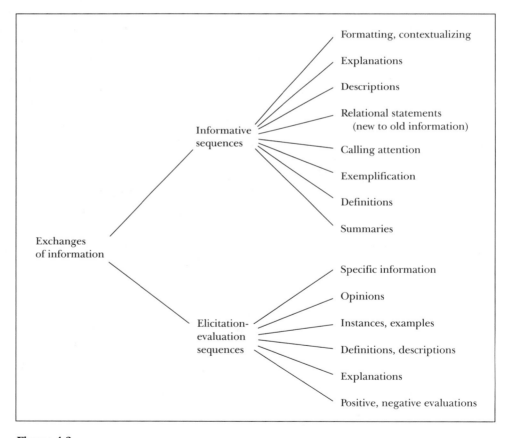

Figure 4.2
Instructional language used by teachers that students need to comprehend during whole-class teaching
Source: From "Language Minority Students and School Participation: What Kind of English Is Needed?" by L. Wong Fillmore, 1982, *Journal of Education, 164,* p. 150. Reprinted by permission.

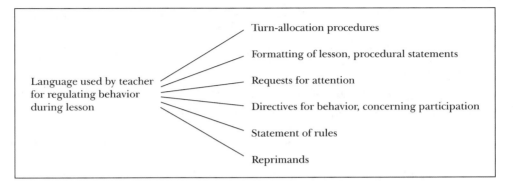

Figure 4.3
Regulatory language used by teachers that students need to comprehend during whole-class teaching
Source: From "Language Minority Students and School Participation: What Kind of English Is Needed?" by L. Wong Fillmore, 1982, *Journal of Education, 164,* p. 150. Reprinted by permission.

prehend in order to follow along and participate in the lesson. Figure 4.3 indicates the kinds of regulatory language students need to comprehend during the lesson. From our perspective, the figures also present the kinds of language that we use routinely to exchange information via knowledge structures and to move students through the lesson.

We can see in Figure 4.2 that the language used in exchanges of meaning includes all of Mohan's six knowledge structures, plus the kinds of language we use to set up and call attention to features within knowledge structures. While the informative sequences deal with information we present to students and therefore with the knowledge structures they have to comprehend, the elicitation-evaluation sequences have to do with requests for and evaluations of information from and by students. For example, during an explanation of how circus elephants are cared for when they are not in shows, students may also be asked for and helped to give examples of the kinds of food elephants eat or to provide an opinion about the care the elephants receive. Thus students have to understand the explanation of the material, which may be organized around the discourse of sequential information and description, and that what the teacher has solicited is information concerning examples and evaluations.

In addition to comprehending information sequences and sequences concerning requests and evaluations of what students produce, students also have to understand language used for regulating behavior. Wong Fillmore (1982b) gives an example of regulatory language to set up the format of a lesson using procedural comments:

And now I will ask you today to do this. Take a partner. Make sure it's a friend. You don't want to work with an enemy. And, you find somebody that you can work together with to do some word problems using addition and subtraction. (p. 151)

This kind of language is important for students because it lays out the procedures to be followed during the learning activity (Edelsky, 1991, Wong Fillmore, 1982b). Other kinds of regulatory language provide students with information about how turns for talk are allocated and about rules for participation during the lesson. Students have to comprehend the myriad functions of the language we use during lessons to benefit from the experience. The greater the understanding we have about the instructional language students have to comprehend, the more prepared we are to make adjustments in how we teach to increase students' comprehension and, ultimately, their active participation and expression of knowledge.

Language in Content. The last feature of language that we can notice in planning and conducting lessons is the vocabulary and grammatical structures of the content, including regulatory language, that we present to our students. Clearly, part of what second-language students have to comprehend within instructional language, be it informational or regulatory exchanges, has to do with surface language features. For example, a seemingly simple description of an elephant bathing himself may prove to be quite difficult for the second-language student:

After filling his trunk with water from the pool, Benny the elephant flipped his trunk back and squirted water all over his back and me!

What do you think are some vocabulary items that second-language students might have difficulty comprehending? To begin, the sentence involves a cause-and-effect relationship signaled by the temporal conjunction *after.* So to comprehend the sentence, students will have to understand that first the elephant filled his trunk with water, and then he flipped it over his head. Moreover, they have to understand that the subject of the adverbial participial clause "After filling his trunk . . . " is Benny, who is not identified until the main clause of the sentence. Then there are the two meanings of *back,* as in "to the rear" and "the rear part of his body," the former being an adverb, the latter a noun.

The point here is not that we need to consider *all* of the language that we use to exchange information and regulate student behavior, but rather that by paying attention to the vocabulary and grammatical structures that we expect students to comprehend and eventually produce, we can anticipate some of the difficulties that students might have. The sentence above does not necessarily need to be simplified or otherwise changed to make it easier for second-language students. Students comprehend language by attending to major propositions and vocabulary that is meaningful to them. They don't need to understand every word said to them to be able to comprehend a message! If we are aware of certain kinds of structures and vocabulary items that are likely to be conceptually difficult and unfamiliar to second-language learners, we can plan our lessons to highlight key vocabulary and adapt our discourse so that the ideas that are bound up in difficult grammatical structures are repeated, rephrased, and recycled throughout the lesson.

Table 4.1 contains a general list of vocabulary and grammatical structures that might be difficult for second-language students, depending on the amount of contextual support provided along with them and the proficiency of the students who may need to understand them. We can use this list for preparing learning activities. For example, we can take existing content information that students will be experiencing during a lesson and look for core and specialized vocabulary items and marked grammatical structures that are critical for understanding the lesson. We

Table 4.1
Selected list of potentially difficult vocabulary items and grammatical structures for English-as-a-second-language learners in all-English classrooms

Vocabulary items
- collective nouns, quantifiers, and mass nouns
- homonyms
- idiomatic expressions
- low-frequency and abstract words
- prepositions of place
- pronouns
- slang
- specialized vocabulary within each content area
- unusual descriptors

Grammatical structures
- comparatives and superlatives
- indirect speech
- passive sentences
- sentences beginning with *There* and *It*
- sentences containing cause-and-effect and sequential connectors
- sentences containing temporal conjunctions: *before, after, until, while, when,* and *since.*

can then plan our lessons to emphasize key vocabulary and to support complex grammatical structures. How we do this and adapt our lessons to facilitate the exchange of information and second-language acquisition is the topic of the next section. Within specific content areas, we can pay attention to technical language in math, science, and social studies. We can also be on the lookout for ordinary language that has different meanings in the particular content area. For example, in math, we have *square* and *take away;* in science, there are *table* and *mass;* and in social studies, *past* and *branches of government.*

Adapting Teaching Discourse

Once we have learned to notice the language of content instruction in terms of the dimensions and aspects presented above, we are ready to take on the second special ability involved in language-sensitive content teaching: adapting our teaching discourse so that students can comprehend the content by listening and reading and express knowledge about it by questioning, writing, and exchanging ideas. Achieving this ability depends on how well we incorporate the following two practices into our teaching routines: (1) making teaching language comprehensibly inviting for second-language learners of all levels, yet relevant and interesting for native English speakers, and (2) enabling students to express their knowledge in ways that are appropriate to their levels of English and the academic task at hand. Before presenting specific strategies to use with each practice, however, let's take a brief look at what needs to be present for learners to develop proficiency in a second language. This will help us understand the significance of these two practices for facilitating second-language acquisition and participation during content instruction.

Facilitating Second-Language Acquisition. Research in second-language acquisition gives us the following scenario: In every case of successful second-language acquisition, learners had been exposed to regular and substantial amounts of *modified language input* and *modified verbal interaction* (Ellis, 1990; Faltis, 1990; Long, 1987; Scarcella, 1990). Modified language input is more widely known as *comprehensible input,* oral and written language addressed to the learner that has in some way been adjusted to accommodate his or her needs (Krashen, 1982; 1985). According to Krashen (1982), comprehensible input is necessary for second-language acquisition because it supplies meaningful language to the learner. Krashen (1982) explains that learners move from one stage to the next higher stage by understanding the language of the next higher stage. If a learner is at stage i (the current level of competence), our job is to provide language that is at i plus 1, or slightly above the learner's current level of competence. Learners understand the i plus by paying attention to extralinguistic context and by using what they already know about how language works in interaction. When learners understand language addressed to them, the language-acquisition device in their head can operate on it, and if the device receives enough comprehensible input, it creates the rules that enable the learner to use language for communication.

Another way to understand modified language input is what I refer to as *comprehensible invite*, which, like comprehensible input, is language that we adjust to the learner's needs, but for a different purpose. The goal of comprehensible invite is to acquire the learner by inviting him or her into the new language at the same time as we invite him or her into the new knowledge system. Like comprehensible input, comprehensible invite includes language that is a bit beyond the learner's current ability, but for different reasons. First, we know that learners can understand more and communicate better in interaction with adults and more capable peers who invite them to exchange ideas than they can when they study those same ideas on their own (Vygotsky, 1978). Second, language that is a bit beyond the learner's current ability and that invites the learner to interact encourages the creative construction of knowledge within academic discourses or knowledge structures. For example, suppose you were talking with the whole class about pachyderms and asking students to figure out their distinguishing features by comparing and contrasting them with other animals. Comprehensible invite on your part included lots of visuals, a Venn diagram (two intersecting circles), some talk, some short reading, a quick write, and lots of exchanges of ideas. The purpose here was to enable English learners to receive comprehensible invite in both oral and written forms, and at the same time for them to use the language and other sources of invite to construct their understanding of pachyderms in the whole-class setting by using various discourse devices to build knowledge.

Support for the role of comprehensible invite in second-language acquisition stems from research on *caregiver speech*, simplified language used by Western caregivers to invite young children into culturally appropriate ways of being (Clark & Clark, 1977; Faltis, 1984; Hatch, 1983) and on *foreigner talk*, the modified language that native speakers use with nonnatives to invite into discourse exchanges (Ferguson, 1975; Long & Sato, 1983). Caregivers simplify their speech to young children, not to teach language explicitly, but rather to engage them in talk about situations that are in the "here and now," topics in full view of both participants. Many caregivers read dozens of storybooks to young children, pointing to pictures and modifying their speech as they move through the text. The combination of simplified speech with topics tied to the here and now provide linguistic as well as extralinguistic supports that invite the child to understand and participate in what is going on, even when it is clear that the child cannot participate at the level of the caregiver. Examples of the kinds of speech modifications that caregivers make in invite participation include *pronunciation* (slower rate, clearer articulation, longer pauses), *vocabulary* (high-frequency words, fewer pronoun forms, marked definitions, gestures and visuals to accompany words), and *grammar* (shorter, simpler sentences, topic fronting, repetition and rephrasing) (Hatch, 1983).

Although caregiver speech is simplified in the sense that it relies less heavily on complex linguistic structures than does speech occurring between fully competent speakers, it is not finely tuned to the child's exact level of linguistic competence. Rather, caregiver speech is roughly tuned to the child's current level of competence. According to Krashen (1985), roughly tuned caregiver speech offers the following advantages in a child's first-language acquisition:

1. It ensures that language slightly beyond the child's level is provided.
2. It provides a built-in review, since with continued communication, the necessary input will occur and reoccur. (pp. 23–24)

I would also add that roughly tuned caregiver speech invites young children to participate in culturally specific identity-building activities. Thus, when a small children is invited into a storybook about a hungry caterpillar, the child is also being invited to learn colors, shapes, animal names, and many other items of culturally relevant information.

Adult native speakers have also been found to modify their speech while conversing with second-language learners in a fashion remarkably similar to the adjustments caregivers make (Long, 1981). First, as in the case of caregiver speech, modifications are made for the purpose of communication, to invite the learner to understand the meaning of the conversation. Second, foreigner talk is roughly tuned to the learner's level, not to a finely tuned level. Accordingly, in attempting to communicate with a second-language learner, a helpful native speaker uses slower rates of speaking, clear articulation, simple vocabulary, and repetition and rephrasing, as in the following example given by Scarcella (1990):

Native English Speaker: Do you want the book?
Nonnative English Speaker: What?
Native English Speaker: Book. Book. Big red book. Do you want this book? (picks up book and hands it to nonnative speaker) (p. 68)

Finally, in both caregiver speech and foreigner talk, native speakers use contextual support such as gestures, visuals, paraverbal expressions, and knowledge of the world to help support verbal language, especially when the child or learner is perceived not to understand the message (Krashen, 1982).

In summary, modified language input supplies learners with comprehensible language. When that language invites the learner to participate by thinking, guessing, talking, and writing, language acquisition is bound to occur.

Full participation in a second language by children who must learn it in school, however, requires that the children whom we invite to participate actually use the second language regularly for a variety of communicative purposes. Wong Fillmore (1985) provides a pretty good reason for the importance of using language steadily for second-language acquisition:

> . . . learners have to be in a position to engage in interactions with speakers in a variety of social situations, since this is what allows them to figure out what is being said, how language is structured, and how it is used socially and communicatively by its speakers. (p. 26)

This brings us to the second part of second-language acquisition: *modified interaction*. Once English learners are invited to interact, they need to have some way of knowing if their meaning is clear and if they understand what is being said or written to them. This is one of the most intriguing parts of second-language acquisition. Here's why. When learners are invited to participate in exchanges, they have to work to come up with meaning that is precise, coherent, and appropriate. In other words, they have to negotiate meaning with the teacher or peers. The negotiation of meaning encourages them to try out new language as well as to notice the gap between their existing language and the language they need to more clearly and precisely express themselves. Moreover, the negotiation of meaning sustains the discourse and resupplies comprehensible invite.

Modified interaction also "pushes" learners to use their developing language and discourse structures (Swain, 1985; Lemke, 1990). Through interaction with native speakers, learners may be obliged to produce language that increasingly approximates English, especially if the native speakers are asking for clarification, checking for understanding, and rephrasing learner language to confirm understanding. The learner's efforts to produce exacting language may force him or her to test hypotheses about or pay attention to the structure of the language, rather than relying primarily on semantic knowledge and inchoate language structures. Being pushed to try out developing language does not promote the acquisition of new language, however. What it does is confirm to the learner how language that is almost acquired works so that it now becomes fully acquired and used to talk about topics that matter.

Teaching for Comprehensible Invite.   Now that you have an idea about the role of comprehensible invite and modified interaction for facilitating second-language acquisition and participation, you are ready for the nitty-gritty of language-sensitive content teaching: adapting your pedagogical discourse to invite all students to participate in understanding and expressing knowledge about content and the connections between content and their personal lives. In the whole-class setting, participation involves the presentation of content plus sequential interaction between you and the students. During the presentation of content your goal is to make language understandable and relevant on at least two levels: first, by adapting the way you invite students to understand content information, and second, by inviting them to interact with you and with their peers about the content under consideration. Recall that we are also striving for a balance of rights of participation so that you and the students will be sharing the three dimensions of participation (refer to Chapter 3).

Lesson Markers.   An important goal in adapting the way you present information and ideas to students in a whole-class setting is to emphasize understanding. Students understand the language of content best when they are focusing on content without having to figure out where they are in the lesson and when you provide multiple sources of context.

There are a number of features in how you organize and present content during whole-class teaching that you can manipulate to ensure that students, especially second-language learners, are with you throughout the lesson. These features, which we refer to as *lesson markers* (Wong Fillmore, 1985), are signals that you provide to students to let them know where they are in the lesson at all times. For example, you can mark the beginning and ending of the lesson with explicit cues, such as "Okay, let's begin by . . . " and "That's all for now; let's put our books away." You can also mark the signal movement through the phases of the lesson by telling students exactly what you are doing, how it relates to what you have done before, and what you will be doing. For second-language students, lesson markers serve a very important purpose, as Wong Fillmore (1985) points out:

> "Once [second-language learners] learn the sequence of subactivities for each subject, they can follow the lesson without having to figure afresh what is happening each day. They know what they are supposed to do and what they should be getting out of each phase of the lesson; thus they are ahead of the game in figuring out what they are supposed to be learning each day. (p. 29)

Discourse Markers.   While lesson markers signal lesson boundaries, you can also work toward shaping the specific styles of language that you think are required of students during the academic task at hand. In this case, what is important is to help students participate in the discourse of the content area in ways that resemble the discourse of more capable members. For example, suppose you were working with the entire class on how to write a letter to various zoos throughout the United States. The purpose of the letter is to inquire about the kinds and numbers of elephants that are in the zoo and to ask some questions about their daily behaviors. You may wish to highlight different ways of organizing the letter and then encourage students to begin composing their drafts. Another opportunity might occur when students are setting up science experiments; you can assist them in using terms that more experienced members of science discourse would use automatically, such as *steps, hypotheses,* and *conclusions.*

Contextualizing Whole-Class Discourse.   In addition to helping students follow the instructional content by marking phases and boundaries, you can also contextualize your teaching by supporting it through paraverbal, nonverbal, and visual means, also known as *extralinguistic support.* As we learned from the Cummins framework, extralinguistic support facilitates the understanding of new information and knowledge structures to which the information is bound. There are three major ways to provide extralinguistic support to the language you use in teaching content in a whole-class setting:

1.   *Paraverbal support.* Paraverbal support has to do with the ways you emphasize and use sounds and change the pace of your speech as you talk and invite students to participate in the lesson. There are many occasions, for instance, when you can illustrate the meaning of emotions, feelings, and senses through vocal sounds. As you say "A rose smells goooooooood," you can sniff and emphasize the word *good* by stretching it out with rising intonation. A story about a mean giant might call for a deeper voice with punctuated vocalization of key words in order to convey just how mean the giant really is! Turning the volume of your speech up and down also communicates meaning. Using whispers and howls to describe changes in the wind helps students understand vocabulary that might otherwise go unnoticed.

Another way to support instructional language through paraverbal means is to pay attention to the rate and clarity of your speech as you describe, explain, exemplify, elaborate, question, and evaluate. Speaking too quickly during the presentation of key concepts and vocabulary may cause you to lose second-language learners at a critical part of the lesson. Abnormally slow speech, on the other hand, can also cause nonunderstanding, since students rely on the rhythm of your speech to make sense of what you are saying. As a rule of thumb, the rate and clarity of your speech should resemble what you normally use in more casual conversation, with the proviso that you enunciate clearly. Lastly, humming and singing are wonderful ways of providing paraverbal support for learning words and phrases.

2. *Nonverbal support.* Many teachers, particularly in the primary grades, routinely use their hands along with facial expression to illustrate meanings of concepts, notions, and actions. When there are second-language learners in the classroom, bodily and facial gestures are indispensable for making input comprehensible. It is amazing how much meaning support can be generated from gestures such as pointing, waving, joining fingers, holding up fingers, and marking space with your hands. Some meanings can easily be portrayed through bodily movement. Can you, for example, think of ways to pantomime a baby elephant desperately searching for his mother or a cowgirl gracefully galloping on a horse? How about dressing up as Charlie Chaplin once a week to pass out special words—words that your students give you to share with the class. You act out and the children try to guess them.

As the need arises, you can also combine facial expressions with physical gesticulations to indicate surprise, anger, joy, sadness, disappointment, disgust, astonishment, and wonderment. While the facial expressions you use to convey emotions may not be entirely cross-cultural, with repetition and support from other contexts, students soon learn to interpret their meanings in ways that you have intended. Finally, facial expressions coupled with gestures can show students that you are listening to them, that you are interested in what they have to say, and that you will stay with them in their efforts to express their knowledge (Enright and McCloskey, 1988).

3. *Visual and sensory support.* Visual aides are especially useful for organizing and displaying content information. For example, a picture or a diagram can be used to tie in and build background knowledge about a topic and then again later to synthesize new information gained from talking about the topic (Early, 1990). Visual aides can also be used to help students experience the different ways that knowledge is organized in structures (Mohan, 1986). A sequence, for example, can be made visible by using a timeline. A globe or a map provides visual evidence of the distance between Africa and Asia, two regions where elephants live in the wild. A web of ideas concerning elephant features can serve as a springboard to creative classification. Students can test hypotheses about whether concepts are similar or different by using a Venn diagram. All of

these suggestions are examples of graphic organizers, ways of representing different kinds of thinking processes (Alvermann, 1986; Dunston, 1992). You can use graphic organizers to organize the lesson or theme with students. You can also teach students to construct their own graphic representations of the classroom content (Jones, Pierce, & Hunter, 1989). Other ways of providing support for information within knowledge structures include photographs, slides, videodiscs, and videocassette movies.

In a joinfostering classroom we want students to experience lots of realia, or real-life objects, to feel and smell them, and to hear the sounds they might make. Realia are the ultimate visuals because they allow students to use all five senses to experience them. For example, suppose your classroom decided to "adopt" an elephant at the local zoo. As part of the project, your students would have to learn about the elephant's eating habits both in the wild and in the zoo. Visual aides could help them illustrate and classify foods that elephants eat. Students could also prepare a treat of roasted peanuts to send to their adopted elephant!

Print is also a form of visual support. Fill the walls, ceilings, doors with sayings, symbols, and announcements: "An elephant never forgets" "Slow down, elephants crossing" "Don't buy ivory products." Classroom furniture can be labeled for, as well by, the students. As students' literacy abilities improve, print can be used as visual support to teach songs and poems.

Inviting Student Participation. In addition to marking lesson boundaries and providing extralinguistic support to make lessons and activities comprehensible, we need to facilitate student participation by providing opportunities for second-language students to indicate and express understanding when they exchange and share information during the development of the lesson. The balance-of-rights perspective reminds us that we should constantly monitor our teaching discourse to ensure that we do not monopolize the topic, amount, or manner of talk during whole-class instruction. Thus, while we should be concerned with providing extralinguistic support to our discourse as we teach, we also need to encourage students to participate verbally; in the case of second-language learners, we may even need to "push" them gingerly to use their developing language to express meaning and show understanding (Swain, 1985).

Getting students to interact with you in a whole-class setting is a delicate task, requiring multiple strategies for both soliciting talk and responding to what students say. There are basically two ways to get students to talk: (1) ask them directly and (2) pique their curiosity. Asking them directly is the easier of the two. Here are five basic techniques for asking students to talk in a whole-class setting (Enright & McCloskey, 1988):

1. *Ask the question—call on a student.* In this technique, you simply pose a question and then immediately call on a student by name, without the student having to bid for a turn at talking. If you overuse or use this technique unwittingly with English learners, it can be ineffective because some students may be too embarrassed to express themselves in English while the whole class listens to them.

2. *Ask the question—students bid for the floor.* In this case, you ask a question and the students bid for an opportunity to talk by raising their hands. This technique works best when all students understand how to gain access to the floor. If only a handful of the same students raise their hands following a question, participation is not likely to be equitable. Also, in this technique, you need to keep a mental tally of which students have gained the floor and the kinds of questions that these students have responded to (Faltis, 1986).

3. *Ask a question—any student can answer.* There may be times when you pose an open-ended question to which anyone in the class might have an individual answer. To be effective, the students must understand that you want them to speak up without having to bid for the floor.

4. *Ask a question—the entire class responds.* In this case, the entire class responds chorally to your directive or request to recite words, phrases, or long stretches of language, such as poems and important documents. Choral repetitions allow second-language students to practice controlled language use safely within the group.

5. *Ask a question—students take turns responding.* There are certain times when you may want several students to answer the same question, one by one in a patterned sequence. For example, you may ask every fourth student what kind of food he or she would like to prepare for the elephant the class has adopted.

Each of these solicitation techniques has both advantages and disadvantages, but in order to maximize the advantages, it is essential to use all five techniques during whole-group teaching. Variety helps ensure that all of the students, regardless of their English proficiency, are given the opportunity to participate at least some of the time.

A joinfostering classroom should be a place where students are constantly thinking and taking pleasure in using their intellect (Edelsky, 1991). While asking students questions can be helpful for some occasions, there are many times when you should provide only minimal help until the students first do some thinking. One way to get students to participate is to challenge them with thought-demanding projects. They will ask the questions about how to tackle the problem. You can also model that working hard is serious fun. When you pique their curiosity about amazing things, they will talk with you.

It should go without saying that when you ask a question of or solicit a response from a second-language student, you should allow sufficient time for the student to answer. You can also give students an extra chance by repeating the question. If you feel that the student either does not understand the question or lacks the oral language proficiency to respond to it, you may also use alternate question forms. For example, in the following communicative exchange the student, Aucencio, appears not to understand the question. The teacher rephrases the question, making it more concrete. When this doesn't work the teacher uses a choice question and sustains the interaction:

T: So, what do you think the elephant will do next? Aucencio, what do you think? (gives time to answer)
S: Next? Elephant?
T: Yes, what will the elephant do when he finds the water?
S: I think he's going there [pointing to a picture of a pond].
T: Yes, Aucencio, that's where the elephant is going. Do you think he will take a bath or look for trees?
S: I think he's . . . take a bath.
T: Yes, you're right. He will jump right in the water and take a nice, cool bath. Elephants love to bathe in the water.

When Aucencio was unable to answer the second, rephrased question, the teacher could instead have used a yes/no question: "Will the elephant take a bath?" This question is a bit easier to respond to because it does not necessarily call for a verbal response; a nod of the head would also have indicated understanding. The point here is that we can vary our solicits for student participation according to the student's oral language proficiency. Accordingly, for beginning second-language learners, a nonverbal response such as a nod, a smile, or pointing to an object may be acceptable, while more advanced students should be pushed to use words and extended discourse. As students become more proficient in English and adjusted to the interaction patterns used during whole-class instruction, your goal is to help them improve the accuracy of their communicative abilities. One way to nudge your second-language learners to use language communicatively is to utilize discourse strategies in which you negotiate with students the meaning of responses to your questions, either to confirm that you have understood what you heard or to request additional information to clarify what you heard. Two strategies for negotiating meaning with second language students are *confirmation checks* and *clarification checks* (Long, 1987; Schachter, 1984).

Confirmation checks are expressions by the teacher that confirm to the learner that his or her utterance has been correctly understood or correctly heard. Confirmation checks are invariably in the form of a raising question and always repeat part or all of the learner's preceding utterance (Schachter, 1984). Interestingly, confirmation checks not only help to confirm understanding, but they also may model in a nonthreatening manner the correct way to say an utterance. Day, Chenoweth, Chun, and Luppescu (1981, in Schachter, 1984) provide an example of a confirmation check that also models the correct grammar:

Learner: All the people think the Budda is the people same.
Native Speaker: Same as the people?
Learner: Yeah. (p. 173)

Here the dialogue is continued because of the native speaker's effort to confirm the learner's meaning. More language could be generated by a follow-up question on the learner's original message.

Sometimes learners, in response to a solicit for information, produce language that is incomprehensible or in need of clarification. When this happens, we can ask the learner to furnish new information or to rephrase the information just given in order to clarify meaning. Ordinarily, clarification requests are in the form of information questions (what, where, who, how, when, why, etc.) or yes/no questions, but they can be expressed in other ways as well (Schachter, 1984). Clarification requests, such as the ones in the following exchange (Pica, 1987, p. 6), enable the learner to make their initially unclear messages meaningful:

Learner: And they have the chwach there.
Native English Speaker: The what? (clarification request)
Learner: The chwach—I know someone that—
Native English Speaker: What does it mean? (clarification request)
Learner: Like, um, like American people they alway go there every Sunday.
Native English Speaker: Yes?
Learner: You know—every morning that there pr- the American people get dressed up to go to, um, chwach.
Native English Speaker: Oh, to church—I see.

By negotiating meaning with the learner, the native English-speaker in this excerpt helped push the learner to use additional language to clarify meaning, an effort that resulted in sustained interaction as well.

Clarification requests can also come from the learner when the language used by the teacher is beyond the learner's comprehension. In this case, the learner may ask for a clarification, resulting in the teacher's adjusting his or her language to make it comprehensible to the learner and thus providing comprehensible input through negotiation. Enright and McCloskey (1988) point out that teacher-initiated confirmation checks and clarification requests should be used with care because they "can make students feel that they have made some kind of mistake or that they are on the spot in front of class." However, if much of what you do in whole-class teaching involves genuine exchanges of meaning, there is little chance that these two strategies will produce negative results.

CONCLUSION

The major focus of this chapter has been on the development of language-sensitive content teaching and interaction strategies for whole-class settings. An important goal in the joinfostering classroom is to facilitate second-language acquisition and invite participation during content instruction so that students can learn academic discourse. Accomplishing this two-fold goal depends a great deal on learning to notice the language of content teaching and interaction and on knowing the conditions under which second-language acquisition and participation are most likely to occur. We have learned about several strategies for providing comprehensible invite and modified interaction to second-language learners, language that assists participation in oral as well as written communicative exchanges. In the next chapter, we will turn our attention to the social contexts of teacher-led and teacher-delegated small-group work. Much of what has been covered in this chapter will also apply to small-group learning, but we will also be looking at ways to socially integrate second-language learners with native speakers, to facilitate communicative exchanges in small-group work, and to foster cooperative learning during group work.

ACTIVITIES

1. Find or develop your own activities for a thematic unit and place the activities within one of the four quadrants developed by Cummins (1981). Next, show how you can adjust the cognitive complexity and contextual support to make the activities easier or more difficult, and more or less supported by contextual clues. See Gianelli, 1991, and Enright & McCloskey, 1988, for examples of thematic units and how to construct them.

2. Select one science and one social studies textbook used for elementary-school children. Next, for both

books, choose a chapter toward the middle and the end to analyze for the kinds of knowledge structures (using Mohan's six knowledge structures) that the author uses to present information. Compare and contrast the knowledge structure used in the two books and discuss the kinds of difficulties a second-language learner might face in having to comprehend the material in each of the textbooks.

3. Using one chapter from each of the above textbooks, select what you would consider difficult vocabulary and grammatical structures for second-language learners. Justify your choices and suggest how you might present the vocabulary either before or during the lesson to make sure that the second-language learners understood the meaning.

4. Observe and, if possible, tape an all-English classroom containing second-language learners during whole-class instruction time. The observation should be for at least 20 minutes. During the observation, jot down the kinds of informative and elicitation-evaluation exchange sequences the teacher uses in talking to the students as well as the kinds of regulatory language used. After completing the observation, tally the results and write up a snapshot description of the kinds of language exchanges and regulatory language that second-language students would need to understand to follow the lesson. Remember that any time you set foot on school grounds you

need to check in at the main office before going to the classroom in which you plan to observe.

5. Arrange to interview a 3rd-, 4th-, or 5th- grade second-language learner for about 15 minutes. Introduce yourself and tell the student you are interested in learning about what he or she does every day in school. Then, using the adaptation and negotiation strategies presented in this chapter, try to elicit as much conversation from the student as you can. Immediately after the interview, once the student is no longer present, write down what you think worked best and also what you think you could have done better.

6. Enter the debate between Edelsky and Cummins over the nature of language in school. Read Edelsky et al. (1983) and Cummins and Swain's (1983) response. What follows is a poem written in defense of Edelsky's position. Write your own poem in response to this one based on what you understand of the Edelsky-Cummins debate.

A Whole in My Head

In '79 I was but 10 years old
The bilingual community was to be told
About a whole new thought-train
Birthed by Cummins and Swain
And to it teachers 'round the world
    would be sold.

"Bilingual education! Let's drop all the
    labels!

We have icebergs now not just graphs
and tables!

From Shuy we have the icebergs and
Oller, global dimensions,

Donaldson's data with Scots, Kangas'
and Toukamaas' work with Finns.

Celebrate! We'll now classify with fact
not fables!!

There are two types of language for an
easy fix

Smartly labeled CALP and BICS.

Oh let's not pretend, there are many
that'll doubt

Our practices, and scream and shout

But they can't get by us despite their
tricks."

So the education world was content

And bilingual conference moneys were
spent.

They went by the thousands to see the man

Day by day was the birth of a new fan.

When Cummins' name was mentioned,
many an ear was bent.

But uh-oh, what was to happen in '82?

There came a challenge to the bilingual
guru!

Her name was Carole and she wasn't out
to dis.

What she wanted to say is—"We've got
to change this!

How can we assess language on the basis
of IQ?

When working with theory it's easy to label

With kids it's harder to put your cards
on the table.

When qualifying with standardized tests

You dwell on the 'worst' and throw out
the 'best.'

Your idea of 'deficit position' seems far
from stable.

Home and school language are widespread on your map

But we in Whole Language want to close
that gap.

CALP seems to result only from direct
skill instruction,

Introduce it to intercommunication and
it means destruction!

Is this how we fall into the deficit trap?

Your classifications seem so black and
white

It's precisely this that gives me such a
fright.

What ever happened to a qualitative study?

Observing scores and not the whole
child seems kinda cruddy

And to consider test scores as true reading just isn't right.

I'll tell you, Mr. Guru, there's something
else I fear

It may not happen tomorrow, or even
within the year

But with your deficiency terms are an
abuse of testing.

Any future racial discrimination has no
hope of resting

And as an educator you know there's no
room for that here.

I'm not saying that of your whole theory
we must be rid

But let's think of doing what's best for the kid

The child-learner is complex and should be seen as a whole

That in itself, should be our ultimate goal.

So throw out those rigid tests and fasten the lid."

With those last words, Carole put her paper to bed.

A mere four months later Cummins replied, and was he seeing red!

What ensued was essentially, three long years of hell,

With attacks on Carole and others they tried to quell.

But may we never forget by whom the revolution was led.

by Karina Méndez, 1995

REFERENCES

Alvermann, D. (1986). Graphic organizers: Cuing devices for comprehending and remembering main ideas. In J. Baumann (Ed.), *Teaching main idea comprehension* (pp. 210–226). Newark, DE: International Reading Association.

Brown, G., & Yule, G. (1983). *Teaching the spoken language.* Cambridge: Cambridge University Press.

Clark, H., & Clark, E. (1977). *Psychology and language: An introduction to psycholinguistics.* New York: Harcourt Brace Jovanovich.

Coelho, E. (1982). Language across the curriculum. *TESL Talk, 13,* 56–70.

Cummins, J. (1981). The role of primary language development in promoting educational success for language minority students. In California State Department of Education, *Schooling and language minority students: A theoretical framework* (pp. 3–49). Los Angeles: Evaluation, Dissemination and Assessment Center, California State University, Los Angeles.

Cummins, J. (1979). Linguistic interdependence and the educational development of bilingual children. *Review of Education Research, 49,* 222–251.

Cummins, J., & Swain, M. (1983). Analysis-by-rhetoric: Reading the text or the reader's own projections? A reply to Edelsky et al. *Applied Linguistics, 4*(1), 23–41.

Day, R., Chenoweth, A., Chen, A., & Luppescu, S. (1981). *Native speaker feedback to ESL student errors.* Paper presented in AAAL Symposium at the 1981 ACTFL annual conference.

Dunston, P. J. (1992). A critique of graphic organizer research. *Reading Research and Instruction, 31*(2), 57–65.

Early, M. (1990). Enabling first and second language learners in the classroom. *Language Arts, 67,* 567–575.

Edelsky, C. (1993). Whole language in perspective. *TESOL Quarterly, 27*(3), 548–550.

Edelsky, C. (1991). *With literacy and justice for all: Rethinking the social in language and education.* New York: The Falmer Press.

Edelsky, C., Altwerger, B., & Flores, B. (1990). *Whole language: What's the difference?* Portsmouth, NH: Heinemann.

Edelsky, C., Hudelson, S., Flores, B., Barkin, F., Altwerger, B., & Jilbert, C. (1983). Semilingualism and language deficit. *Applied Linguistics, 4*(1), 1–22.

Ellis, R. (1990). *Instructed second language acquisition.* Oxford: Basil Blackwell.

Enright, D. S., & McCloskey, M. L. (1988). *Integrating English: Developing English language and literacy in the multilingual classroom.* Reading, MA: Addison-Wesley.

Faltis, C. (1990). Classroom language use and educational equity: Toward interactive pedagogy. In H. P. Baptiste, J. Anderson, J. Walker de Felix, and H. C. Waxman (Eds.), *Leadership, equity, and school effectiveness* (pp. 109–126). Newbury Park, CA: Sage Publications.

Faltis, C. (1986). Sway students in the foreign language classroom. *Foreign Language Annals, 19*(3), 195–202.

Faltis, C. (1984). A commentary on Krashen's input hypothesis. *TESOL Quarterly, 18,* 352–357.

Faltis, C., & Merino, B. (1992). Toward a definition of exemplary teachers in bilingual multicultural school settings. In R. Padilla & A. Benavides (Eds.), *Critical perspectives on bilingual education research.* Tempe, AZ: Bilingual Review Press.

Ferguson, C. (1975). Toward a characterization of English foreigner talk. *Anthropological Linguistics, 17,* 1–14.

Gee, J. P. (1992). *The social mind: Language, ideology and social practice.* New York: Bergin & Garvey.

Gianelli, M. (1991). Thematic units: Creating an environment for learning. *TESOL Journal, 1*(1), 13–15.

Goodlad, J. (1984). *A place called school: Prospects for the future.* New York: McGraw-Hill.

Hatch, E. (1983). *Psycholinguistics: A second language perspective.* Rowley, MA: Newbury House.

Hudelson, S., & Rigg, P. (1994/95). My *abuela* can fly: Children's books about old people in English and Spanish. *TESOL Journal, 4*(2), 5–10.

Irujo, S. (1990). *How to plan content-based teaching units for ESL.* Paper presented at the TESOL '90 Conference, San Francisco, California.

Jones, B. F., Pierce, J., & Hunter, B. (1989). Teaching students to construct graphic representations. *Educational Leadership, 46*(4), 21–25.

Krashen, S. (1982). *Principles and practice in second language acquisition.* New York: Pergamon Press.

Krashen, S. (1985). *The input hypothesis: Issues and implications.* New York: Longman.

Lemke, J. (1990). *Talking science: Language, learning, and values.* New York: Ablex.

Long, M. (1987). Native speaker/non-native speaker conversation in the second language classroom. In M. Long & J. Richards (Eds.), *Methodology in TESOL* (pp. 339–354). New York: Harper & Row.

Long, M. (1981). Input, interaction, and second language acquisition. In H. Wintz (Ed.), *Native language and foreign language acquisition* (annals of the New York Academy of Sciences No. 379, pp. 259–278). New York: Academy of Sciences.

Long, M., & Sato, C. (1983). Classroom foreigner talk discourse: Forms and functions of teacher questions. In H. Seliger & M. Long (Eds.), *Classroom oriented research in second language acquisition* (pp. 268–285). Rowley, MA: Newbury House.

Mohan, B. (1986). *Language and content.* Reading, MA: Addison-Wesley.

National Science Teachers Association. (1991). *Scope, sequence, and coordination of secondary school science.* Washington, DC: Author.

Penfield, J. (1987). ESL: The regular classroom teacher's perspective. *TESOL Quarterly, 21*(1), 21–39.

Pica, T. (1987). Second-language acquisition, social interaction, and the classroom. *Applied Linguistics, 8*(1), 3–21.

Ramírez, J. D., & Merino, B. J. (1990). Classroom talk in English immersion, early-exit and late-exit transitional bilingual education programs. In R. Jacobson & C. Faltis (Eds.), *Language distribution issues in bilingual schooling* (pp. 61–103). Clevedon, England: Multilingual Matters Ltd.

Rigg, P., Kazemek, F., & Hudelson, S. (1993). A bibliography of books with non-stereotypical views of the elderly. *Rethinking Schools, 7,* 28–29.

Scarcella, R. (1990). *Teaching language minority students in the multicultural classroom.* Upper Saddle River, NJ: Prentice-Hall.

Schachter, J. (1984). A universal input condition. In W. Rutherford (Ed.), *Language universals and second language acquisition* (pp. 167–181). Philadelphia: John Benjamins Publishing.

Schinke-Llano, L. (1983). Foreigner talk in content classrooms. In H. Seliger & M. Long (Eds.), *Classroom oriented research in language acquisition* (pp. 146–168). Rowley, MA: Newbury House.

Short, D. (1994). Expanding middle school horizons: Integrating language, culture, and social studies. *TESOL Quarterly, 28,* 581–608.

Sirotnik, K. (1983). What you see is what you get—Consistency, persistency, and mediocrity in classrooms. *Harvard Educational Review, 53*(1), 16–31.

Solomon, J., & Rhodes, N. (1995). *Conceptualizing academic language.* Santa Cruz, CA: The National Center for Research on Cultural Diversity and Second Language Learning.

Spanos, G., Rhodes, N., Dale, T., & Crandell, J. (1988). Linguistic features of mathematical problem solving: Insights and applications. In R. R. Cocking & J. P. Mestre (Eds.), *Linguistic and cultural influences on mathematics learning.* Hillsdale, NJ: Lawrence Erlbaum.

Spindler, G. (Ed.). (1982). *Doing the ethnography of schooling: Educational anthropology in action.* Prospect Heights, IL: Waveland Press.

Swain, M. (1985). Communicative competence: Some roles of comprehensible input and comprehensible output in its development. In S. Gass & C. Madden (Eds.), *Input in second language acquisition* (pp. 235–253). Rowley, MA: Newbury House.

Swain, M. (1988). Manipulating and complementing content teaching to maximize second language learning. *TESL/Canada Journal, 6,* 78–83.

Trueba, H. (1988). English literacy acquisition: From cultural trauma to learning disabilities in minority students. *Linguistics and Education, 1,* 125–152.

Vygotsky, L. (1978). *Mind in society: The development of higher psychological processes.* Cambridge, MA: MIT Press.

Wong Fillmore, L. (1982a). Instructional language as linguistic input: Implications of research on individual differences for the ESL teacher. In L. Cherry Wilkenson (Ed.), *Communicating in the classroom* (pp. 283–296). New York: Academic Press.

Wong Fillmore, L. (1982b). Language minority students and school participation: What kind of English is needed? *Journal of Education, 164,* 143–156.

Wong Fillmore, L. (1985). When does teacher talk work as input? In S. Gass & C. Madden (Eds.), *Input in second language acquisition* (pp. 17–50). Rowley, MA: Newbury House.

Chapter Five

Facilitating Communication for Learning in Small Groups

OVERVIEW

In previous chapters, we learned that in addition to teacher-led whole-class teaching, language and content learning in a joinfostering classroom also can occur through (a) teacher-led small-group interaction and (b) teacher-delegated small-group work in which students work together on their own in pairs or in groups of three to five students. Each of these two social contexts can supply second-language learners with myriad opportunities for authentic communication about subject matter content and issues of social consciousness (Linfors, 1989). But because of their complexity and the fact that both social contexts favor a balance of rights in which students often control not only the opportunities for discussion but the topic of discussion as well, many teachers are reluctant to incorporate them as an integral part of their students' daily learning experiences. In other words, for many teachers, small-group work represents a yielding of power to students, and that can be threatening.

A major goal of this chapter is to present ways of integrating the two kinds of small-group work into your classroom as a way to reinforce joinfostering conditions and to do so without compromising your need to have a well-organized and smoothly run classroom. Small-group work is a good place for students to exchange thoughts and feelings about serious topics as well as topics that bring pleasure and understanding.

In an all-English classroom containing second-language learners, the incorporation of small-group teaching and learning means at the very least that the second-language learners must be socially integrated with native English-speaking students and must actively participate in ways that necessarily enable them to listen to, read, and use authentic discourse as they work. Part of your ability to accomplish this depends on how well students are and have been invited into the kinds of language uses, knowledge structures, and social requirements involved in small-group work. To no small measure, successful small-group work depends on our ability to guide and assist student participation so that as students move through a task or a set of literacy-based activities, they gradually assume total responsibility for carrying out the task on their own, regardless of their English-language proficiency. Moreover, the way we arrange our classrooms both physically and socially to allow students to talk and work together comfortably and productively without hindering the efforts of others also influences the success of small-group work.

Most teachers incorporate small-group *teaching* as a means to work on special needs while the rest of the class works on assignments individually, but a significantly small number of teachers delegate authority to students for their own *learning* in small groups (Sirotnik, 1983; Ramírez & Merino, 1990). Assigning students of mixed English-language abilities and/or social skills to collaborate and cooperate in small groups makes many teachers uncomfortable (Penfield, 1987). One of the real concerns is that the native English-speaking students, particularly the higher-status students, will end up doing most of the talking as well as most of the work and will consequently receive the greatest benefit from the learning experience (Cohen, 1986). In a joinfostering classroom, it really helps to prepare students for small-group learning and to make it a beneficial experience for all students.

Teaching effectively to students in a small-group context means that we are relying primarily on teaching strategies that enable every student in the group

to participate from the outset of our interaction with them. The strategies we choose should provide temporary assistance that is adjusted to the students' language and learning needs (Cazden, 1988). Likewise, when we delegate authority to students for their own learning in small groups, we need to make sure that they know how to work in groups, that they have the social abilities that promote continuous interaction and collaboration, and that they see themselves linked together positively as members of a group.

Teaching and learning in small groups is complex compared to whole-class teaching because in small-group work, students teach and are taught by peers of differing English-language, social, and academic abilities. The knowledge that they construct through interaction stems from not only their own experiences, but the experiences of others who, like them, are learning the discourse of the task at hand. This is one of the best reasons to place students into pairs and small groups (Calderón, 1994). No other classroom context intentionally or unintentionally offers this degree of interactional complexity or authenticity. That small-group learning is complex and provides a relatively safe and authentic context for language use and that small-group learning benefits all students, and most especially second-language learners, are realities that Julia has discovered as a result of using small-group teaching and small-group learning on a daily basis since the beginning of the school year.

Incorporating small-group learning wasn't easy for Julia at first. She experi-

mented with different group composi-
tions, different group assignments, and
different lengths of time that students
would stay in one or more groups. Over
time, she noticed that some students work
better in a small-group setting than others, depending on the kind and duration
of the task. By watching students as they
worked, she also became aware of which
students needed additional assistance
before being ready to assume greater
responsibility for their own learning. And
most important, Julia became convinced
that small-group work is an ideal setting
for the second-language students to hear
and use lots of authentic discourse, especially when reading is involved.

Let us now look briefly into Julia's
classroom as she works with a group of
four students while the rest of the class is
working in groups on a social studies
project. Following this episode, we will
learn about the kinds of specific teaching strategies we can use for small-group
teaching when one or more of the students in the group is a second-language
learner. This will be succeeded by a
detailed discussion on small-group
learning; specifically ways to plan, organize, and implement small-group work
in which students of varying English-language proficiency talk and work
together without the presence of the
teacher. As you will see, the section is
highly structured, and you may wish to
adjust the level structure to suit your
own tastes about how to incorporate
small-group learning.

EPISODE 5: MAKING TEACHING AND LEARNING IN SMALL GROUPS WORK

By this time in the year, Julia realizes totally that second-language students are capable of participating in and benefiting from all social contexts for learning. She has become much more aware of the extent to
which language and literacy play a role in classroom participation and
learning. She habitually takes notice of her own language use, so that
much of what she says to students throughout the day is adapted in one
way or another to ensure that they understand her and are given the
opportunity to talk if necessary. The seven second-language students are
well adjusted to classroom life and attuned to the language of the classroom. Although all still receive extra help in English as a second language, the amount of time they spend out of class has dropped considerably. Their English-language progress is variable, but all have improved
their speaking and writing abilities from the beginning of the school year.
As we have seen, there are several reasons for their success, not the
least of which is that Julia expects all of her students to do well and has
made adjustments in her teaching and classroom organization to realize
this expectation. The fact that a student is learning English as a second

language is NOT a problem in Julia's class. Her students are provided with many opportunities to be curious, to question social injustices, and to show that they are capable of understanding and creating new knowledge. One of the contexts in which Julia enables students to learn and to question is having students collaborate on tasks in groups while she works with a small group of students, as in the following scenario:

Most of students are chattering away, conversing with classmates who are working with them at their tables. Julia has reggae music playing softly in the background. Only a few children are up and about; one is heading to the paper shelves, another is conversing with a friend near the pencil sharpener, and another is at the world map looking for a particular country. At this time of the day, for approximately 35 minutes, five groups of four students per group collaborate on assignments that involve various amounts of reading, writing, drawing and coloring, and lots of social interaction. The groups, each of which contains one second-language student, are spread throughout the classroom in areas with clearly marked physical boundaries. Today two of the groups are putting the finishing touches on their skits about ways to preserve elephants in the wild. Each group has written a short skit about some aspect of elephant preservation. The skits contain a short poem, some facts and figures, and a two-way dialogue. Several of the skits are modeled after the Dr. Seuss storybook in which Horton the Elephant saves the day. Julia and the students have read the Horton story and other Dr. Seuss books, and she has encouraged students to incorporate some aspect of Horton and his outlook into their skits.

Julia also invited the school librarian into the class to read two other children's books that feature elephants. Each group has also created a poster and a written background for their skit, which will be presented to the class and to parents on Back to School Night. One of the books that the librarian read was *Babar,* the story about a young elephant who becomes civilized by a rich lady who adopts him after a hunter has shot and killed his mother. Julia was disturbed by the messages in the Babar stories. The rich lady is portrayed as good in the story because she has money and the power to transform Babar into a human, teaching him human ways of eating, dressing, bathing, and counting. To become "good," Babar has to give up his old ways of being unclothed and uneducated. Once he becomes civilized, he returns to his elephant jungle abode and is eventually named the king because he has "learned so much living among men" (Kohl, 1995). The elephants themselves are portrayed as legitimizing the value of wealth and power that Babar has come to symbolize.

Julia discusses the Babar story with the class. The students immediately see how the story pits rich people against poor people (represented by the elephants) and how it glorifies the hunter who kills elephants as sport. The students decide to study the Babar stories to learn more about how the author, Jean de Brunhoff, develops the idea that Western civilization is superior to ways of living in Africa. They want to learn how children's books might promote racism in subtle and often undetected ways. To help them get started, Julia does a lot of reading about Babar and relies heavily on Herbert Kohl's book, *Should We Burn Babar?* (Kohl, 1995). For the first task, the children study how Babar becomes distinguished from other elephants. Each group studies the story and generates a list of items and events for discussion later in a whole-group setting.

While the groups are at work on their Babar and skit projects, Julia is attending to four students who need help with reading for comprehension. Two of the students in this group are second-language learners; the other two are native speakers of English. In today's activity, the students are discussing and reading a story that one of the students chose about a small fish named Swimmy (Lionni, 1963). In this story, Swimmy joins a school of fish who are also small; together they form the outline of a large fish, which enables them to swim about safely, without being bothered by bigger fish.

Julia follows a relatively set procedure of first drawing out what students already know about the topic of the text, using assisted dialogue techniques. She consciously incorporates extralinguistic support and varies her requests for information according to student ability. At the outset of the lesson, Julia invites the students to interact and negotiate not only with her but also with peers. In this manner, she and the students listen to and use one another's comments for discussion. For today's lesson, Julia wants the children to begin by thinking about personal experiences with and general knowledge about fish and then move the discussion to how working together enables individuals to accomplish tasks that would be impossible alone.

Following a lively discussion on how big fish eat little fish and how sometimes the bigger kids pick on the smaller ones during recess and in the cafeteria, Julia asks the students to read the story silently. Their objective is to find out how Swimmy and his friends are able to swim out to places that had previously been off-limits to them. Students are encouraged to help each other with unfamiliar words and with any difficult passages. When all of the students finish the story, Julia asks a number of questions about it, including questions that were brought up in the discussion prior to the reading and questions that pull out certain facts found in the story that guide the discussion toward a higher level analysis of the meaning of the story. In this final phase, Julia again varies her requests for participation and continues to encourage students to interact with each other and to use their background experiences, their cultural knowledge, and their interpretive skills for understanding the text. Throughout her interaction with the students, she tries to encourage them to talk about the story in ways that reflect the way a more capable member of story discourse would discuss it.

While Julia is teaching with her group, she is also monitoring what the rest of the class is doing in their small groups. Occasionally, when the noise level becomes too high, she raises her hand, which immediately triggers a few and then eventually all students to do likewise. This is the signal that is used to indicate that everyone needs to work at a much quieter level. It works! If one or two of the students start to dance to the beat of the reggae music, that's okay too, as long as it doesn't disturb others or get way out of hand.

Julia plans most of her small-group learning activities so that each member of the group has a particular role and a set of responsibilities. She has done lots of team-building activities to help students see the value of different perspectives and to feel comfortable working together in a team for the longer, more complicated group activities. In addition, she frequently models, and has students practice, ways of asking questions, ways of talking about the assignment, ways of inviting others to talk, ways of responding to ideas, and ways of being polite about disagreeing with someone. This is about all of the planning Julia does for her groups to work together well. A lot of what goes on in small-group work is unplanned, and that is what makes it so valuable for learning.

By this time in the year, Julia is feeling much better about how the class is progressing. She has arranged with Jake to have the second-language students work on activities from her class while they are in their special language class and vice versa. For example, Jake was eager to work with students on the Babar critical consciousness project. Through constant watching how the students are participating in whole-class and small-group work settings, Julia senses that she is improving her teaching in exactly the areas that concerned her most at the beginning of the year.

To expand upon what Julia has done to make her work with groups work, let's spend some time thinking about (1) small-group conversing strategies for engaging students in purposeful dialogues about ideas and content that come from texts and talk and (2) ways to plan and implement teacher-delegated small-group learning. Throughout these sections, it might be wise to refresh your memory and review the joinfostering principles presented in Chapter 1.

TEACHING AND CONVERSING IN SMALL GROUPS

Teaching to a small group of students while the rest of the class works with another adult (a teacher aide or a parent or grandparent volunteer), an older peer, with peers in small groups, or individually enables you to interact with students in ways that no other social context can provide. When you are working with a small group of students, not only can you contextualize your academic discourse through paraverbal, nonverbal, and visual as well as sensory support (see Chapter 4), you can also incorporate dialogue strategies to jointly construct conversations about knowledge and experiences that relate to knowledge. The dialogue strategies that we will discuss are based on principles of social interaction and learning in school settings, particularly on the work of L. S. Vygotsky. It is to Vygotskian theory that we now turn.

Vygotskian Principles of Teaching and Learning

The role of social interaction between children and more capable conversants in the development of knowledge was first explored over three score years ago by Lev Semenovich Vygotsky (1896–1934), a Soviet sociohistorical psychologist. He proposed that the learning process for children and youth depends on the presence of four interrelated preliminary components (Faltis, 1989a, 1990; DeVillar & Faltis, 1991), which are:

1. The presence of an adult or a more capable peer (MCP)
2. The occurrence of two-way communication between the learner(s) and the adult or MCP
3. That the communication be carried out in a language comprehensibly inviting to both the learner(s) and the adult or MCP
4. That the adult or MCP temporarily provide discourse assistance within the learner's area of potential development or zone of proximal development

Small-group teaching necessarily invokes only the first component; the remaining three require the desire and ability to implement them. In a joinfostering classroom, we know that we can effectively satisfy the second condition by inviting second-language students to converse and by responding authentically to what they have said. Likewise, we can meet the third condition by actively providing comprehensible invite through extralinguistic support, using modified speech to get second-language students to talk, and by responding to and extending their initiations. In other words, we invite students into the discourse, and they construct the meaning by drawing on their past experiences in terms of the task at hand and the language and literacy that support it.

Before we can satisfy the fourth condition, however, we need to gain an understanding of how, in the Vygotskian framework, learners, through the experience of joint interaction followed by individual practice either alone or with others, come to learn academic meanings and participate in academic discourses.

Learning as Other Regulation to Self-Regulation.   In Vygotskian theory, learning entails a two-phase process that first requires the learner to receive assistance through social interaction with significant others before individual meaning making can take place. By talking through a problem with someone who fully understands it and then practicing it through talking, writing, or manipulating objects, the student ultimately internalizes the ability to solve similar problems unassisted. However, he or she does not merely internalize the adult's or MCP's higher-level ability, but rather reconceptualizes it into a novel form of understanding and knowledge based upon prior and present experiences. In other words, the learner gains an internally organized, new way of responding to and solving problems similar but not identical to those used by the adult or MCP (Díaz, Neal, & Amaya-Williams, 1990). Vygotsky (1978) refers to this social, two-phase process as moving from other-regulated to self-regulated learning (see Figure 5.1).

Other-regulated learning

1.   Adults or more capable peers assist learner's performance.
2.   Adults or more capable peers negotiate meaning with the learner.
3.   Adults or more capable peers supply comprehensible invite in the context of negotiated interaction.
4.   Assistance provided is temporary and adjusted to learner's needs and abilities.

Self-regulated learning

1.   The learner practices and applies understanding of tasks similar to those provided through other-regulation.
2.   The learner plans, guides, and monitors new tasks.

Figure 5.1
Other-regulated to self-regulated learning

Other-regulated learning enables learners to converse about and perform tasks that are beyond their individual capability at the time of their introduction. For example, with assistance from an adult or MCP, a second-language learner may be able to identify and discuss the motivation of characters in a story or explain how and why a hot-air balloon rises. Self-regulation, on the other hand, is when the learner is able to plan, guide, and monitor problem-solving activities similar to those once performed jointly, without adult or MCP assistance (Díaz, Neal, & Amaya-Williams, 1990). Using the same two examples, now the second-language learner would be able to identify and comprehend the motivation of characters in a range of contexts and be able to solve similar problems involving the scientific principles underlying hot and cold air exchanges.

From a Vygotskian perspective, the adult initially regulates the learning activity in order to create a level of *intersubjectivity,* the redefinition of the problem situation by the learner in terms of the adult perspective (Wertsch, 1984). Once intersubjectivity has been accomplished, the goal of subsequent interaction then becomes to gradually and increasingly transfer the responsibility for problem solving to the learner.

Working in the Zone of Proximal Development.   One of Vygotsky's most important social learning principles is that jointly constructed social interaction that begins with intersubjectivity and works toward self-regulation must fall within the learner's *zone of proximal development.* Vygotsky (1978) proposes that problem solving in collaboration with adults or MCPs provides learners access to new areas of learning potential beyond what they can accomplish alone. He refers to these areas of potential as the "zone of proximal development," stating that each learner has an actual developmental level, which can be assessed through individual tests, and an immediate potential for development, which may result with assistance through joint interaction (Tudge, 1990). Thus, the zone of proximal development is the difference between actual and potential levels of learning. In Vygotsky's own words, the zone of proximal development is "the distance between the actual developmental level as determined by independent problem solving and the level of potential development as determined through problem solving under adult guidance or in collaboration with more capable peers" (Vygotsky, 1978, p. 86). (See Figure 5.2 for a schematic representation of the zone.)

The zone of proximal development is a function of both the learner's level of development and the nature of the instruction involved. To the extent that the adult or MCP provides discourse assistance so that the learner can be a participant (understand and initiate talk or writing) from the beginning, the adult or MCP is working within the learner's zone of

Figure 5.2
The zone of proximal development
Source: From "Spanish for Native Speakers: Freirian and Vygotskian Perspectives" by C. Faltis, 1990, *Foreign Language Annals, 23*(2), p. 122. Reprinted by permission.

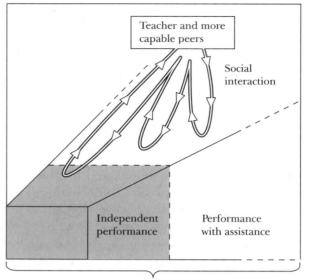

Zone of proximal development

proximal development. For both first- and second-language learners to participate from the outset requires that the assistance given be presented through discourse that is suitably tuned to the learner's zone of proximal development and done for the purpose of assisting conceptual understanding. Such discourse must also be both *adjustable* and *temporary* (Cazden, 1988). As learners gain conceptual understanding through discourse and practice, the boundaries of the zone gradually expand into new areas of knowledge, in terms of both what can be done independently and what can be done with assistance. (See Figure 5.3 for a representation of the development of problem-solving ability in the zone of proximal development.)

You might have wondered at this point what the difference is between comprehensible input, which Krashen (1985) argues is responsible for second-language acquisition, and the zone of proximal development. As was presented in Chapter 4, according to Krashen, a necessary condition for language acquisition is that learners understand language that is a bit beyond their current level of competence. Providing learners with language slightly in advance of their current ability provides a built-in review and introduces new areas of language as well.

Comprehensible input as Krashen (1985) characterizes it is both similar to and different from Vygotsky's conception of the zone of proximal development (DeVillar & Faltis, 1991). The two concepts are obviously similar in that development depends on the extent to which language input is made comprehensible to the learner by an adult or MCP. Moreover, both concepts underscore the importance of adjusting to the learner's language and learning needs. The important difference between comprehensible input and the zone of proximal development lies in the emphasis each concept places on the role of language in learning (DeVillar & Faltis, 1991). Comprehensible input is concerned primarily with adjusting speech a bit beyond the learner's linguistic level of competence. According to Krashen (1985), learners acquire language when they can have repeated opportunities to understand new language. From his theoretical perspective, learner output has no direct role in language acquisition. Contrarily, the goal in working in the zone is to adjust speech around the learner's interactional level of competence, where output is indispensable for showing academic discourse abilities. In fact, the adult or MCP utilizes the language produced by the student as a means to direct subsequent interaction toward getting the student to assume discourse style characteristic of the knowledge structure that underlies the task at hand.

Vygotsky's ideas about how learning takes place support two of the five joinfostering conditions: (1) a high incidence of two-way communicative exchanges and (2) the thoughtful integration of second-language acquisition principles with content teaching. In addition, Vygotskian ideas are particularly well suited to small-group work where second-language students are socially integrated with native English-speaking students. However, Vygotskian theory does not necessarily promote critical con-

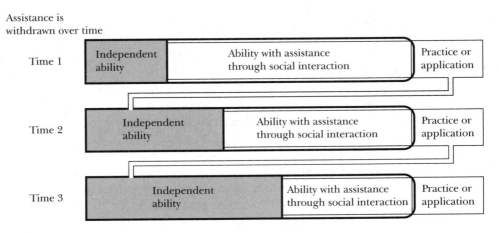

Figure 5.3
Problem solving in the zone of proximal development

sciousness. Students do that. You do that. For example, when students talk about and listen to others talk about how Babar buys into a social hierarchy that favors rich Europeans over poor "uncivilized" African elephants (people), the only thing Vygotskian about that is that it is conducted within the students' zones of proximal development. The critical consciousness comes from thinking and talking about equity, compassion, and social hierarchies.

Small-group work as a social structure can also bring out issues of equity in terms of who gets to talk and when. We know from research on small-group work that students who are good readers (of English) often control the talk in small groups even when reading is not required for the task (Cohen, 1986). We also know that students are concerned about issues of fairness and that small-group interaction is a good time for exchanging ideas about fairness and justice.

In the next section, we will examine some small-group strategies for assisting interaction and performance that are geared toward working in the zone of proximal development and in some cases for encouraging critical consciousness.

Conversing with Scaffolds and Dialogue Strategies

Teaching to students in small groups is very much like conducting a grand conversation (Eeds & Wells, 1989) because it involves multiple channels of talk about topics that are tied together by the experiences of the group. For our purposes, we can learn to sustain and adjust small-group conversation within the zone of proximal development through the use of (1) scaffolding and (2) dialogue strategies.

Scaffolds and Scaffolding. *Scaffolding* refers to visible and audible support that an adult or MCP temporarily supplies to a learner, making it possible for him or her to participate in problem-solving activities from the very beginning that otherwise might be too difficult (Cazden, 1988). It might help to think of a scaffold in its ordinary sense, as a way for workers to reach higher levels when they need to. Furthermore, scaffolds used by workers come down when they are no longer needed. Likewise, in the context of small-group teaching, scaffolding enables you to assist performance in the zone that would be beyond the learner's individual ability. When you have second-language learners in the small group, for example, at times it may be necessary to assist students with certain language constructions, providing vocabulary and grammatical and functional support so that they can participate in exchanges. At other times, you might find yourself helping students become aware of the different ways of talking about concepts. For instance, you can provide direct reference to how to say something a certain way. On most occasions, however, the assistance you provide will be aimed at helping students clarify their meaning so that together you and they can move ahead and participate fully in the dialogue. One way to do this is by using *assisting* and *assessing* questions (Tharp & Gallimore, 1988). Assisting questions aim to move students through the discourse and at the same time enable them to talk in ways that are recognized by members of the discourse. The purpose of an assisting question is to engage students in talk or writing that they could not or would not produce alone. Assessing questions enable you to gauge comprehension and to discover whether additional assistance is needed. Often it is difficult to distinguish between an assessing and an assisting question, since you may be doing both at once.

When you use scaffolds for either assistance or assessment to interact with second-language learners during small-group work, you should use them selectively to accomplish the following three goals:

1. As support, to remove the discourse responsibility that would normally be shouldered by the students
2. As a tool to guide learners who are on the scaffold to new areas of knowledge
3. As an extension of your range as a teacher so that you can sustain a dialogue with the second-language learners, a dialogue that would be impossible without the assistance your scaffolds provide

Dialogue Strategies.   Good extended dialogue is the result of the students contributing to the conversation what they can and you doing the rest (Resnick, 1985). Students can enter into a dialogue in one of two ways: (1) The students themselves can initiate a conversation, or (2) you can begin by orienting them to a particular topic that you would like them to pursue further. Regardless of who initiates the conversation, your role is to sustain it so that as the dialogue progresses, you talk less and the students talk more. As in scaffolding, dialogue requires you to remove your assistance so that the student takes over the construction of the discourse. In the following sections, you are introduced to five dialogue strategies Joan Tough (1985) offers to cover both situations. The strategies can be considered as scaffolds for conversing with students in their respective zones of proximal development about topics that might otherwise be difficult to discuss. However, it is worth while to mention that you can also engage in good dialogue with students that is not so structured. The strategies that are offered here are for you to consider and try out. If they help you sustain dialogue, use them as needed. Otherwise, a good rule of thumb is to listen carefully, be interested, and encourage talk through questions and queries.

Strategy Number 1: Orienting. The first step in entering a dialogue with students is to establish the interpersonal and contextual foundation from which the dialogue will unfold. You can accomplish this by introducing a topic through statements and comments and then asking questions that invite students to think in a particular way about the topic. You have probably done this many, many times around storybooks. The statements and questions should be open-ended in the sense that they allow students a wide range of choices or options. You also want to let the students know from the outset that they can make a major contribution to the dialogue, so be encouraging and praise their efforts. Here is an example of a teacher inviting a second-language student named Kyung to tell the group what he knows about circuses:

T: [Holding up a picture of a circus act inside a tent] Kyung, what's happening here? Tell us about this [pointing to a circus elephant balancing on a ball].
K: Elephant . . . The elephant is on the ball.
T: [Looking around to members of the group] Yes, can you believe it! Have you ever been to a circus with elephants, and clowns, and all kinds of fun things to watch? [All of the students in the group nod their heads enthusiastically.] A lot of people work in the circus, and today we are going to read about what they do in their jobs. Kyung? [inviting him to comment]
K: Oh yes, a circus. I know what is a circus. I went to a circus with my uncles. We saw many funny things. I liked the clowns and I see the people swinging high in the air, in that circus. I like that.

The teacher follows this up with similar questions to other students in the group, signaling that the main topic of discussion is the circus, in particular, the kinds of jobs that people have in the circus. Later on in the dialogue, the teacher will introduce the issue of treatment of animals.

Strategy Number 2: Enabling. On the basis of how students respond to orienting requests, you can decide how much and what kind of assistance to provide in subsequent exchanges. When students respond with less expression of thought than you know they are capable of, you can use several questioning strategies to assist them to elaborate in the direction of the topic introduced in the orienting discussion and hence move the dialogue forward. Here are three enabling strategies for generating long as well as short exchanges from second-language students:

Follow-through questions. These are assisting questions that follow the student's response to an open-ended request for information. Follow-through questions aim to expand the student's ability to express ideas more fully. Typically, a follow-through question asks the student for more detail, more explanation, or for a justification of an opinion or a statement. When you ask a follow-through question of a second-language student, be sure to vary your requests for more information according to the student's language proficiency and social style (Enright & McCloskey, 1988). For example, for one second-language student, the simple response "because I like it" might be appropriate to a follow-through question, whereas with another student you might feel a need to "push" for more information by requesting a fuller, more explicit explanation. Two useful rules of thumb to follow in varying your requests to second-language students are (1) a straight description is easier than narrating the events of a story and (2) it is harder for students to justify an opinion than it is to give one (Brown & Yule, 1983).

Focusing questions. In responding to your questions or in initiating talk about the topic at hand, students inevitably say things that, with your assistance, could result in a more effective or appropriate response. Used carefully, focusing questions can direct a student's attention to a particular feature in something that was just said, for example, a fact or an event that was overlooked during the orienting and follow-through exchanges. Answers to focusing questions should be simple and short.

Checking questions. These questions are identical to the clarification requests that we read about in Chapter 4, and they are assessing questions as well. Checking questions invite students to think again about what they have said and to clarify their meaning. Usually they are asked in the form of a *wh-* question (what, where, when, who, why, etc.), but there are numerous other ways of asking for clarification, for example, yes/no questions, choice questions, and directives. Yes/no questions are questions that can be answered with a simple "yes" or "no." Choice questions are inquiries in which the answer is one of the choices you present, for example, "Do you mean that the man doesn't hurt the lions or that the man does hurt the lions?" Choice questions are good to use because they usually enable the student to continue the dialogue. Directives are simple commands, such as "Tell me what you mean by 'the clowns have scary face'" and "Talk to me about what you said about 'mens and womens on swings go high'."

Strategy Number 3: Informing.   Informing strategies make up a large part of your contribution to dialogue with students. Basically, informing strategies can be divided into ways of (1) providing new content information to students and (2) giving corrective language information. As teachers, we are constantly providing students with new information about academic content. For example, we describe persons, places, and events; we present facts and details; we suggest and use analogies; we relate narratives; we summarize events; we make guesses; and we provide explanations. We not only model these discourse structures for our students, we also want them to understand and use them themselves as they become proficient members of the academic discourse.

The ways that we inform students depend both on the purpose of the information and the knowledge structure that underlies it (see Chapter 4), although most information can be presented through a variety of knowledge structures. Students need to hear a wide range of ways for organizing and expressing information because part of what you want them to internalize is the discourse of various knowledge structures, or academic language (Solomon & Rhodes, 1995). Moreover, it is important at times to identify what you are doing as you inform. For example, you can let students know when you are summarizing the main steps in an experiment or comparing types of clouds with common household objects. This not only furnishes them with information, but it also teaches them a metaterm for how content information is organized.

Using informing strategies in small-group teaching requires a sensitivity not only to how information is organized, but also to how you are presenting it. You should take care to adapt your language linguistically and extralinguistically so that students can comprehend and express their understanding of the information you share with them. Remember that your goal is to establish intersubjectivity and then move the conversation forward.

Second-language learners also need your assistance and guidance in the appropriate use of English. Thus, included in informing strategies are ways to extend vocabulary use and to correct errors that interfere with comprehension and communication. Strategies for extending vocabulary use include checking on the meaning of a word, for example, *"belly* is another word for *stomach"* or giving several definitions of a word that students are having trouble understanding. For example, suppose that a second-language learner in your group of students has confused the meaning of *crosswalk* with *sidewalk* and that the distinction is critical for understanding a passage. One informing strategy would be to stop the discussion immediately and give one or two definitions of each concept, using extralinguistic support such as drawings and pictures. Even better is to encourage other students in the group to talk about the meanings; then you can add a drawing or a picture as needed.

Error correction in informing strategy should be done very carefully during authentic interaction, and when it is done, its focus should be mainly and most often on *global errors* (Burt & Kiparsky, 1972). Global errors are violations of grammatical rules governing the organization of connected speech. An error is considered global when it affects the overall comprehension of an idea at either the sentence or discourse level. Thus, global errors can range from improper word order within one sentence to the illogical sequencing of ideas across sentences.

Considerably less attention should be given to *local errors,* minor mistakes, usually at the word or phrase level, that have little affect on comprehension or communication (Burt & Kiparsky, 1972). You may want to correct a local error when the mistake could potentially cause embarrassment or shame, for example, if a student were to write "By in large, most Americans speak only one language" or say "My friend María, she have to go pee."

Let's consider a sentence that contains a global error and two local errors and see how correcting the global error improves comprehension. "They started to learn English as childrens, because they speak very good." In English *because,* a causal conjunction, is always attached to the event that happened first. However, in this sentence, *because* is incorrectly attached to the second event, making the overall meaning of the sentence unclear. By correcting the global error, the sentence is comprehensible at once, even though the sentence still contains the two local errors *childrens* and *good*: "Because they started to learn English as childrens, they speak very good." You should leave the local errors alone because they occurred during authentic conversation, and they do not interfere with the meaning of the sentence.

An effective way of informing students about global errors is to first alert them to the error by telling them that you don't understand something that they have just said. Next, tell them how the language works in this particular case, using modified input and simple terms, and then give them a concrete, here-and-now example to illustrate the rule. Then quickly return to the dialogue in progress. Stevick's (1986) "5-second rule" tells us that if it takes more than 5 seconds to explain a rule to a learner during a meaningful dialogue, it is probably not worth the effort.

Remember that all students make errors, that errors are essential to learning, and that correcting them doesn't mean learning has occurred. You may have to call attention to something several times before the student begins to reconstruct his or her developing language.

Strategy Number 4: Sustaining.   When students have initiated talk or are responding to your questions, you can encourage them to continue talking and at the same time let them know that you are interested in what they are saying. Nonverbal expressions of agreement, such as smiling and nodding your head, looks of amazement, and vocal expressions of appreciation signal to the student that you are listening and you want the talk to keep going. Sustaining implies that you are using minimal scaffolding support. However, you should be listening for opportunities for re-employing scaffolds and enabling strategies according to the new language and conceptual needs that students display.

Strategy Number 5: Concluding.   While continued talk is important for developing students' language and reasoning abilities, at some point you will need to draw the conversation to a close or move on to a new topic. Concluding strategies are statements to students that you are about to end the conversation or to change the topic. Marking the end of a dialogue is important because it prepares the students for what comes next.

As you use these dialogue strategies coupled with modified input and negotiated interaction, you should always remember that your assistance should be adjustable and temporary. If you feel that a student is capable of contributing more, raise the scaffold and propel the student to a new zone of proximal development. Likewise, if students are using language creatively and independently, remove the scaffolds until you are ready to draw the conversation to a close.

DELEGATING STUDENTS TO LEARN IN SMALL GROUPS

Small-group work can also be planned and implemented so that students of generally equal abilities but with differing language and skill preparation join together to talk and work among themselves in small groups of two to five students per group. In this section, we will discuss ways to delegate authority for learning to students as they collaborate in pairs and small groups, ways that incorporate Vygotskian principles of assisted learning and promote second-language acquisition as well. To these ends, you will learn how to develop in students the social skills needed for continuous interaction and cooperative collaboration. But before embarking on the "how" of small-group work, let's examine briefly why peer interaction is well suited to a joinfostering classroom.

Benefits of Peer Interaction

Vygotsky (1978) affirms the importance of peer interaction on learning in his definition of the zone of proximal development, referring specifically to the function "more capable peers" can have in assisting others to develop new conceptual understanding. In the context of small-group learning, a more capable peer is "a student who, similar to the teacher, possesses certain skill preparation that is particularly appropriate to assisting a fellow student in the completion of a task that is within that student's zone of proximal development" (DeVillar & Faltis, 1991, p. 20). From a Vygotskian perspective, peers benefit from one another by internalizing the thinking processes implicit in their talk with others. Several critical features of higher-level thinking occur during peer dialogues; among them are the planning of strategies in advance, the verification of ideas, and the confrontation of opposing points of view (Damon, 1984). For Vygotsky, then, the value of having students engage in peer dialogue comes from the means by which ideas and conflicts are discussed and eventually resolved, namely, interaction and communication in the zone of proximal development. Eventually, after repeatedly engaging in dialogues in which performance is assisted by more capable peers, students begin to take on or internalize the cognitive and communicative procedures needed for a range of problem solutions (Damon, 1984). At this point, peer assistance is no longer essential for learning; the student can now solve similar problems alone.

Small-group learning is also advantageous to second-language learners because it provides many of the favorable ingredients for successful second-language acquisition (Johnson, 1994; McGroarty, 1993). To begin, peer learning provides second-language learners with an acquisition-rich environment, an environment in which meaning is accessed through language that has been adjusted consciously or unconsciously to accommodate second-language learner's needs. Talk that occurs in small-group work gives second-language learners greater exposure to contextualized language and thus more opportunities to build comprehension. Input generated from peer interaction also provides a natural context for greater redundancy in communication as students exchange information (McGroarty, 1993). Second-language learners are helped to understand new language when they hear key words and ideas being repeated and rephrased in different contexts.

Another benefit for second-language learners stemming from peer interaction in small groups is the increased practice opportunities it provides (Johnson, 1994). When students are collaborating in small groups, there are substantially more and more-varied opportunities for using language to express and generate meaning, opportunities that are absent in both whole-class instruction and individual seatwork. Peer interaction is an ideal "practice field" where students can try out expressions and negotiate meaning with a familiar audience without having to worry about getting everything right or adhering to external norms of correctness. These opportunities to practice language also help students develop interactional competence—knowledge about when, where, and how to produce language to get things done, as well as knowing what to say (Enright, 1991). Such practice prepares students for the other social contexts of learning in the classroom.

Small-group learning benefits second-language students in another way, one that is often overlooked in the literature. Learning in small groups is intrinsically enjoyable! When students talk with one another they are using language for authentic purposes. In other words, they are engaged in language use that is genuinely meaningful and that serves a functional purpose in completing the task at hand.

Last, peer interaction in small-group work is beneficial for second-language students because it meets the joinfostering conditions of providing multiple opportunities for authentic two-way communicative exchanges, of socially integrating second-language students with native English-speaking students, and of integrating second-language acquisition and participation principles with content learning. It can also be a setting in which critical awareness about social inequities can be developed safely and deeply.

While the above benefits may occur as a result of peer interaction, you would be wrong to assume that second-language acquisition and authentic language practice will occur naturally just because students of mixed language proficiency are physically grouped. There are plenty of instances of second-language students being *physically grouped* with native English-speaking students, but with little or no meaningful interaction taking place among them (Milk, 1980; Edelsky & Hudelson, 1982). Good small-group learning, then, may need to be complemented by features that ensure that all students are contributing through talk and action to the group effort. If you feel the need for structural support to help ensure equitable participation in small-group work, there are four actions that you can plan for. These four actions, which are interconnected and mutually supportive, are:

1. You can work with students on interpersonal and small-group courtesy.
2. You can make sure that your students are face to face when they are in small groups.
3. You can organize the activity so that they depend on each other to complete the tasks at hand.
4. You can make each student accountable for completing the activity (Johnson, Johnson, & Holubec, 1986).

A Word About Group Size and Group Composition

Before we further the discussion on small-group work, it is worth while to consider the size of your small groups and the compatibility and language ability of students you wish to place together to carry out the various activities and roles that you intend to assign to them.

There are a number of factors that you should consider in deciding how many students to place in a group (Johnson, Johnson, & Holubec, 1986):

1. As the size of the group increases, so does the range of abilities and experiences of the members. The larger the group, the greater the number of "more capable peers" who have special knowledge that may be helpful to the group.

2. The larger the group, however, the more important social skills become. In small groups of more than three students, students must have the social skills to provide everyone a chance to interact and to remain on task.

3. The nature of the task and the materials required for the task may also play a role in determining the size of the group.

4. The less time available for group work, the smaller the group should be. Smaller groups are more effective for accomplishing shorter tasks because less time is needed for getting organized, and there is more participation time for each member.

Johnson, Johnson, and Holubec (1986) advise beginning teachers to start with pairs or groups of three and then move on to groups of four and in some instances five, while Kagan (1989) strongly recommends working primarily with groups of four from the outset.

An equally important consideration in forming groups has to do with the compatibility and language proficiency of the students you place together. In a joinfostering classroom, we want second-language students to interact socially with native English-speaking students, and small-group work provides us with an ideal setting for this to take place. But we need to keep in mind that students have different social styles and interests, and that these vary greatly according to the topic and task (Enright, 1991). Moreover, students have all sorts of social relationships with other students in the class, and these can enhance or diminish interaction and learning within an activity depending on the nature of the tasks. For example, it may be unwise to place students who intensely dislike one another together for learning content that is critical for achieving a class grade, but it may be helpful to assign them to work together on a project that is intrinsically interesting. Likewise, placing best friends together may lead to imbalanced interaction during some tasks but well-rounded interaction during others.

Native- and second-language proficiency also affect student interaction and productivity. Every time you place a second-language learner into a group of native English speakers, in addition to social styles and student interests, you should also consider the language proficiency of the student. A general rule of thumb is that the lower a student's English-language proficiency, the more important it is to place him or her with peers who are most likely to work together cooperatively. If you place more than one second-language student in a group, you should also think about whether you want students of the same native-language background together in the group, or whether you want students of different native-language backgrounds. If your goal is primarily language development, it may be best to select two students with different language backgrounds and different proficiency levels in English. If you are more concerned about content understanding and content learning, having two students of the same language background may be beneficial because they can explain ideas to each other in their native language if necessary (DeVillar, 1990).

Preparing for Small-group work

Most students need at least some preparation in interpersonal and small-group relations to be able to collaborate effectively with their peers when you are not directly supervising them. The social interaction required for small-group work operates on the principle that everybody needs to talk and listen, but not all at the same time. Some of your students may not have had the experience of working effectively in small groups, where task completion and, ultimately, learning depend on cooperation and collaboration among group members. In other words, when you assign students to work in groups, they need to be responsible not only for their own behavior in the group, but for group behavior as well (Cohen, 1986).

One of the most important interpersonal and small-group abilities that students need to develop is how to share in the exchange of ideas so that all students contribute more or less equally. Students can learn to distribute talk fairly among themselves by following three basic rules of behavior:

1. Everyone in the group must have an equal chance to talk.
2. Everyone needs to listen when a member is talking to the group.
3. Everyone must contribute ideas, even when they are potentially in conflict with those of others.

The first rule speaks to the need for equitable access to participation; the second, to a key requirement and component of all communicative exchanges; the third, to the need for participation from all.

There are a number of ways to help students internalize and apply these behavioral rules. One way is to teach them the rules directly and then have them practice applying the rules during group work. Following group work, you can also have the students evaluate the group process by having each group member respond to the statements about how well they carried out the rules. Here is an example of how this might be done. At the end of a small-group activity, pass out and read the following statements to all students. They are to respond by circling YES or NO on the sheet. (As a variation, you could use a happy face and a sad face with each statement and have the students circle the face that best represents their opinion.) Once completed, the members of each group share responses. Finally, the group decides which social skill they will work on the next time they meet.

Working and Sharing in My Group

1. I shared with my group today.   YES   NO
2. I encouraged others in my group.   YES   NO
3. Others shared with me.   YES   NO
4. I listened when others were talking.   YES   NO
5. Others listened while I talked.   YES   NO

As always, you can and should adapt your speech and use extralinguistic support as needed to make sure that the second-language students understand the instructions and the purpose of the evaluation. There is no need to conduct this type of evaluation more than two or three times a year.

In addition to explicitly teaching these general rules, you can also model and reinforce them throughout the day as students work in groups. Students appreciate hearing that they are behaving appropriately during group work. For example, to reinforce rule number 1, you might draw the class's attention to a group and publicly announce, "Class, I am really happy about how nicely everyone in Group Three is working together. It is great to see that everyone is getting a chance to talk." On other occasions, to reinforce active listening, you might point out to the class how pleased you are to see that students in a particular group are visibly listening to one another.

Small-group abilities can also be learned by adding a particular structure to the group assignment. The idea is to structure the interaction so that everyone in the group gets to practice carrying out the rules that underlie successful small-group behavior. Here are some examples of structures that you can use to prepare students for small-group learning (these suggestions might be pretty controlling for some of you, but at least try them):

Talking Chips.   This structure distributes talk more or less equally among members of a group. At the beginning of the activity, each student in the group is given some kind of marker, which serves as a talking chip. Every time a student wishes to talk, he or she must place a chip in a central place, usually the center of the table. No one in the group can talk again until everyone has placed a chip in the pile, at which time all the chips are retrieved, and the process begins again (Kagan, 1989). Adding this structure to group work ensures that everyone talks, and that no one student will do all of the talking.

Paraphrase Passport.   The purpose of this structure is to encourage students to contribute to the discussion and to listen as others in the group speak. Access to talking comes from correctly paraphrasing the student who has just spoken. After a member of the group has contributed an idea, the next person to speak must accurately rephrase that idea before contributing a new idea. This structure reinforces group listening and at the same time enables second-language students to hear other ways of saying the same thing. Moreover, when their turn comes, second-language students are compelled to create a new way of saying something without repeating it word for word.

Finally, here are two highly structured small-group activities that allow students to practice all three rules for effective group behavior. Both of these activities are designed for maximum student involvement, and neither should last less than ten minutes.

The Three-Step Interview.   This activity consists of three steps and is best suited for groups of four (Kagan, 1989). In step one, students are assigned to work in pairs, with one student serving as an interviewer and the other as an interviewee. The interviewer's responsibility is to gain as much information from the interviewee by asking as few questions as possible. In step two, the students reverse roles: the interviewee now becomes the interviewer, and vice versa. In step three, each student shares with the group what was learned from his or her interview partner, in a round-robin sequence. The content of the interview can cover a wide range of topics, but a good way to begin is to have students exchange personal experiences related to the topic at hand. For example, after viewing a short movie on the lumber elephants of India, you could have students engage in a three-step interview on what they liked most about the movie and why. You could also ask students to indicate what they thought about the work done by the elephants.

Think-Pair-Share.   A variation of the three-step interview, think-pair-share is also conducted in three steps, preferably in groups composed of four students (Lyman, 1987). In step one, you pose a relatively open-ended question to all groups, usually about a topic all students are currently studying and then allow them a minute or so to contemplate how they would answer it. In step two, pairs of students orally exchange their answers with one another. In step three, students share their partner's answer with the members of the group, again in a round-robin fashion. This third step of sharing responses within the group encourages students to actively participate through talk and to listen for meaning in step two. You can vary step three by asking one member of each group to summarize to the entire class his or her group's response.

Face-to-Face Interaction

One of the simplest yet often overlooked features of small- group learning has to do with how students are physically arranged for small-group work. They need to be within personal talking distance (within 2 feet) and be physically facing each other. For example, if students are seated at a small rectangular or circular table, they need to be positioned so that at least the pairs of students are face-to-face (see Figure 5.4).

Face-to-face interaction ensures that students can hear each other speak and actually see any paraverbal and nonverbal support that may accompany what is being said. Under these circumstances, students are more apt than not to comprehend and actively engage in dialogue generated by members of their group. You may find that some students will need to be physically moved so that they face their partners or team members. If you do have to move students a bit closer to one another, be sure to explain to them that being face to face improves interaction because now, not only can they can see each other better, they can hear each other better as well.

Positive Interdependence

Positive interdependence is the heart and soul of small-group learning. At the individual level, students are positively interdependent when they perceive themselves as linked with their group members in such a way that no one can succeed unless everyone in the group does and realize

Figure 5.4
Face-to-face interaction in small-group work

that the contributions each member makes benefit everyone in the group (Johnson, Johnson, & Holubec, 1986). Without positive interdependence, students placed together to work in groups see little value in helping their fellow students learn, even though they may have had some preparation in social skills development.

When students are not linked together through positive interdependence, an inevitable result is that only certain students benefit from the experience. What typically happens in small-group work sans positive interdependence is that the rich get richer while the condition of the poor either becomes worse or, at best, stays the same. The reason this happens is fairly straightforward: In small-group work, learning is directly tied to the extent to which students participate verbally in the completion of the task. From a Vygotskian perspective, students who participate more benefit more because they use language to mediate their learning. But the relationship between active participation and learning is not merely a quantitative one. By talking more, students are likely to practice a wide range of language functions, such as expressing and finding out about agreement and disagreement, about emotional attitudes (likes and dislikes, surprise, hope, satisfaction), about appreciation, about regret, and about getting others in the group to do things (inviting, advising, warning, and instructing), in addition to describing, narrating, and offering opinions and justifying them. Consequently, it behooves us to promote positive interdependence to ensure that all students participate optimally during small-group learning. Sometimes students are positively interdependent on their own; they just connect with one another. At other times you may need to help them get connected. Here are five simple ways to organize small-group work in ways that promote positive interdependence (Johnson, Johnson, & Holubec, 1986; Kagan, 1989; McGroarty, 1989):

1. *Goal interdependence.* Assign a group product, such as an essay, a mural, a report, or a problem set. You can have students sign their names at the bottom of the product to indicate that they all contributed, and could, if asked, describe and justify its content.

2. *Reward interdependence.* Assign the same reward to each member of the group for completing the task. You can also give bonus points when everyone in the group achieves a certain predetermined score. Or you can calculate the average of individual scores and give a reward when the average reaches a predetermined criterion. A rule of thumb in giving rewards for group work is that the more intrinsically interesting the assignment is, the less need there is for a group reward. Once the motivation for learning becomes apparent, you should probably dispense with the reward.

3. *Labor interdependence.* Divide the task into subcomponents that must be completed sequentially in order to accomplish the overall task. In other words, you might divide the labor involved in a task so that one student has to complete a part of the task before anyone else in the group can move ahead. Labor interdependence is especially useful for small-group learning of programming and problem solving at the personal computer, where one student is in charge of accurately presenting the problem, another types the problem on the screen, and the third serves as the debugger. It can also be incorporated in science projects and other tasks that are organized in a linear fashion.

4. *Resource interdependence.* Provide each member of the group with only a portion of the information, resources, or materials needed to complete the task. Jigsaw (Aronson, Blaney, Stephan, Sikes, & Snapp, 1978) is one of the best illustrations of resource interdependence. In this activity, students are responsible for reading and learning about a topic area that is also broken up into three to five subtopics. Each student in a group becomes an "expert" on one subtopic by working with members from

other groups assigned the corresponding subtopic. When the students return to their group, which now contains experts on all of the subtopics, each expert student in turn teaches the group, and then all students are assessed on all areas of the general topic. Other ways to promote resource interdependence include limiting the resources given to a group so that members must share them, and assigning writing activities in which students share in the writing of stories, reports, or poems.

5. *Role interdependence.* Assign complementary and interconnected roles that give each student a responsibility that the group needs in order to function successfully (Johnson, 1994). Examples of roles that give everyone a part to play are (a) a *group leader* to answer any questions about the task and to see that everyone gets the help they need to complete the task; (b) a *recorder* to write down the group's ideas and answers; (c) a *checker/encourager* to make sure that everyone in the group is participating and has completed all of the work and that everyone understands what is being agreed upon; (d) a *setup/cleanup* person who is responsible for setting up all of the required materials, and/or also for putting away materials properly and cleaning off the table; and (e) an *evaluator* to keep track of how well the group members are working together.

In addition, you can boost the strength of positive interdependence by playing cooperative games during recess and physical education time and by exposing your students to children's literature in which characters solve problems through positive interdependence and demonstrate their concern for helping one another (Faltis, 1989b; Barone & Faltis, 1990). Some excellent sources for cooperative games are Orlick (1978; 1982), Gregson (1982), and Sobel (1983). *Swimmy* by Lionni (1963) is a good example of a storybook that reinforces the value of positive interdependence (Barone & Faltis, 1990). Other examples are *Squares Are Not Bad* (Salazar, 1967) and *The Case of the Dumb Bells* (Bonsall, 1966). See Appendix A for an annotated bibliography of children's storybooks that promote the value of cooperation among characters. The more opportunities students have to see the value of positive interdependence in other contexts, the more likely they are to make sure that their peers are participating optimally during small-group work.

Student Accountability

A primary purpose of small-group learning organized to promote positive interdependence is to ensure that each student participates so that through the participation of all members of the group, the task is completed and learning is maximized. Occasionally, when you assign small-group learning activities, you will find that some students are not participating to their fullest potential. Unequal participation in small-group work may be the result of multiple factors, making it difficult to know for sure why it is happening. However, even though the material is interesting to most students, and you think you have structured the activity to promote positive interdependence, you may still need to remind students that they are each accountable for their work in small groups.

Creating individual accountability for work completed as a group is especially critical when you place second-language learners with native English speakers. Suppose that each group in your class will receive a team grade for completing their task, but that there is no individual accountability. Some native English speakers may decide to take over the activity to make sure that the second-language learners don't get involved and slow down the process, and the second-language learners may defer to the native English speakers, letting them do the lion's share of the work. However, if the group grade is based on the individual work of every student in the group, it is less likely that any one student will do more or less than others and more likely that students will help one another to ensure that all are participating equally.

You can encourage student accountability by randomly selecting members to explain what they are doing, by having members edit and review each others' work, and by randomly picking from the group the completed task of one student and using that as the grade for the group (Johnson, Johnson, & Holubec, 1986). One cool way to practice individual accountability when students are in either whole-group or small-group settings is to use *Numbered Heads Together* (Kagan, 1989). In this activity, which also promotes teamwork and positive interdependence, students who are in close proximity to one another form groups of four, and count off from 1 to 4. At an opportune time during your presentation, ask the students a question, usually a convergent one, and then say, "Okay, everyone, let's do Numbered Heads Together. I'll give you a couple of minutes to discuss the answer." As this point, the students physically huddle together to talk about the answer, and when once agreed upon it, they consult to make sure everyone understands and has the same answer. When time is up, you choose a number from 1 to 4, and then call on the students who correspond to the number you selected.

Other ways of practicing individual accountability are the Three-Step Interview and Paraphrase Passport. Both of these activities make students accountable for listening to others in their group.

CONCLUSION

This has been a long and rather detailed chapter about teaching and learning in small groups. And there is much more to learn about these exciting contexts and effective ways of integrating second-language learners into the all-English classroom. By this point, if you have understood the assistance you can provide in small-group instruction to make language and content meaningful, you are well on your way to becoming a teacher who is better prepared to work in culturally and linguistically diverse settings. Also, if you comprehend the merits of small-group learning for encouraging communication and critical awareness among students of diverse language and cultural backgrounds, and you feel ready to try it out in your classroom, you will be helping all of your students learn how to collaborate. It is important to keep in mind that it takes some time to develop a classroom community and to develop positive interdependence among students of diverse backgrounds. However, you can be certain that if you prepare students for small-group

learning and engage them consistently, and you monitor and reinforce acceptable group behavior, the quality of their interaction and learning will improve and their ability to work by themselves will become self-regulated over time.

Small-group work helps create a classroom community where students rely on one another for help and learning (Johnson, 1994; McGroarty, 1989). But a classroom community that includes only the students is not enough. We need to extend into the home communities of the students themselves so that the classroom community includes parents and other significant caregivers. In the following chapter, we will learn about ways to improve and expand parental involvement and participation in the home, the classroom, and the school. In this manner, we will prepare for the fourth joinfostering condition: **the involvement and participation of second-language students' parents and other adult caregivers in both classroom- and school-related activities.**

ACTIVITIES

1. Arrange to have a 15- to 20-minute dialogue with an ESL student at a local public school or at the English Language Center at your college or university. For this activity, look for a student who has at least some communicative proficiency. You should audiotape the dialogue. Begin by asking about the student's favorite hobby, story, or movie and try to incorporate as many of the dialogue strategies presented in the chapter; at the same time, try to assist the student so that as the dialogue progresses, he or she is doing most of the talking. An hour or so after the dialogue, listen to the tape and identify the various strategies you used and note any places where you think you could have employed a strategy to further the dialogue.

2. In a group of 4 or 5 students, elect one person to guide the others through a problem using scaffolds and dialogue strategies. The student who serves as a guide reads the following instructions to the group:

Here is the problem that I want you to try to solve: You have 23 coins of exactly the same size, weight, and value, and one coin that is identical to the other 23 in every way *except* that it weighs more. Your task is to determine which coin weighs more than the others by using a balance scale. No other method can be used. And you must be able to pick out the heavier coin in just *three* weighings.

The student teacher's task is to assist the group members by using assessment and assisting questions. The solution to this problem and ways to scaffold the dialogue follow the Activities section.

3. Here is a fun small-group team-building activity presented in Kagan (1989). Organize groups of four. Use a random group assignment procedure: Divide the total number of the class by 4, and then have students count off by the resulting number. For example, in a class of 25, students will count off by sixes, making five groups of 4 and one group of 5. Once in the group, your goal is to come up with at least one *uncommon commonality.* That is, try to find out something that all of you have in common that is truly uncommon. For example, you may learn that you have all been hit by a car when riding a bicycle or that you all have twins in your family and that they all drive Volkswagens!

Once you have generated your uncommon commonality, the next step is to come up with a group name based on your uncommon commonality. How about the Volksy Twins or the Banged-Up Bikers?

If you want to continue, you can invent a handshake to go with the group name. The only rule on the handshake is that everyone in the group has to be connected at one point in the shake.

3. In groups of three, read the children's story by Ellen Levine (1989) called *I Hate English!* and discuss how the author presents the acculturation process. Try to come up with a critical evaluation of the story. What are the hidden agendas? You may also wish to consult Lessow-Hurley's review of the book (Lessow-Hurley, 1991).

4. Visit the children's section at your local public library or in your campus library and look for storybooks in which the characters are able to accomplish feats that they would otherwise be incapable of doing alone. Also seek out children's storybooks in which the characters show a social concern for the welfare of others. As a class, put together an annotated bibliography and share it with classmates and teacher acquaintances.

5. Interview several classroom teachers to learn about the kinds of small-group work that they use in class. Ask about pair-work as well. Do they use dialogue journals? Do they do team-building activities? How do they organize small groups?

ANSWER TO THE SCAFFOLDING ACTIVITY

The solution to this problem rests in the ways you divide the coins for each weighing. You can expect most group members to begin by dividing the 24 coins into two piles of 12 coins and weighing them to reduce the number of coins to 12. This typical first step makes it impossible to solve the problem in three weighings. Allow the students to proceed in the process anyway. In the next weighing they will again probably divide the coins into two groups of 6, and then into two groups of 3. This uses up the three weighings and it is still not possible to pick out the heavier coin.

So what do group members do next? Here is where you can provide some valuable scaffolded assistance through questions. For example, suppose you say something like:

Let's start again with the 24 coins. The first time you divided them into two equal parts, didn't you? Now, is there another way of dividing them?

If they need further assistance, you can continue with:

Is there another way to divide the coins so that you have an equal number of coins on each side of the scale and the same number of coins off the scale?

What you want them to understand here is that they can also divide 24 by 3, giving them three piles of 8 coins, two piles for the scale and one off the scale. If the heavier coin is in either of the piles on the scale, the scale will tip and reveal its location. If it doesn't tip, we know immediately that it is in the pile off the scale.

Next question: So how do you wish to divide up the remaining 8 coins? The goal is to guide the students to divide the 8 coins into 3, 3, and 2: 3 coins on each side of the scale and 2 off the scale. The reason: No matter which pile contains the coin, we can pick it out in the next and final weighing. If the coin is in one of the piles of 3, then in the third weighing we place one coin on each side of the scale and one off. A tipped scale gives us the answer, as does a balanced one. If the coin is the pile of 2 off the scale, then simply place the 2 coins on the scale, and select the heavier one according to which side of the scale tips.

REFERENCES

Aronson, E., Blaney, N., Stephan, D., Sikes, J., & Snapp, M. (1978). *The jigsaw classroom.* Beverly Hills, CA: SAGE.

Barone, D., & Faltis, C. (1990). *Cooperation-fostering beginning literacy events in the linguistically diverse classroom.* Unpublished manuscript, Center for Language and Literacy, University of Nevada, Reno.

Bonsall, C. (1966). *The case of the dumb bells.* New York: Harper & Row.

Brown, G., & Yule, G. (1983). *Teaching the spoken language.* New York: Cambridge University Press.

Burt, M., & Kiparsky, C. (1972). *The gooficon: A repair manual for English.* Rowley, MA: Newbury House.

Calderón, M. (1994). Cooperative learning for bilingual settings. In R. Rodríguez, N. Ramos, & J. Agustín Ruíz-Escalante (Eds.), *Compendium of readings in bilingual education: Issues and practices* (pp. 95–110). San Antonio, TX: Texas Association for Bilingual Education.

Cazden, C. (1988). *Classroom discourse: The language of teaching and learning.* Portsmouth, NH: Heinemann.

Cohen, E. (1986). *Designing groupwork: Strategies for the heterogeneous classroom.* New York: Teachers College Press.

Damon, W. (1984). Peer education: The untapped potential. *Journal of Applied Developmental Psychology, 5,* 331–343.

DeVillar, R. A. (1990). Second language use within the non-traditional classroom: Computers, cooperative learning, and bilingualism. In R. Jacobson & C. Faltis (Eds.), *Language distribution issues in bilingual schooling* (pp. 133–159). Clevedon, England: Multilingual Matters Ltd.

DeVillar, R. A., & Faltis, C. (1991). *Computers and cultural diversity.* Albany: State University of New York Press.

Díaz, R. M., Neal, C. J., & Amaya-Williams, M. (1990). The social origins of self-regulation. In L. Moll (Ed.). *Vygotsky and education: Instructional implication and application of sociohistorical psychology* (pp. 127–154). New York: Cambridge University Press.

Edelsky, C., & Hudelson, S. (1982). Reversing the roles of Chicano and Anglo children in a bilingual classroom: On the communicative competence of the helper. In J. A. Fishman & G. D. Keller (Eds.), *Bilingual education for Hispanics in the United States* (pp. 303–325). New York: Teachers College Press.

Eeds, M., & Wells, D. (1989). Grand conversations: An exploration of meaning construction in literature study groups. *Research in the Teaching of English, 23,* 4–29.

Enright, D. S. (1991). Tapping the peer interaction resource. In M. McGroarty & C. Faltis (Eds.), *Languages in school and society: Policy and pedagogy* (pp. 209-232). Berlin: Mouton de Gruyter.

Enright, D. S., & McCloskey, M. (1988). *Integrating English: Developing English language and literacy in the multilingual classroom.* Reading, MA: Addison-Wesley.

Faltis, C. (1989a). Classroom language use and educational equity: Toward interactive pedagogy. In B. P. Baptiste, H. C. Waxman, J. Walker de Felix, & J. Anderson (Eds.), *Leadership, equity, and school effectiveness* (pp. 109–124). Newbury Park, CA: Sage Publications.

Faltis, C. (1989b). Spanish language cooperation-fostering storybooks for language minority children in bilingual programs. *Journal of Educational Issues for Language Minority Students, 5,*(1), 41–50.

Faltis, C. (1990). Spanish for native speakers: Freirian and Vygotskian perspectives. *Foreign Language Annals, 23*(2), 117–126.

Gregson, B. (1982). *The incredible indoor games book.* Belmont, CA: Pitman Learning.

Johnson, D. (1994). Grouping strategies for second language learners. In F. Genesee (Ed.), *Educating second language children* (pp. 183–211). New York: Cambridge University Press.

Johnson, D. W., Johnson, R. T., & Holubec, E. J. (1986). *Revised circles of learning: Cooperation in the classroom.* Edina, MN: Interaction Book Company.

Kagan, S. (1989). *Cooperative learning resources for teachers.* San Juan Capistrano, CA: Resources for Teachers.

Kohl, H. (1995). *Should we burn Babar? Essays on children's literature and the power of stories.* New York: New York Press.

Krashen, S. (1985). *The input hypothesis: Issues and implications.* London: Longman.

Lessow-Hurley, J. (1991). Review of *I hate English!. TESOL Journal, 1*(1), 35–36.

Levine, E. (1989). *I hate English!* New York: Scholastic.

Linfors, J. W. (1989). The classroom: A good environment for language learning. In P. Rigg & V. G. Allen (Eds.), *When they don't all speak English: Integrating the ESL student into the regular classroom* (pp. 39–54). Urbana, IL: NCTE.

Lionni, L. (1963). *Swimmy.* New York: Alfred A. Knopf.

Lyman, F. (1987). Think-pair-share: An expanding teaching technique. *MAA-CIE Cooperative News, 1*(1), 1–2.

McGroarty, M. (1989). The benefits of cooperative learning arrangements in second language instruction. *NABE Journal, 12*(2), 127–143.

McGroarty, M. (1993). Cooperative learning and second language acquisition. In D. Holt (Ed.), *Cooperative learning: A response to cultural diversity* (pp. 13–27). Sacramento, CA: Delta Systems.

Milk, R. (1980). *Variations in language use patterns across different settings in two bilingual second grade classrooms.* Unpublished doctoral dissertation, Stanford University, Stanford, CA.

Orlick, T. (1978). *The cooperative sports and games book: Challenge without competition.* New York: Pantheon.

Orlick, T. (1982). *The second cooperative sports and games book.* New York: Pantheon.

Penfield, J. (1987). ESL: The regular classroom teacher's perspective. *TESOL Quarterly, 21*(1), 21–39.

Ramírez, J. D., & Merino, B. (1990). Classroom talk in English immersion, early-exit and late-exit transitional bilingual education programs. In R. Jacobson & C. Faltis (Eds.), *Language distribution issues in bilingual schooling* (pp. 61–103). Clevedon, England: Multilingual Matters Ltd.

Resnick, L. (1985). Cognition and instruction: Recent theories of human competence and how it is acquired. In B. L. Hammond (Ed.), *Psychology and learning: The Masser lecture series.* Washington, DC: American Psychological Association.

Salazar, V. (1967). *Squares are not bad.* New York: Golden Press.

Sirotnik, K. (1983). What you see is what you get—consistency, persistency, and mediocrity in classrooms. *Harvard Educational Review, 53*(1), 16–31.

Sobel, J. (1983). *Everybody wins: 393 non-competitive games for young children.* New York: Walker.

Solomon, J., & Rhodes, N. (1995). *Conceptualizing academic language.* Santa Cruz, CA: The National Center for Research on Cultural Diversity and Second Language Learning.

Stevick, E. (1986). *Images and options in the language classroom.* Cambridge: Cambridge University Press.

Tharp, R., & Gallimore, R. (1988). *Rousing minds to life: Teaching, learning, and schooling in social context.* New York: Cambridge University Press.

Tough, J. (1985). *Talk two: Children using English as a second language.* London: Onyx Press.

Tudge, J. (1990). Vygotsky, the zone of proximal development and peer collaboration: Implications for classroom practice. In L. Moll (Ed.). *Vygotsky and education: Instructional implication and application of sociohistorical psychology* (pp. 155–172). New York: Cambridge University Press.

Vygotsky, L. S. (1978). *Mind in society.* Cambridge, MA: Harvard University Press.

Wertsch, J. V. (1984). The zone of proximal development: Some conceptual issues. In B. Rogoff & J. V. Wertsch (Eds.), *Children's learning in the "zone of proximal development"* (pp. 7–18). San Francisco: Jossey-Bass.

RESOURCE LIST

Groups Working Together

Balian, L. (1972). *The Aminal.* Nashville, TN: Abingdon Press.

Patrick finds an animal, which he calls an *aminal.* He tells a friend about his new pet without saying exactly what it is. His friend tells another and so on. Eventually, all of the friends decide that the pet might hurt Patrick. So they all arrive at Patrick's house to protect him only to find that his pet is really a turtle.

Bonsall, C. (1965). *The case of the cat's meow.* New York: Harper & Row.

Snitch is worried that someone will steal his cat, Mildred. His friends assure him that no one will take his cat. However, Mildred soon disappears. The boys work together to find the cat. Eventually, they locate Mildred in the basement with three new kittens. The story concludes with each child taking home a kitten.

Bonsall, C. (1966). *The case of the dumb bells.* New York: Harper & Row.

Skinny, Wizard, Snitch, and Tubby are private eyes. They earn money to buy two telephones and they install them themselves. Unfortunately, they hook up the phone wires to the doorbell. The boys attempt to solve the case of who is ringing the doorbell. When they discover the answer, they are angry at first, but then declare that they "stick together through thick and thin."

Bonsall, C. (1971). *The case of the scaredy cats.* New York: Harper and Row.

The boys' detective club excludes girls. When the girls decide that they also want to be members of the club, a fight ensues, which results in the boys running away. Then the girls discover that Annie is missing. The boys and girls put their differences behind them to join together and find Annie.

Ginsbury, M. (1974). *Mushrooms in the rain.* New York: Macmillan.

Various animals hide under a mushroom for protection from the rain. But one day a fox comes by looking for a rabbit who is hiding under the mushroom. The animals band together to protect the rabbit and divert the fox to another location.

Peet, B. (1972). *The ant and the elephant.* Boston: Houghton Mifflin.

A turtle accidently falls over on his back. He asks various animals for help, but all refuse. After refusing, each animal finds itself in a disastrous predicament. The only animal that does not follow this pattern is an elephant who helps an ant across the river. The elephant then continues to help all of the other animals. At the conclusion of the story, the elephant falls into a ravine. An entire colony of ants, working together, carry the elephant out of the ravine and save him from danger.

Salazar, V. (1967). *Squares are not bad.* New York: Golden Press.

The various shapes—squares, circles, triangles, and rectangles—each live alone and do not like each other. One day the shapes are playing together and they accidently bump into each other.

They discover that they are able to form wonderful new shapes and figures by working together.

Pairs Working Together

Cohen, M. (1971). *Best friends.* New York: Collier Books.

Paul and Jim are usually best friends, but they have some difficulties in this story. When the light goes out in the incubator, the boys work together to fix it and save the baby chicks.

Delton, J. (1974). *Two good friends.* New York: Crown Publishers.

Duck and Bear are friends who have opposite skills. Bear likes to cook and Duck likes to clean. They surprise each other one day by doing their favorite activity for each other.

Johnston, T. (1972). *The adventures of Mole and Troll.* New York: G. P. Putnam's Sons.

Mole and Troll work together to accomplish various goals, as when Mole models for Troll so that he can make a dress for his grandmother.

Lobel, A. (1979). *Days with Frog and Toad.* New York: Harper & Row.

Frog and Toad help each other through many interesting episodes. One example is when Frog offers Toad encouragement as he tries to fly his kite.

Chapter Six

Building Bridges Between Communities and the School

● ●

OVERVIEW

Up to this point, we have concentrated exclusively on providing for learning inside the joinfostering classroom, but for joinfostering to work optimally, the students' parents and communities also must have significant roles in education, both at home and in school. And, once again, your role is critical for building bridges between the community and the school by extending joinfostering principles into your students' homes and enabling family members to reciprocate by becoming involved.

Involving the community, especially non-English-speaking parents and other family members, in educational activities at home and in the school, the fourth joinfostering condition, is no simple matter. There are language barriers to consider in addition to various ways that adult caregivers in different cultures and communities view their role and the school's role in educating their children (Delpit, 1998; Coelho, 1994). Within the Asian immigrant community, for example, many parents feel that they are

solely responsible for their children's learning, particularly how the children should approach learning, both at home and in school (Constantino, Cui, & Faltis, 1995). The school's job is to provide a workplace where children can be exposed to and practice basic skills (Cheng, 1987). In contrast, many recently arrived Mexican families see the school as the sole authority on what needs to be learned and how it should be done (Scarcella, 1990). At home, although parents constantly teach their children to be respectful to elders, to care for family members, and to be accountable for their own actions, they rarely work with their children on school-related activities (Delgado-Gaitán, 1987). For many of these parents, school, not home, is the appropriate place for learning about content and basic skills. Within both cultural groups, parents are deeply concerned about the education of their children (Olsen, 1988; Yao, 1988; Ramos & Santos, 1994; Delgado-Gaitán, 1994). However, in both cases, the ways

159

that parents and other adult caregivers see their role in schooling often differs considerably from the way that mainstream English-speaking communities view their relationship with schools (Leitch & Tangri, 1988).

Parents from mainstream communities, partly because they speak the language used in school and partly because the majority of school personnel are members of their communities, tend to share with schools the view that parental involvement at home and in schools is positively related to school achievement (Epstein, 1991). Consequently, most mainstream parents agree that they are responsible for helping schools do their job and that they can do so by engaging in the following kinds of behaviors: (1) tutoring their children at home, (2) helping them with homework, (3) helping their children sell raffle tickets or candy to neighbors and friends, (4) attending class plays, (5) accompanying children on field trips, (6) attending parent-teacher conferences, and (7) helping out with PTA (Parent-Teachers Association) activities. In addition to these more traditional parental-involvement activities, many mainstream parents also function as *advocates for change* by attending school board meetings, as *co-learners* by attending workshops with teachers where participants learn more about children and schooling, and as *decision-makers* by becoming members of advisory boards or school committees (Chavkin & Williams, 1989).

The fact that great numbers of mainstream parents or other adult caregivers perform these behaviors demon-strates the tremendous degree of familiarity that these adults have with the way schools expect communities to be involved in supporting the education of their children. However, the fact that non-English-speaking parents and adult caregivers do not perform many of these behaviors does not mean that they are any less concerned about their children's education. In all likelihood, the reason that many of them are less involved in school-related activities than their English-speaking counterparts has as much to do with the school's unfamiliarity with non-English-speaking communities as it does with these communities' unfamiliarity with the schools.

In this chapter, you will learn about ways to help your students' parents and other significant caregivers become increasingly familiar with how they can be more involved in schooling matters. At the same time, you will also learn about how to become involved in your students' communities and to pay attention to the kinds of activities that parents and others feel comfortable doing in school and at home. A few words of caution are in order, however, before we continue.

It is important to understand that parental involvement in the joinfostering framework necessarily moves you out of the classroom and into the communities you serve. This may come relatively easily in some cases, but may cause feelings of anxiety and insecurity in others. Moreover, building home-school relationships may also move you into school-level politics, due to the fact that some of the strategies that we will advocate may require support from your principal and other school-level authorities. Thus, you can expect many different kinds of resistance. For example, using a language other than English to invite parents to school functions or making sure that information about bus schedules is available in the parents' native language are political stances. Garnering support for these kinds of actions may require you to get into some potentially bitter battles with colleagues and non-school people who do not share your perspective. Choose your battles wisely and don't expect to fight or win every one. Instead, look for ways to advocate for actions that you believe are clearly needed to improve education for all students and that you know your parents also support. Work with other teachers and with parents who share your views about joinfostering and the need for greater involvement of parents in the school and of the school in the

community. Lastly, rely on your personal stance to help your students and their communities join in the education process at home as well as in school.

With these caveats in mind, let us now proceed directly to Julia's classroom to learn how she is going to inform parents about the upcoming presentations her students have prepared on ways to preserve elephants in the wild. Following this final episode in Julia's classroom, we will examine a structured two-way approach to parental involvement that divides the process of parental involvement and participation into four levels such that at each level the involvement of parents in the school increases proportionately to the school's involvement in the communities it serves. For each level of involvement, we will discuss specific strategies and activities for teachers and parents alike.

EPISODE SIX: ALMOST ALL OF THE PARENTS SHOWED UP!

Back to School night is next Wednesday from 7:00 to 9:30 P.M. This gives Julia and her students less than one week to finish rehearsing their skits before presenting them to an audience of parents, family, and friends! The principal of the school selected Wednesday night after learning from a majority of both second-language and English-speaking parents across the grades that this was the best night for them to come to school. Julia and several other teachers, with the support of the principal's office, made sure that the general invitations to Back to School night were written and sent out in the language of the home at least one week before the event, with a short reminder going home with students on Monday. Each invitation also asked for the parents or other family members to bring one item of food or a beverage.

Julia's students also sent out a personal invitation to their parents and other family members to come to the auditorium on the evening of Back to School night to listen to and watch the students in her class present their skits and supporting materials to the entire school. Along with the invitation, she sent an accompanying letter written by the students of her class, explaining the purpose of Back to School night and the kinds of activities that they could expect. Since the letters were composed in English by the students, Julia hoped that the students would be able to read and translate them to their parents and other family members as needed. Julia knew that all of her second-language parents spoke and understood very little English, but was not sure about their English reading abilities.

With the help of Jake, the bilingual resource teacher, and one of the teacher aides, Julia also located and talked with community workers who spoke the four non-English languages in her class: Spanish, Korean, Chinese, and Vietnamese. She explained to them about the presentations her students would be making and about other events that were planned for Back to School night. Julia also inquired about the appropriateness of someone in place of the teacher contacting parents by telephone and inviting them to Back to School night. All of the community workers felt certain that the parents would understand and would most likely welcome the invitation.

Julia asked the community workers to make one other request of the parents. On the general invitations, each household was asked to bring one item of food. One of the English-speaking mothers had already volunteered to help Julia call the English-speaking families and find out what they would be bringing. Julia wanted the community workers to let parents know that she hoped they would bring a typical food from their respective country. She also asked the community workers to share the telephone numbers of bilingual compatriot parents in other grades who they knew for certain were bringing food, with the hope that the parents would talk among themselves about the meaning and purpose of the Back to School night.

On Wednesday afternoon, Jake and three 6th-grade students go to the cafeteria to help Julia finish setting up the posters and the cardboard backgrounds for the skits. That evening, Julia's and her helpers' efforts paid off! Virtually all of the parents of Julia's students showed up for the performance and most stayed afterward to visit her classroom to learn about the kinds of activities that their children were doing. Julia realized that this was quite an accomplishment for many of the parents. For some of the second-language parents, this was the first time that they had attended a school function. Her next goal was to get her parents to feel comfortable contributing to classroom as well as school-level activities and eventually to school-wide decisions. To reach this goal, Julia knew that she had to continue her involvement with her students' families and communities and keep the families involved in school.

In the following sections, let's consider the kinds of things that you might do if you were in Julia's place with her enthusiasm to build bridges between the home and the school and ultimately to give parents a voice in helping improve education for their children.

A TWO-WAY PARENTAL-SCHOOL INVOLVEMENT MODEL

> Refugee parents are frustrated. On the one hand they want to push their children academically, to become someone in society, to work hard and study well. On the other hand, they cannot effectively intervene in the educational process. They cannot attend school functions, PTA meetings, even school conferences because of language and not understanding the process. *The relative solution would be two-sided. Parents have to be educated on how to access the system, how to be influential, what to go to. And on the other hand, the school itself needs to outreach to bring in the parents of the new students in the system, because unless the parents work cooperatively with the schools we will not get an education for the children that they need.*
>   Vu-Doc Vuong, Public Testimony, San Francisco, CA, in Olsen, 1988, pp. 82–83
>   (emphasis mine).

Most of the research on the relationship between parental involvement and academic achievement reports that parents who participate in the schooling experiences of their children have a positive impact on attitudes toward schooling and, ultimately, on school success (Bermudez & Padrón, 1987; Epstein, 1991; Solomon, 1991). The relationship between parental involvement and school success is based on the assumption that children whose parents participate in school-related activities become more invested in school because their parents talk with them about the value of schooling for success in life. The fact that parents are participating in school-related activities, however, presumes a familiarity with schools and a belief that schools provide access to a variety of professions and occupations in society (Ogbu, 1983). Accordingly, parental involvement is perceived as a one-way venture, from the parents to the school. That is, the school does not need to reach out to parents since parents implicitly understand the value of being involved in schooling matters. However, in the case of parents of second-language students and particularly immigrant parents, there may be little understanding about the way U.S. schools work (Olson, 1990), and the parents may not share the belief that schools prepare all children equally (Torres-Guzmán, 1991). The following statement by a Honduran mother captures the essence of these concerns:

My son needs an education here. That is the way for him to have a good life. I fear for him, though. Here the teachers don't keep an eye on the children. He misses school and the teacher doesn't discipline him. He says the teacher doesn't care if he does his work. I try to teach him respect for his teacher, but he says that is not how it is here. (Olsen, 1988, p. 82)

What can this parent do to allay her fear that her son is not getting a good education? And what could we do as representatives of the school to enable this parent to turn these concerns into action that would benefit not only her children, but other children as well?

A Multilevel Approach to Home-School Relationships

Building bridges between the home and the school inevitably rests on the cooperative efforts of the school, the teachers, and the parents. But teachers have the primary responsibility for initially getting parents involved in schooling matters. Reluctant parents won't get involved in schooling simply because the principal wants them to. They may get involved, however, if their child's teacher reaches out to them and gives them multiple opportunities to become involved at home and in school. The key to involving parents within the joinfostering framework, therefore, is to strike a balance between learning about the home environments of your students, while the parents of your students also learn about school-oriented activities and programs.

We can work toward this balance of involvement by dividing the process of building bridges between the home and the school into four levels. This multilevel approach to parental and teacher involvement is based on the works of Petit (1989) and Rasinski and Fredericks (1989). The approach is especially well suited for working in a culturally and linguistically diverse classroom because it begins with the teacher learning about the parents' community support systems and about stress factors related to living in a new environment and ends with the parents actively contributing to curricular decisions. Figure 6.1 presents a visual representation of the four levels of teacher and parental involvement.

Level I.   Your objectives in Level I are (a) to learn about your parents' daily experiences and the community in which they live; (b) to initiate individual contact with the parents and other adult caregivers through informal chats, get-togethers, and home visits; and (c) based on (a) and (b), to begin to work with parents and other caregivers to show them ways to monitor their children's progress in school.

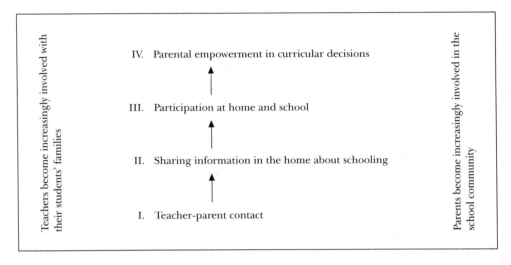

Figure 6.1
A multilevel approach to teacher and parental involvement
Source: From "Dimensions of Parent Involvement" by T. Rasinski and A. Fredericks, 1989, *The Reading Teacher,* November, 181. Adapted with permission.

The most effective way to develop and establish rapport with parents and to learn about their community is through a home visit, which enables you to gain firsthand knowledge of some of the constraints that parents may face. For example, many second-language parents live in crowded conditions with little room for study in isolation (Olsen, 1988). Children are often attended to by siblings and extended family members (Delgado-Gaitán, 1987); parents work long hours and sometimes have two or more jobs.

Begin scheduling your home visits early in the year and continue them on a regular basis, not just when a problem arises. Every visit you make should have a specific purpose, and the parents as well as the student should be aware of that purpose before the visit (Gestwicki, 1987). In addition, before you visit second-language parents, you should make inquiries about any special protocol or taboos that you should be aware of. Likewise, you will have a more successful encounter if you learn about greeting and leave-taking rituals and politeness formulae. (See Hoskins, 1971, for Vietnamese families; Scarcella & Chin, 1993, for Korean families; Kang, Kuehn, & Herrell, 1994, for Hmong families; Yao, 1988, for Asian families; Delgado-Gaitán, 1987, for Mexican families; Wong Fillmore, 1990, for Latino families; and Delgado-Gaitán, 1994, for Russian families). If there is not an adult in the household who can serve as an interpreter, bring a trusted translator from school. But before you visit, talk with the translator about how you would like your interaction with the parents to be translated. Do you want paraphrased translations or word-for-word translations? It is important to have a translator who can translate literal information as well as cultural nuances. The translator may also be able to provide you with valuable information about the community and answer questions about appropriate cultural behavior.

In addition to making contact with parents through home visits, you should also be learning about the community-based organizations that provide information and support services for different ethnic and language communities. Make an appointment to talk with a community worker or counselor at the local community-based organization. In the meeting, try to learn as much as possible about the services the organization provides and talk about the ways that you would like to involve parents over time. The community workers should be able to provide you with lots of information about the needs of the community. You should also ask about places in the community where families might shop for ethnic food and music and where they go for entertainment. Inquire about native-language religious services and places of worship. You might even attend a church service or visit a marketplace to get a better feel for the community.

Learning about the community enables you to tap into the "funds of knowledge" that families rely upon for their daily experience. Greenberg (1989) refers to funds of knowledge as an "operations manual of essential information and strategies households need to maintain their well-being" (p. 2). These funds of knowledge may be useful to you in getting information out to the community and for developing thematic units around topics that are community-based. (See Moll & Greenberg, 1990, for an example of a community-oriented curriculum project.)

Your efforts to learn about the community and your parents at Level I should help you decide on the kinds of monitoring of schoolwork that you feel is most appropriate for parents. For example, suppose you learn that many of your second-language parents work at jobs that require long hours and that they have relatively little time to monitor children's schoolwork at home. And you also find out that a local neighborhood center offers after-school and weekend peer tutoring services. What you might do is inform parents about the services and help them set up a ride-share program if needed. Next, you can suggest a plan whereby you or students from a higher grade check their child's homework three days a week, and the parents or other caregivers check it two days a week. You might also ask parents to spend at least 3 minutes every evening talking with children about schoolwork and any homework that they might have. You can even suggest the kinds of questions they might ask. Obviously, if you do not speak the language of the parents you will need to work with a bilingual liaison to assist you in your communication with parents.

In summary, your primary goals at this level are to establish contact with parents, to begin learning about the community, and to let parents know that you are there for them and that you will continue to support them throughout the school year. As you gain their trust, you can begin suggesting ways to monitor schoolwork assignments done at home. You will increase the likelihood of getting parents involved in their child's schoolwork to the extent that your suggestions take into account the constraints under which the family operates.

Level II.   The second level of involvement broadens the kinds of communication that you have with parents. From your perspective, Level II involves informing parents through written sources, telephone calls, and informal conferences about their child's progress, about classroom activities that may involve their community, about upcoming events, and about basic school policies. From the parents' perspective, the communication might range from providing you with feedback on how the child is responding to schoolwork at home to inquiring about holidays and bus routes.

At this level, involvement is tantamount to information sharing, so that parents begin to feel comfortable relying on you for information about school policies and activities, while at the same time you increase your personal contact with them. Here is a list of some of the kinds of information that you might wish to share with parents:

1. Important school dates (workshop days, half-days, holidays, registration days, report card days);
2. Information about school events and meetings that parents should attend;
3. Information about the school board and the kinds of issues it is currently addressing;
4. Summary of the minutes of school board meetings with a schedule of the next meeting;
5. Information about changes in bus or school-day schedules;
6. Information about and telephone numbers of bilingual liaisons who work for the school and the community;
7. Information about community-based organizations;
8. Information about upcoming television programs about the parents' community and/or country of origin;

9. Information about local community events, such as music festivals, plays, carnivals, art displays, and speakers;

10. Tips about the kinds of academic help that parents can provide at home.

To the extent possible, all of this information should be provided in the parents' native language, preferably by individuals who are native speakers and writers of the language. You will probably need the help of bilingual liaisons working in the school or the district office. But as the year progresses, you may find that there are a number of parents who would be interested in helping with this kind of information sharing.

Another way to inform parents about classroom and school activities is to send home a weekly newsletter based primarily on ideas generated by your students. The easiest way to produce a newsletter is to set aside a few minutes one day a week and, in a group meeting format, generate news items from students, which you then immediately write out on a ditto master. News items can range from students discussing what they are studying or what they liked about something they read or experienced in class to the kinds of issues they would like to tackle in the coming weeks. In terms of format, the newsletter should have a name, (e.g., *Bruner Bobcat Weekly News)*, a volume number, and a date at the top of the page. Most of the space on the paper should be reserved for student ideas. As the year progresses you may need to add a second page from time to time. You can also use 8 x 14 legal-size paper for an occasional longer edition.

The newsletter can also serve as a means to briefly announce upcoming field trips and special events; other reminders to parents and adult caregivers can be placed in a small rectangle toward the bottom of the page, under the heading of *Community News*. In addition, the newsletter can devote a small space to a special phrase written in the native language of one of the groups represented in your class. For example, in a classroom such as Julia's, where there are four languages in addition to English, each week Julia would write out a saying in one of the four languages and repeat the cycle at the end of every fourth edition. Gertrude Moskowitz's (1978) *Caring and Sharing in the Foreign Language Class: A Source Book for Humanistic Techniques* offers an extensive list of wonderful sayings in several different languages. And, in collaboration with your school librarian, you can also make suggestions about age-appropriate storybooks written in the native language being highlighted for that particular week.

Finally, you can appoint two students a week to write a kind sentence about their family or their community. You can label this special section something like "People in Our Community" and let the students write the sentences in their own handwriting on the master sheet for Xeroxing later on.

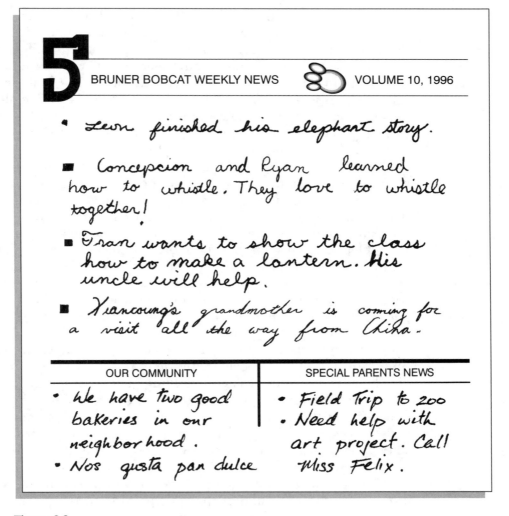

5

BRUNER BOBCAT WEEKLY NEWS   VOLUME 10, 1996

- Leon finished his elephant story.

- Concepcion and Ryan learned how to whistle. They love to whistle together!

- Tran wants to show the class how to make a lantern. His uncle will help.

- Xiancoung's grandmother is coming for a visit all the way from China.

OUR COMMUNITY	SPECIAL PARENTS NEWS
• We have two good bakeries in our neighborhood. • Nos gusta pan dulce	• Field Trip to zoo • Need help with art project. Call Miss Felix.

Figure 6.2
Newsletter example: Bruner Bobcat Weekly News

Some schools may even have computer software programs that allow students to choose the format for their newsletter. When the newsletter finally comes out it should look something like like the example shown in Figure 6.2.

A weekly newsletter is a good way to get parents and other family members and caregivers involved in schooling. Students enjoy reading about their classmates to just about anyone who will listen. Moreover, Hakuta (1990) has shown that bilingual children from the 3rd grade on up are very capable of translating from English to their native language and vice versa. Thus, your second-language students should be delighted to translate the newsletter for their parents and other family members!

You can also strengthen your relationship with parents and adult caregivers by writing occasional personal notes and making telephone calls. In the personal notes addressed to the parents, you should share personal observations or anecdotes about how well the child is doing in class, especially in subjects that are of concern to parents and adult caregivers. The notes should be brief and written in clear English or in the parents' or adult caregivers' native language. (You need to find out early on if there are adult family members who can read English. This will save you from having to rely so much on a translator.) Personal notes take less than 5 minutes to write. If you send out approximately ten notes a week, each student in your class will take at least one home every three weeks.

Telephone calls may be a bit more complicated because if you need a translator, you will also need a special telephone system set up for conference calls. Telephone contact may be the only way for you to personally contact some parents and adult caregivers, however, so you may want to put forth the effort. Before you start making phone calls, you should find out about any special telephone protocol that might be required in the cultural groups represented in your classroom. For example, in Latin American culture, it is considered rude to telephone someone and immediately go right to the reason for calling. The appropriate behavior is to exchange relatively lengthy greetings and to ask about the health and well-being of the family. Once you have completed this opening ritual, it is then acceptable for you as the caller to state the purpose of the call. The bilingual liaison or community worker for the various language communities are probably aware of any special telephone protocol.

To summarize your goals in Level II, you should be working toward broadening the information that you provide to the parents and adult caregivers of your students through several kinds of personal contact. At the same time, you should be slowly but steadily encouraging parents and adult caregivers to reciprocate by getting more involved with their children in terms of the information and schoolwork that you send home. Moreover, in Level II, parents and adult caregivers should begin to sense that school is not such a foreign place as they might have thought.

Level III.   You can begin to invite parents and adult caregivers to participate in your classroom and in school-related activities as soon as you sense that they are responding favorably to your efforts to contact and inform them of schooling and community-related activities. Your primary objective in Level III is to get parents and adult caregivers into the classroom to informally observe and eventually help with classroom activities and school events. At the same time, you also want them (with your guidance) to take on increasing responsibility for monitoring their child's study skills and work habits at home (Rasinski & Fredericks, 1989). In essence, you want the parents' and adult caregivers' experiences in school to serve as a model for the kinds of support and monitoring that they can provide for their children at home. That is, as a result of working in a joinfostering classroom environment, you want parents and adult caregivers to try out strategies that they see occurring in the classroom when they assist their children with school tasks at home.

It is important to understand that while you may have contact with 100% of your parents and adult caregivers as a result of your efforts in Levels I and II, in all probability there will be some who may resist becoming involved at this level for any number of reasons. For example, second-language parents and adult caregivers who do not speak or understand English may feel uneasy about coming into your classroom or participating in school activities. Others may have work schedules that simply prohibit them from participating during school hours. These reasons should not deter you from maintaining contact with them or from offering suggestions for improving their involvement in schoolwork at home. One of the other adult family members who is bilingual might be able to participate on their behalf. Moreover, there are activities that do not require interactive English proficiency and school events that take place on weekends and in the evening.

Let's consider some of the kinds of help that parents and adult caregivers might provide in your classroom and for your school in Level III.

One of the first ways to get parents and adult caregivers into a classroom is to invite them to observe for a few minutes throughout the school day. For example, you can invite those who drop their children off to stay a few minutes in the morning and those who pick up their children to visit a few minutes before the school day ends. For families who live far from the school and have their children bussed, you can still set aside special parent visit days. You can work with parents and adult caregivers who drive their children to organize ride-sharing programs so that parents or other family members who live far away can come in for a brief visit on key days.

You can also invite parents and adult caregivers to come to special events involving their children. Throughout the year you may put on a play, present a musical extravaganza, or have a storybook/poetry reading session. Before and after the presentation, you can have students show their parents and adult caregivers around the room and talk about art, writing, science, and social studies projects that the class is currently undertaking. *These kinds of informal involvement can be done in any language!* In fact, you should encourage parents and adult caregivers to speak with their children in their native language in your classroom just as you should encourage them to do so in their homes.

In addition to the sheer enjoyment that parents and adult caregivers receive from watching their children in your classroom, you can also help them become more aware of how learning takes place there by giving them a few tips on the kinds of actions and events to look for. For example, you can have them pay attention to the different kinds of verbal and written interaction that the students engage in. Have them watch you teach to the whole class or to a small group. Encourage them to notice the type of visual and nonverbal support that you provide as you teach. Both before and after they observe your teaching, you might ask them to look for certain kinds of events and actions that you plan to emphasize in the lesson. Their observations of your teaching may give them ideas to improve interaction with their children at home. If you know ahead of time that second-language parents or adult caregivers are coming to visit your classroom, try to have another bilingual parent or a bilingual liaison there to help you communicate with them.

As you learn more about your students' families, you are bound to uncover the wealth of experiences parents and other families members have. In fact, you may even wish to engage your students as budding anthropologists to learn about the "funds of knowledge" that adults in their household rely on for any number of functions within their communities. Heath (1983) and Moll, Vélez-Ibáñez, and Greenberg (1989) present ways for teaching students to use ethnographic techniques for studying community funds of knowledge. For example, Heath tells how students learned from local gardeners about the best time to plant and harvest vegetables and then compared that with what the science books said. Moll and his colleagues had students discover what community members knew about banking and other important business concepts and then developed curricula around the information.

One of the many benefits of gathering data and information from parents and other family members is that students learn about new sources of information in their own communities. Doing so elevates the status of community-based knowledge and makes it easier to invite family members into the classroom to share their personal knowledge about how things work and how things are done. For example, suppose your class were interested in finding out how people acquire sense about directionality (north, south, east, and west), and you collected lots of information from parents and family members. You could then invite several parents and adult caregivers in to share with the class how they tell about directions, and students could try out the various methods.

Parents and adult caregivers who speak a language other than English can of course also be invited to share their knowledge of directionality or whatever practice, through a translator. It is the knowledge that is important and the fact that the parent is participating in the class. There is an additional benefit to having non-English-speaking parents present a demonstration of a particular practice in their native language: Students get to hear different languages and they find out that teaching and learning can occur in any language!

There is one possible drawback to using ethnographic techniques to bring community knowledge and, ultimately, parents and other family members into the classroom. There are some kinds of community knowledge that adult members do not want children to bring into the school. To illustrate this point, Lipka (1989) tells a poignant story of a group of well-meaning educators and curriculum developers who were bent on developing a school curriculum that was responsive to the needs of the Yup'ik Eskimo community of Bayup in rural Alaska. One of the teachers involved in the project guided a group of students in producing a questionnaire to find out how the community survived in the bitter winter months and how they gathered food. According to Lipka (1989), here's how the community responded:

> . . . as soon as students began interviewing parents throughout the village, concerned community members got on the C.B. [radio] and warned everybody not to fill out the questionnaire. (p. 223)

The parents later explained that they felt threatened by attempts to take certain kinds of cultural knowledge outside the community and place them into the school. Their objection was essentially that "if *kass'at* [white people] teach our culture to the students, then what is left for us? Our culture belongs to the community" (Lipka, 1989, p. 223).

What Lipka and his colleagues learned subsequently, however, was that the native community did respond to efforts to construct curricula that dealt with contemporary issues of concern to the community. For example, community members were eager to work with the school on issues of land use and land management. Lipka learned from this experience that the information we gather from the community has to be relevant and purposeful to that community. In other words, rather than the community just being a resource for the school, the school has to become a resource to the community. For our purposes, this means that when we invite parents and other adult caregivers in to speak about their knowledge and practices, we also need to consider ways that we can become resources for their needs as well.

Another way of involving parents in the classroom is to have certain parents or adult caregivers help with making bulletin boards and other kinds of decorations and building projects. For example, if you decorate your classroom around thematic units and festivities, parents and adult caregivers can help you. You can set aside several locations in your classroom for non-English-language bulletin boards. If you use the ceiling for decorations, as was suggested in Chapter 3, you can have a crew of parents help you put the students' work up and then add their own creations around a particular theme.

Parents and adult caregivers can also help in the preparation of classroom materials. They can come to the classroom to work on assembling a stage for a play, or they can sew and cut materials for a cooperative game. There are many activities they can help with regardless of their English-language proficiency.

Finally, at the school level, parents and adult caregivers can observe and help with many of the same kinds of activities that they did in your classroom. They can attend school functions, assemblies, and parties. They can be enlisted to help with food preparation and serving at these events. They can help set up and take down tables before and after the functions, assemblies, and parties. You need to be there, however, to support them and make them feel comfortable as they are learning to get involved in the school.

In summary, your goals in Level III are to get parents and adult caregivers to participate in your classroom and in school, doing many different kinds of activities, while you improve and increase your communication with them and show them how schools work. They will participate in your classroom and in school when they start to feel that the school is a comfortable place to be and that it is potentially a resource for them.

Level IV. In this fourth and highest level of parental, adult caregiver, and teacher involvement, the goal is to enable parents and adult caregivers to play a more decisive role in school decisions and policies and at the same time to increase the level of confidence and trust that they have in you as the teacher. This level is what Rasinski and Fredericks (1989) refer to as the "empowerment" level. To achieve this highest level of involvement, you and the parents and adult caregivers must have experienced each of the first three levels. Accordingly, Level IV is clearly not for every parent or adult caregiver and, in fact, few attain it. Reaching the level of empowerment depends in great part on the mutual trust and bond that forms between you and certain parents and adult caregivers who want to invest extra time and effort in the schooling process (Rasinski & Fredericks, 1989). Those who do reach Level IV often become community spokespersons to whom you and the school can look for both advice and support. In other words, due to their intense involvement in schools they become your colleagues in matters of curriculum and education in general. As such, you can ask for their opinions on classroom ideas and, as their participation progresses, for their advice on curricular decisions at the school level.

Your involvement with parents and adult caregivers at this level is tailored primarily to providing suggestions to them with the confidence that they will implement the suggestions. So, for instance, if you suggest to Level IV parents or adult caregivers that they organize a get-together to discuss community opinions about school plans to decrease the number of contact hours for art and music or to require all teachers to acquire an endorsement in teaching English as a second language within five years, you can be certain that they will do it. Moreover, because of your commitment to the various communities represented in your classroom, you may be asked to attend meetings and offer opinions at community-based organizations or you may be even be asked to give rides to parents who lack means of transportation.

An excellent example of what empowered parents and teachers can accomplish is the Pajaro Valley Experience (Ada, 1988), a family literacy program designed by Spanish-speaking parents with the help of teachers in the Pajaro Valley School District near Watsonville, California. Sixty to 80 Spanish-speaking parents come together each month to discuss children's literature in Spanish and to read the stories that their children have written in Spanish. Over time, the parents join in to write stories and poems along with their children. Parents also learn how to talk about books with their children and eagerly share the fruits of these discussions with fellow parents at the following monthly meeting. Ada points out that the program worked because a few parents worked to get others involved and because a few teachers helped with invitations, transportation, and book selections.

The establishment of a family literacy program is one of many kinds of activities that empowered parents and adult caregivers can engage in. They can also set up after-school tutoring programs. Padilla (1982) reports that parents in many communities throughout the Southwest have organized *escuelitas* (little schools) to provide help with schoolwork, to promote Spanish-language development, and to reinforce Mexican culture. The *escuelitas* are run by parents and other students who volunteer to work with young children. Trueba, Moll, and Díaz (1982) discuss a similar effort by Mexican immigrant parents in California who organized *Cafés de Amistad* (Friendship Coffees) for interested parents to come and share their concerns and knowledge about school.

Parents and adult caregivers can also organize Parent Advisory Committees and work toward affecting change in school. Parent Advisory Committees represent the voice of the community on issues that concern their children. To be effective, parents who become involved in these committees must "be informed not only about the legal realities but also about the attitudes and activities of the local policy makers" (Curtis, 1988, p. 291). Moreover, the school district needs to be made continually aware of the parents' position on certain issues, just as the parents and adult caregivers need to be apprised of their rights and of their power to impact school policy (Curtis, 1988).

As was mentioned above, due to the intense nature and relatively narrow focus of efforts, only a few parents or adult caregivers participate in Level IV activities. The fact that some may eventually become involved in curricular and other schoolwide decisions does not mean, however, that you can lessen your communication and commitment to other parents or adult caregivers. You still need to maintain contact with all of them and continue to encourage their involvement in school-related activities both at home and in your classroom.

In summary, your main goal at Level IV is to involve parents and adult caregivers from the language groups represented in your class in advising, planning, and developing programs that they and you feel are needed for their children. Level IV parents and adult caregivers have transversed the first three levels of involvement and are committed to working with you on improving education for their children. At this level you and the parents and other adults work with many people ranging from school board members and the school principal to fellow parents and local community leaders. Level IV involvement is intense and usually long-term, but the benefits are also rewarding and long lasting.

CONCLUSION

This chapter began by emphasizing how difficult it may be to involve parents and other adult caregivers from diverse language and cultural backgrounds in school-related activities. In addition to language barriers, the ways that parents and adult caregivers from different cultures view their role and the school's role in educating their children may be quite different from the expected pattern of school involvement. Despite language and cultural differences, however, there are ways to involve parents and other adult caregivers in schooling matters that minimize the barriers that language and cultural differences can create. The multilevel approach to home-school relationships is one such way to minimize barriers and instead build bridges between the home and the school. The success of this approach rests on you, parents, caregivers, and the community working in tandem to learn about each other's worlds and, as a result, get involved in helping the children make it in both.

As we witnessed in Julia's classroom, it takes lots of time and effort to bring about the social and pedagogical conditions that drive a joinfostering classroom. But joinfostering in the classroom is not complete unless parents and adult caregivers are involved in schooling at home and in the school. The reason for this is that joinfostering means that the teachers, students, and the community are inexorably connected in the process of education. From this perspective, no one should be left out of the education process due to a language or a cultural barrier. The multilevel approach to home-school relationships presented above gives you a means to complete the joinfostering mission of providing all parents and adult caregivers variable access to and participation in schooling.

ACTIVITIES

1. Contact a local elementary school and ask for a copy of the parents' handbook. Review the handbook and determine which sections might be difficult for second-language parents and rewrite them, using scaffolds, visuals, and other kinds of support. Work with an adult bilingual native speaker of one of the languages represented in the school and translate the section you rewrite.

2. Using the parents' handbook as a guide, prepare a video in English and in the other major languages represented in the school to explain registration day and school policies concerning absences, the school lunch program, bus services, and discipline.

3. Contact a local Parent Advisory Committee and interview one of the members. Find out how the committee works and what some of the major issues have been in the last couple of years. Ask about committee membership of bilingual parents.

4. Visit a community-based organization serving a language-minority community and interview one of the community workers. Find out about the history of the community, about major community events, and where the people in the community shop, worship, and go for entertainment. On the basis of what you learn about the community, attend an event or ceremony and notice (a) the roles that men and women play, (b) how and the extent to which children are involved, and (c) whether and under what conditions

English is used for communication among members attending.

5. Interview two parents from the same non-English-speaking background to find out their perceptions of parental involvement. Try to find one parent who has minimal involvement in the school and one who is intensely involved in the school. Using the multiple-level approach to guide the interview, ask each parent to comment on how parents and the school can build better bridges at each level of involvement. Compare and contrast the responses given by each parent.

REFERENCES

Ada, F. A. (1988). The Pajaro Valley experience: Working with Spanish-speaking parents to develop children's reading and writing skills through the use of children's literature. In T. Skutnabb-Kangas & J. Cummins (Eds.), *Minority education: From shame to struggle* (pp. 223–238). Clevedon, England: Multilingual Matters Ltd.

Bermudez, A., & Padrón, Y. (1987). Integrating parental education into teacher training programs: A workable model for minority parents. *Journal of Educational Equity and Leadership, 7*(3), 235–244.

Chavkin, N. F., & Williams, D. L., Jr. (1989). Community size and parent involvement in education. *The Clearing House, 63*(4), 159–162.

Cheng, L. R. (1987). *Assessing Asian language performance.* Rockville, MD: Aspen Publishers.

Coelho, E. (1994). Social integration of immigrant and refugee children. In F. Genesee (Ed.), *Educating second language children: The whole child, the whole curriculum, the whole community* (pp. 301-327). New York: Cambridge University Press.

Constantino, R., Cui, L., & Faltis, C. (1995). Chinese parental involvement: Reaching new levels. *Equity and Excellence in Education, 28*(2), 46–51.

Curtis, J. (1988). Parents, schools and racism: Bilingual education in a Northern California town. In T. Skutnabb-Kangas & J. Cummins (Eds.), *Minority education: From shame to struggle* (pp. 278–298). Clevedon, England: Multilingual Matters Ltd.

Delgado-Gaitán, C. (1987). Parent perceptions of school: Supportive environments for children. In H. T. Trueba (Ed.), *Success or failure? Learning and the language minority student* (pp. 131–155). New York: Newbury House.

Delgado-Gaitán, C. (1994). Russian refugee families: Accommodating aspirations through education. *Anthropology and Education, 25,* 137–155.

Delpit, L. (1988). The silenced dialogue: Power and pedagogy in educating other people's children. *Harvard Educational Review, 58*(3), 280–298.

Epstein, J. (1991). Paths to partnerships: What we can learn from federal, state, district, and school initiatives. *Phi Delta Kappan, 72*(5), 344–349.

Gestwicki, C. (1987). *Home, school and community relations: A guide to working with parents.* Albany, NY: Delmar Publishers.

Greenberg, J. B. (1989). *Funds of knowledge: Historical constitution, social distribution and transmission.* Paper presented at the annual meeting of the Society for Applied Anthropology, Santa Fe, New Mexico.

Hakuta, K. (1990). Language and cognition in bilingual children. In A. M. Padilla, H. H. Fairchild, & C. M. Valadez (Eds.), *Bilingual education: Issues and strategies* (pp. 47–59). Newbury Park, CA: Sage Publications.

Heath, S. B. (1983). *Ways with words: Language, life and work in communities and classrooms.* Cambridge: Cambridge University Press.

Hoskins, M. W. (1971). *Building rapport with the Vietnamese.* Washington, DC: Government Printing Office.

Kang, H-W., Kuehn, P., & Herrell, A. (1994). The Hmong literacy project: A study of Hmong classroom behavior. *Bilingual Research Journal, 18*(3/4), 63–84.

Leitch, M. L., & Tangri, S. S. (1988). Barriers to home-school collaboration. *Educational Horizons,* Winter, 70–74.

Lipka, J. (1989). A cautionary tale of curriculum development in Yuk'uk Eskimo communities. *Anthropology and Education Quarterly, 20,* 216–231.

Moll, L., Vélez-Ibáñez, C., & Greenberg, J. (1989). Community knowledge and classroom practice: Combining resources for literacy instruction. *Year one progress report.* College of Education, University of Arizona.

Moll, L., & Greenberg, J. (1990). Creating zones of possibilities: Coming social contexts for instruction. In L. Moll (Ed.), *Vygotsky and education: Instructional implications and applications of socio-historical psychology* (pp. 319–348). Cambridge: Cambridge University Press.

Moskowitz, G. (1978). *Caring and sharing in the foreign language class: A source book on humanistic techniques.* Rowley, MA: Newbury House.

Ogbu, J. (1983). Minority status and schooling in plural societies. *Comparative Education Review, 27*(2), 168–190.

Olsen, L. (1988). *Crossing the schoolhouse border: Immigrant students and California public schools.* San Francisco: A California Tomorrow Report.

Olson, L. (1990). Misreading said to hamper Hispanics' role in school. *Education Week, 9*(32), 4.

Padilla, A. (1982). Bilingual schools: Gateways to integration or roads to separation. In J. A. Fishman & G. D. Keller (Eds.), *Bilingual education for Hispanic students in the United States* (pp. 48–70). New York: Teachers College Press.

Petit, D. (1989). *Opening up schools.* Harmondsworth: Penguin Press.

Ramos, N., & Santos, R. (1994). Promoting community-school partnerships in bilingual education. In R. Rodríguez, N. Ramos, & J. A. Ruiz-Escalante (Eds.), *Compendium of readings in bilingual education* (pp. 267–273). San Antonio: Texas Association for Bilingual Education.

Rasinski, T., & Fredericks, A. (1989). Dimensions of parent involvement. *The Reading Teacher,* November, 180–182.

Scarcella, R. (1990). *Teaching language minority students in the multicultural classroom.* Upper Saddle River, NJ: Prentice Hall.

Scarcella, R., & Chin, K. (1993). *Literacy practices of two Korean-American communities.* Research Report No. 8. Santa Cruz, CA: The National Center for Research on Cultural Diversity and Language Learning.

Solomon, Z. (1991). California's policy on parent involvement: State leadership for local initiatives. *Phi Delta Kappan, 72*(5), 359–362.

Torres-Guzmán, M. (1991). Recasting frames: Latino parent involvement. In M. McGroarty & C. Faltis (Eds.), *Languages in schools and society: Policy and pedagogy* (pp. 529–552). Berlin: Mouton de Gruyter.

Trueba, H. T., Moll, L., & Díaz, E. (1982). *Improving the functional writing of bilingual secondary school students.* (Contract No. 400-81-0023). Washington, DC: National Institute of Education.

Wong Fillmore, L. (1990). *Latino families and the schools*. Remarks prepared for the Seminar on California's Changing Face of Race Relations: New Ethics in the 1990's. Sponsored by the Senate Office of Research. State Capitol, Sacramento, California, May 1.

Yao, E. L. (1988). Working effectively with Asian immigrant parents. *Phi Delta Kappan, 70*(3), 223–225.

Chapter Seven

Toward Becoming the Kind of Teacher You Want to Be

The joinfostering framework challenges you to become a teacher who can restructure the social organization of your classroom so that all of your students and their adult caregivers can participate in and benefit from schooling. Becoming this kind of teacher is a never-ending process. In no small measure, the quest to become the kind of teacher you want to be is what leads to better teaching. Becoming a better teacher does not occur in a vacuum, however. As teachers, we need a social, critical, and pedagogical foundation from which to grow and generate new ideas. And much of what is advocated in this book is against the grain (see Cochran-Smith, 1991). Accordingly, a significant part of becoming the kind of teacher you want to be involves teaching against the grain (Simon, 1992), which is an affirmation about what matters in school and in the lives of the students that make up the school. Teaching against the grain ranges from engaging students in the critical study of chil-

dren's literature to resisting English-only policies in school (Shannon, 1995).

As the ethnolinguistic makeup of schools changes toward diversity, we can no longer rely on traditional ways of teaching that too narrowly define the role of social interaction and critical consciousness in learning, prohibit students from non-mainstream backgrounds from participating fully and critically in the classroom, and maintain the status quo, which favors social stratification and inequitable schooling (Hudelson & Faltis, 1993). As we have already seen, all-English classrooms that organize teaching around whole-class instruction and individualized content spell failure for second-language students. All-English classrooms that separate students along cultural and language lines discriminate against second-language students. All-English classrooms that are insensitive to language and cultural differences favor mainstream English-speaking students. All-English classrooms that ignore social injustices in and out of school maintain the status quo. And all-English class-rooms that ignore the parents and communities of second-language students deny these parents and communities access to schooling.

Joinfostering, which goes against the grain of these practices, provides a stark contrast to what happens in many classes. In a joinfostering classroom, the social context of learning is expanded to provide multiple opportunities for students to hear and use language and literacy in varied settings about critical historical and present-day topics. Native English-speaking students are socially integrated with second-language students to share knowledge and experiences through talk and collaboration. Language and cultural differences serve as input for the creative construction of authentic curriculum. Teaching is language-sensitive and based on an understanding of how language and literacy are acquired. And last, parents, adult caregivers, and teachers interact at many levels, regardless of the language of the home.

 ## JOINFOSTERING AND THE EMPOWERMENT MODEL

In this final chapter, following Torres-Guzmán (1990), I present joinfostering conditions and the strategies to support them from the perspective of Jim Cummins's minority empowerment model (Cummins, 1986). In a manner similar to the joinfostering framework, Cummins's model focuses on the relationships between students and teachers and between schools and communities. He argues that minority empowerment is first and foremost a matter of teachers personally redefining the way they interact with the students in their classrooms and with the communities they serve (Cummins, 1986). In other words, teachers play a major role in empowering or disabling members (students, parents, and adult caregivers) of cultural and language minority groups. At the heart of Cummins's model is that interactions between the school and the communities it serves are mediated "by the implicit or explicit role definitions that educators assume in relation to four institutional characteristics of schools" (Cummins, 1986, p. 21). Accordingly, the four characteristics that empower or disable minority groups are the extent to which:

1. teachers incorporate minority students' language and culture into the school program;

2. teachers facilitate minority community participation as an integral component of children's education;

3. the pedagogy teachers use promotes intrinsic motivation on the part of students to use language actively in order to generate their own knowledge; and

4. professionals involved in assessment become advocates for minority students rather than legitimizing the location of the "problem" in the students. (Cummins, 1986, p. 21)

Each of these characteristics can be placed on a continuum, with one endpoint promoting student and community empowerment and the other, students who are disabled and a community without a voice. The continua are presented in Figure 7.1. To the extent that teachers stay on the left side of the continua, students become empowered with the ability to incorporate and express divergent world views as well as to acquire and create knowledge (Torres-Guzmán, 1990).

The question that we will address in this section is the extent to which the joinfostering framework equips you with the kinds of support in each of the four major areas that would most likely lead to student empowerment. See Table 7.1.

As you can see, the joinfostering framework incorporates all of the major features of the empowerment model except one, the intense use of

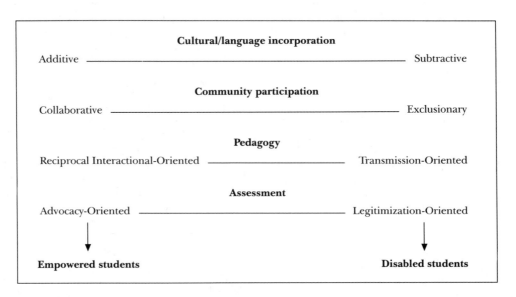

Figure 7.1
Characteristics that contribute to the extent to which minority students are empowered or disabled

Source: From "Empowering Minority Students: A Framework for Intervention" by J. Cummins, 1986, *Harvard Educational Review, 56*(1), p. 24. Copyright 1986 by the President and Fellows of Harvard College. All rights reserved. Reprinted by permission.

Table 7.1
A comparison of the empowerment model with the joinfostering framework

Empowerment model	Joinfostering framework
1. Cultural/language incorporation	
A. The second language (L2) is added to the students' native languages (L1); students' native languages are reinforced through intensive L1 instruction.	A. Teaching is done in ways to facilitate L2 acquisition along with content learning; all of students' native languages are incorporated in bulletin boards, invitations, and newsletters; native language use during recess and on playgrounds is not discouraged. Since joinfostering occurs in an all-English classroom, L1 instruction does not occur.
B. Students' cultural identities are reinforced.	B. Students' culture is celebrated; students are encouraged to tie back to cultural experiences; many activities tie into students' cultures.
C. Instructional patterns are adjusted to take into account cultural variations in learning style preferences.	C. Social contexts of teaching and learning are varied to include whole-group, small-group, and individual learning. Students engage in multiple ways of interacting with materials and peers; all five senses are promoted.
D. Teachers define their roles in relation to the incorporation of minority students' languages and cultures.	D. Teachers draw on students' languages and cultural experiences to facilitate language and content learning. Teachers understand that students need to use their languages and cultural experiences for making sense of interaction and learning tasks.
2. Home-School Interactions	
A. Minority parents are involved as partners in their children's education.	A. Joinfostering uses a multilevel approach to home-school relationships; parents and teachers work together to improve each other's involvement in the process of education at home and in school.
B. Teachers work to develop collaborative relationships with parents.	B. Through home visits, personal notes, and phone calls, teachers help parents better monitor their children's schoolwork at home. Parents are invited to observe and participate in classroom and school events.

the students' native language for instruction. Obviously, this particular feature, while a critical one in bilingual classrooms, does not apply to an all-English classroom.

However, it is important to point out that the joinfostering framework values bilingualism by providing support for a student's first as well as second language. That is, in the all-English classroom, when possible, a second-language student's native language is used for expressions and for

Table 7.1
continued

Empowerment model	Joinfostering framework
3. Pedagogy	
A. Teachers aim to empower students by engaging them in tasks that enable them to be generators of their own knowledge and understanding.	A. The balance of rights of participation promotes student-generated talk and topics; students are in control of their learning in small groups. Teachers assist students in expressing their own ideas verbally; students talk and write authentically to multiple audiences.
B. Teachers use a reciprocal interaction model for teaching to students.	B. There is a high incidence of two-way comunicative exchanges between the teachers and the students and among students, regardless of their oral English proficiency. Teachers negotiate for meaning with students. The physical environment of the classroom is organized to facilitate and support reciprocal talk.
4. Assessment	
A. Professionals become advocates for children by critically scrutinizing the societal and educational contexts within which minority students have developed rather than locating "problems" within the students.	A. Students' knowledge is assessed in multiple ways; language development is viewed holistically as opposed to the mastery of discrete structures. Students assess each other through revision and self-evaluation.
	B. Language and literacy acquisition are viewed as resulting from opportunities to understand and create meaning. Errors are evidence of learning.
	C. Teachers become "kid watchers," constantly assessing students' understanding and their ability to apply new information.

communicating with parents. Moreover, the bilingual student's *second language* is regarded as equally important as the first for promoting social and academic learning (see Pease-Alvarez & Winslow, 1994; Shannon, 1995). The third joinfostering condition is that teachers integrate second-language acquisition principles with content instruction so that as second-language students experience and practice new subject matter, they develop oral and written language as well. In a joinfostering classroom teachers have an understanding of how children acquire language socially and are able to create social contexts in which their students understand and use language to mediate learning. Like Julia Felix and many other teachers who are committed to children, we can make it our responsibility to implement the physical and social conditions needed to facilitate language acquisition, critical consciousness, and content learning.

Building Upon Our Students' Strengths

In an essay titled "Transforming Deficit Myths About Learning, Language, and Culture," Flores, Cousin, and Díaz (1991) challenge the assumption that children who come from non-mainstream and non-English-speaking backgrounds are necessarily at risk of failing because of their backgrounds. They propose that we turn the whole idea of language and cultural differences upside down and instead look for new ways of viewing the strengths that language-minority children bring to the classroom, for example, an ability to talk and write about their experiences. Learning to see children as users of language and literacy promotes the assumption that "children need opportunities to learn language in rich, integrated settings and [they] can be successful in regular classroom programs" (Flores, Cousin, & Díaz, 1991, p. 373). Moreover, it resists the status quo, which fragments language and literacy and presents them as exercises. Their against-the-grain view of the kind of settings needed to facilitate language and learning corresponds closely to the joinfostering framework and reflects elements of Cummins's empowerment model as well. In combination, these perspectives lead us to a strong conclusion: Second-language students can be successful in all-English classrooms given the appropriate conditions.

Flores, Cousin, and Díaz (1991) echo one other point that is central to becoming the kind of teacher that you want to be. Assuring the success of students who come from non-English-speaking backgrounds will not come about merely by changing a few practices in our classrooms, but rather by developing a strong perspective to guide our decisions about the kinds of social contexts and learning activities that students need to experience for developing critical awareness of social injustices as well as language and academic content. This point is well taken in the joinfostering framework, where how we and our students use language to communicate ideas plays a critical role in organizing instruction to promote social justice, social integration, two-way interaction, language acquisition, and parental involvement.

CONCLUSION

If your goal is to become the kind of teacher who can empower students, who questions the status quo of many classrooms, who wants to teach against the grain, then you must learn to teach in ways that enable students to build on their experiences and knowledge through social interaction and you have to believe that all students can succeed. You can reach this goal by working toward creating a joinfostering classroom environment in which all students have multiple opportunities to learn regardless of language and cultural background. You can facilitate this goal by getting to know your students' parents, adult caregivers, and community and involving them in the process of schooling. To repeat Cummins's words, we can either disable minority students or we can empower them; the choice is fundamentally ours: "The required changes involve *personal redefinitions* of the way classroom teachers interact with the children and communities they serve" (Cummins, 1986, p. 18).

In closing, this book is an attempt to prepare teachers who are committed to the latter by enabling second-language students and their parents to join in the educational process fully, critically, and in multiple ways. Moreover, this book is about joining in with your students and their communities to advocate for and provide equitable and quality education for all children. Finally, this book is about pedagogical optimism, that with hard work and a firm stance all children can be successful, and with a commitment to social justice, we can improve teaching and learning in the all-English multilingual classroom.

REFERENCES

Cochran-Smith, M. (1991). Learning to teach against the grain. *Harvard Educational Review, 61*(1), 279–310.

Cummins, J. (1986). Empowering minority students: A framework for intervention. *Harvard Educational Review, 56*(1), 18–36.

Flores, B., Cousin, P. T., & Díaz, E. (1991). Transforming deficit myths about learning, language, and culture. *Language Arts, 68,* 369–379.

Hudelson, S., & Faltis, C. (1993). Redefining basic teacher education: Preparing teachers to transform education. In G. Guntermann (Ed.), *Developing language teachers for a changing world* (pp. 23–42). Lincolnwood, IL: National Textbook Company.

Pease-Alvarez, L., & Winslow, A. (1994). Cuando el maestro no habla español: Children's bilingual language practices in the classroom. *TESOL Quarterly, 28*(3), 507–536.

Shannon, S. (1995). The hegemony of English: A case study of one bilingual classroom. *Linguistics and Education, 7*(3), 175–200.

Simon, R. T. (1992). *Teaching against the grain: Texts for a pedagogy of possibility.* New York: Bergin and Garvey.

Torres-Guzmán, M. (1990). *Voy a leer escribiendo* in the context of bilingual/bicultural education. In C. J. Faltis & R. A. DeVillar (Eds.), *Language minority students and computers* (pp. 145–171). New York: The Haworth Press.

Index